Polish Americans

AN ETHNIC COMMUNITY

To Larry Maher,
With best wishes always
to a good friend and colleague.

James Pula

Twayne's Immigrant Heritage of America Series

Thomas J. Archdeacon, General Editor

Polish Americans

AN ETHNIC COMMUNITY

James S. Pula

TWAYNE PUBLISHERS
An Imprint of Simon & Schuster Macmillan
New York
Prentice Hall International
London Mexico City New Delhi Singapore Sydney Toronto

Polish Americans: An Ethnic Community
James S. Pula

Copyright ©1995 by James S. Pula

Twayne Publishers
An Imprint of Simon & Schuster Macmillan
866 Third Avenue
New York, New York 10022

Library of Congress Cataloging-in-Publication Data

Pula, James S.
  Polish Americans : an ethnic community / James S. Pula
      p.   cm.—(Twayne's immigrant heritage of America series)
  Includes bibliographical references and index.
  ISBN 0-8057-8427-6.—ISBN 0-8057-8438-1 (pbk.)
  1. Polish Americans—History.   I. Title.   II. Series.
E184.P787 1995
973'.049185—dc20   94-20514
                                                                CIP
                                                                 AC

The paper used in this publication meets the minimum requirements of American National Standard for Information Sciences—Permanence of Paper for Printed Library Materials, ANSI Z39.48-1984. ♾ ™

10 9 8 7 6 5 4 3 2 1 (hc)
10 9 8 7 6 5 4 3 2 1 (pb)

Printed in the United States of America.

For Marcia and Michael
so they will know their heritage

Contents

Preface

The history of a people should capture not only their chronology but, more important, the essence of their cultural being, the shared ideas and values that compose their unique worldview. Indeed, group historical studies usually progress through various stages before a level of analysis and synthesis can occur that make it possible to paint such a group portrait.

The first serious attempt to pen a history of Polish America—often referred to by the appellation "Polonia"—dates to 1908 when Rev. Wacław Kruszka completed publication of his thirteen-volume *Historja Polska w Ameryce* (History of the Poles in America). Relying on extensive correspondence with parish priests, organizations, and individuals, as well as consulting newspapers, archival collections, and other sources, Kruszka amassed a monumental amount of data and information. He organized his work into two parts, the first constituting a topical overview of Polish America and the second a detailed description of each Polish American community and parish. While ambitious in scope, Kruszka's work is primarily descriptive, lacking both the analysis and the synthesis required of an integrated group history. Although the first part of his work focuses on such topics as ethnic newspapers, clergy, businesses, and organizations, the book, with the exception of its treatment of religious issues, reads more like a catalogue of Polish American achievements than an in-depth exploration of Polish American history.

Similarly, works by Mieczysław Haiman (*Polish Past in America 1608–1865*, 1939), Joseph Wytrwal (*America's Polish Heritage: A Social History of the Poles in America*, 1969; *Behold! The Polish Americans*, 1977), and Bogdan Grzeloński (*Poles in the Unites States of America 1776–1865*, 1976) represent a chronicle of names and dates devoid of interpretation and lacking in historical perspective that would place the development of Polish America within its proper Polish and American contexts.

Among the works that move beyond the descriptive and cataloguing stages are several collections of essays that begin to view aspects of Polish American history as topics for analysis and understanding rather than mere description and preservation. These include Frank Mocha's *Poles in America. Bicentennial Essays* (1978), Stanislaus A. Blejwas and M. B. Biskupski's *Pastor of the Poles: Polish American Essays Presented to Right Reverend Monsignor John P. Wodarski in Honor of the Fiftieth Anniversary of His Ordination* (1982), and Frank Renkiewicz's *The*

Polish Presence in Canada and America (1982). Yet each of these works consists of a series of loosely organized articles rather than an integrated history of Polish America.

The most recent attempt to interpret Polish American history is John Bukowczyk's *And My Children Did Not Know Me: A History of the Polish-Americans* (1987). A stimulating effort that employs the Marxian methodology of the new labor history to develop an analytical portrait of the Polish American worker, Bukowczyk's contribution opens new avenues for exploration into the Polish American experience but does not constitute a survey of the group's historical roots. Rather, it offers one possible interpretation of selected themes within labor and social history.

The purpose of this modest volume is to lay the foundation for an understanding of the complexities of Polish American history and culture by focusing on central themes that have bound Polish Americans into an identifiable community—"Polonia." For the purposes of this work, the terms "Polonia" and "Polish Americans" are defined, as Rev. Kruszka articulated them so well in his pioneering work on the Poles in America, as "a collection of people with a common origin and heritage." Thus, the focus of the work is not on the individual but on "Polonia" as a collective, identifiable community. In this sense it is intended as neither a recitation of the names and contributions of famous Polish Americans nor a partisan espousal of a particular theoretical viewpoint, but as an introductory synthesis of the extant work of scholars delving into the Polish past in America.

While no work of this size can hope to be either inclusive or comprehensive, the author hopes it will provide a context for better understanding Polish American history and culture and suggest topics for further research.

Acknowledgments

Naturally, this volume is the sum total of contributions made by a great many people. In addition to the scholars whose works are cited in the following pages, I should like to extend my sincere appreciation to M. B. Biskupski, Stanislaus A. Blejwas, Eugene E. Dziedzic, John Kromkowski, Lesley Poliner, and Robert Szymczak, who offered particular assistance and guidance on various chapters, to Thomas J. Archdeacon, who read and provided valuable comments and suggestions on the entire work, and to India Koopman, whose editorial skills added greatly to the final publication.

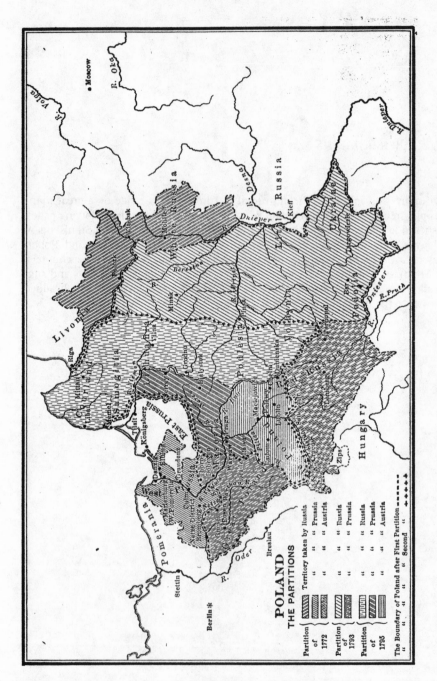

Map of Poland giving the general location of the three partitioned areas as they existed during the late nineteenth century. Polish immigrants in America often referred to one another by the part of the Old Country where they originated.

one

A *Common* Past

History, a common shared and remembered past, is a key element in defining a people and shaping their collective actions, values, and worldview. This can be seen clearly in the characteristics that Poles brought with them to America and instilled in their descendants. These characteristics, transplanted to the New World, became the recurring themes of the Polish experience in America: an affection and concern for their ancestral homeland, a deep religious faith, and a sense of shared cultural values.

Although individual Poles, and even a few small groups, migrated to the United States throughout the antebellum period, the migration that formed permanent Polish American communities did not begin in significant numbers until after the American Civil War. By that time, Poland, once a powerful European force, had been eliminated from the political face of Europe by Austria, Prussia, and Russia in the "Partitions" of 1772, 1793, and 1795. Because of this occupation by foreign powers, all of whom, to a greater or lesser extent, sought to suppress Polish language, heritage and culture, the Poles who migrated to America in the nineteenth century generally held a very emotional attachment to their homeland and a strong desire to see its independence regained. This commitment to the "Polish cause" was a common theme throughout Polish America until the reestablishment of an independent Poland after World War I and, to a great extent, during the period of Nazi-Soviet dominance between 1939 and 1989.

The second important value of Polish immigrants was a firm commitment to Catholicism. In *Stary Kraj*, the Old Country, the peasantry was at the mercy of both invading armies and the vicissitudes of nature. In this peasant world, religious belief provided a means for coping with the challenges of everyday life. There were religious ceremonies to ask for a good harvest, to offer thanks for good fortune, and to address most every other imaginable occurrence. Social life tended to be organized around the Church, with religious holidays, weddings, births, funerals, national or local celebrations, and ceremonies to assist with planting, harvesting, and other critical events forming the cornerstone of community life. In this setting, the Church served as the focal point for both religious *and* social life.

The attachment of Poles to religion—Catholicism in particular—was affirmed and strengthened during the nineteenth century when they found themselves ruled by foreign occupiers intent on limiting or eliminating Polish culture and tradition. Faced with varying demands to conform to the dominant culture of the occupying powers, Poles sought to preserve their language, history, and culture through clandestine activities often undertaken in conjunction with, or under the protection of, the local Catholic parish church. Indeed, during the nineteenth century the bond between Polish patriotism and the Roman Catholic religion became so complete that to many being Polish became synonymous with being Catholic. It was this sense of religious attachment, both spiritual and secular, that formed the central focus of Polish community life in the United States, where, in the immigrant generation, the parish became the center of community life and a lasting influence on succeeding generations.

Finally, the cultural values Poles brought to America and instilled in their offspring derived from their experience in rural agricultural society. Among the more prominent traits that Poles brought with them were traditional extended family structures, a desire for property ownership and social status, and a belief in self-help. Polish immigrants transplanted these values to America by developing a complex system of social and fraternal organizations that provided opportunities for leadership and status through election as officers, by donating generously to the construction of churches that became sources of both individual and community pride, and by dedicating themselves to support the fight for an independent homeland.

Although the first Poles to migrate to America arrived as early as the first years of the Jamestown colony in Virginia, the history of Polish America prior to the American Civil War was generally a movement of individuals whose primary contribution to the formation of "Polonia" was the establishment of an early history in North America that could be pointed to with pride by later generations. Of these early arrivals, Tadeusz Kościuszko and Kazimierz Pułaski were certainly the most important. As historian Joseph Wieczerzak explained, they not only "engendered pro-Polish sympathies in the American public through the nineteenth century and afterwards" but also provided later Polish immigrants with "surrogate roots in the American past that psychologically lessened their feelings of being 'strangers' to America."[1]

Only three times prior to 1860 did relatively large groups migrate to America. Some 234 exiled revolutionaries arrived in New York following the failure of the Polish November Uprising against Russian rule in 1830–31, several hundred political exiles migrated to America in the years following the abortive Mierosławski revolution of 1846, and about 800 poor Silesian peasants followed Rev. Leopold Moczygęba to a colony in Texas in 1854.

The Political Emigrés

On the night of November 29, 1830, cadets from the Warsaw Military Academy attacked the royal residence in Warsaw, beginning the November Uprising against foreign occupation. Word of this new revolt reached America on a packet ship arriving in New York harbor on January 31, 1831. Despite a certain amount of isolationist sentiment, Americans generally greeted news of the Polish insurrection with enthusiasm and the press provided considerable coverage of the event. Literary giant William Cullen Bryant published a strong case for American support for Poland, and the April 2, 1831 New York *Commercial*

An allegorical depiction by Arthur Szyk of the establishment of the Polish colony at Panna Marya, Texas, by Rev. Leopold Moczygęba in 1854. Kościuszko Foundation.

Advertiser advised its readers that "there is no nation upon that continent in whose behalf the sensibilities of the American people are more awakened." The oppression of Poland was, it continued, "unrivalled in atrocity in modern history," concluding "every friend to justice, the rights of men, and the independence of nations, will most cordially wish [the Poles] abundant success in their present struggle for emancipation."[2] In a similar light, the May 20, 1831 New York *Evening Post* told its readers that "the cause in which this gallant people are engaged appeals so strongly to the sympathies of Americans, and the recent brilliant success which has crowned their holy efforts has imparted such a thrill of joy to this whole community, as, in the opinion of the undersigned to justify a public manifestation of their feelings; they therefore take leave to ask a meeting of all such fellow-citizens as may be disposed to unite in such an expression of the public sentiment at the Merchants' Exchange, at half past 7 o'clock on Monday evening."

Nor was American support only verbal. Immediately upon the outbreak of the revolt the American community in Paris formed, through the influence of the Marquis de Lafayette, an American-Polish Committee. James Fenimore Cooper, president of the new organization, wrote a stirring "Appeal to the American People" calling on them for support. In the United States, a committee of prominent citizens sponsored a meeting in New York City, and the editor of the *Advertiser* called on Americans to "lend all the aid consistent with the law of nations and the faith of treaties, which it is in their power to yield to the brave asserters of the rights of men, and of their own national rights." The widespread publication in the American press of James Fenimore Cooper's appeal stimulated further American interest. Many prominent Americans responded with personal involvement, while others offered moral and financial support.

Despite its ultimate failure, the November Uprising of 1830–31 released a wave of *Polonophilia* throughout Jacksonian America. Orators extolled the virtues of Poles, while others collected funds for the Polish cause. The press continued its sympathetic portrayal of Poland, and in 1832 Joseph Hordyński published in Boston his *History of the Polish Revolution and the Events of the Campaign*. The first "Polish" book published in the United States did much to keep alive the interest and enthusiasm of the American public. So obvious was the support for Poland that the Russian chargé d'affaires in Washington lodged several strong protests with the State Department. The Russian found it difficult to comprehend the American concept of freedom of the press, assuming that the outpouring of sentiment for Poland mirrored official government policy. In fact, according to Joseph Wieczerzak, the chargeé's protests only "served to increase sympathy for the Poles among the American public" and to greatly strain U.S.-Russian relations. So serious did the diplomatic flap become that the Russian chargé d'affaires was recalled at the request of the Jackson administration, "which considered him an arrogant *persona non grata* guilty of offending the President."[3]

Following the end of the revolt some exiles escaped to Austria, but the Austrian government became increasingly wary of their presence when their revolutionary activities appeared undiminished. Concerned about possible international ramifications that could result from its harboring of the exiles, Austria signed agreements with Russia and Prussia in 1833 in which it promised to carefully control the exiles' activities. As a result of these agreements, Austria interned some 400 exiles in the Fortress of Brno in Moravia. When it became apparent that the exiles were busily planning for an extensive guerilla war, Austrian authorities determined to deport them lest their country be drawn into conflict with Russia, or itself become the target of the revolutionaries' plans. The exiles hoped to be sent to France, but the French government of King Louis Philippe declined owing to growing apprehension about the large number of Polish political revolutionaries already in its domain.

Following their refusal by France, the exiles were given the choice of returning to Russian rule under a czarist amnesty or being deported to America. They chose the latter and were sent to Trieste, from which the deportations began on the night of November 21–22 when 234 were loaded aboard the Austrian warships *Hebe* and *Guerriere*. Prior to embarking the Poles pledged to remain loyal to a single Polish Committee. Once in America, this committee became the first Polish organization in America, the immediate purpose of which was to elect a national representative to speak for the Poles arriving in New York. Under its chair, Captain Ludwik Banczakiewicz, the group established its headquarters in the city's Union Hotel, continuing its activities until 1840.

The Austrian warships that arrived in New York harbor on March 28, 1834, carried the first large group of Poles to migrate to the United States. Once in New York, the Poles quickly became objects of curiosity, but the language barrier often prevented effective communication. Nevertheless, popular support for Poland remained high and an American Assistance Committee formed in New York with Albert Gallatin, the Swiss-born former senator and secretary of the Treasury, as its chair. The committee raised funds by sponsoring dinners, receptions, and theatrical performances, as did organizations in Philadelphia, Boston, Baltimore, and other cities.

Nearly all of the Poles arriving on the Austrian warships initially believed their stay in America would be temporary; they planned to return to Europe to continue the struggle for a free Poland. As the months dragged on, it became increasingly apparent that there would be no immediate return. Rather, it was necessary for them to find employment and earn a living. The various committees helped them to find jobs and housing, and gradually they dispersed by ones and twos and in small groups. More than 30 emigrés went to Albany, Troy, and other locations in upstate New York, 25 to Philadelphia, and more than 30 to Boston. By mid-1834 the Poles, who then numbered some 425 with the addition of other deportees, were dispersed over a wide area from Washington, D.C., to Boston and as far west as Ohio. About one-third of that number remained in the New York City area, but by the end of the year all of the committees except that in Boston were defunct and the Poles were virtually on their own.

To assist them in earning a living and to provide a means for the exiles to remain together, the Polish Committee in 1834 drew up a memorial to Congress asking for a grant of land on which to settle. Responding favorably to the Polish request, Congress took the unprecedented step of authorizing a grant to the Poles in a township of their choice in either Illinois or Michigan. On June 30, 1834, President Andrew Jackson signed the bill into law, granting the Poles land at $1.25 per acre. Under the terms of the law they could pay for the land on a long-term basis, but had to furnish their own transportation and farm implements and had to settle within a certain time period. Further, the land could be granted only to the original 234 exiles who arrived in March 1834. The offer would not be extended to those coming later.

The land grant, which might have formed the basis of a "New Poland" in America, came at a time of great strain within the exile community. Some had already left New York, and internal squabbling split the group into two or three factions with a second organization, the Polish National Committee, formed under the leadership of Dr. Charles Kraitsir. A Hungarian closely associated with the Poles, Kraitsir seems to have wielded a divisive influence among them. His group accepted the lands granted by Congress and dispatched two people to select a parcel and solicit funds to cover the purchase price and associated expenses.

Ludwik Chłopicki selected land along the Rock River in northern Illinois and was successful in convincing local residents to take up a collection on behalf of the Poles for tools, seed, and other necessities. Unfortunately for the exiles, this promising beginning soon collapsed in shambles. First, one of the people soliciting funds absconded with the collection and went to Europe. Then the colonists ran into squatters who enjoyed strong support from the local congressman, orchestrating a smear campaign against the newcomers. Discouraged, most Poles chose not to move to the new lands. In 1840 the Polish National Committee again attempted to claim the land, but its appeal went unanswered. The land was then declared in forfeiture and later sold by the State of Illinois. Although the dream of a Polish colony was not dead, most of the exiles experienced a profound sense of "disillusionment and demoralization."[4]

Despite their sometimes difficult existence, the Polish political exiles retained a vigorous interest in politics, continuing to plan for the eventual liberation of their homeland. To accomplish this, they made every attempt to publicize the continuing plight of Poland "to gain the moral, if not diplomatic or financial, support of the American government and American people for the case of Polish independence." In this they were bitterly disappointed that the U.S. government maintained a strict policy through the years between Andrew Jackson and Abraham Lincoln that the Polish question was an internal affair of the Russian Empire.

As the years passed, many found prolonged life in America to be more difficult than they had imagined. In 1834 an exile wrote "amid the greatest despair" to explain his "job at the tanner's." At the beginning, he wrote, "I worked even though blisters grew on my hand, that was a minor thing, but now they tell me to crawl on roof tops, and stretch the stinking hides from roof to roof, and when I fell to the ground I became so pained that I cast it all aside and now I am like a madman without lodging and without food, and if I knew that I would be of some use to the Motherland I would chance this miserable existence, there are several of us in this position, we suffer the same, on meeting each other our first greeting is 'Did you eat today?'"[5] Another expressed a growing fear that the exiles, once dispersed, would gradually lose their identity in a sea of Americans. "It seems to me," he lamented, "that the force of absorption in this country prevails over an impact of any nationality, especially of one so small in numbers like ours. We have nothing here to live for except as colonists committing an act of national suicide."[6]

Despite these misgivings, and the hardships that some endured, within a few years the exiles from the November Uprising were well on their way to taking control of their futures. Some determined to return to Europe, or moved on to Mexico or South America. Those who chose to stay generally began life in their new country as manual laborers, but within a few years most started to climb the socioeconomic ladder. Language was an initial barrier, but this could be overcome by learning English. As members of Poland's gentry, most were already educated and many had professions or skills they could use in America. Some moved quickly into teaching, particularly in subjects such as drawing, dancing, music, and language instruction. Those with a military education taught fencing. Others found employment as surveyors, cartographers, engineers, and musicians. A few went into agriculture, business, or the U.S. Army.

In retrospect, the political exiles of the November Uprising played an important part in the beginnings of Polish settlement and influence in the United States. Their arrival as a group led to the organization of the first Polish American political association, the creation of a relatively stable Polish presence in New York City for the first time, and the beginning, however tenuous, of a Polish publishing tradition in America. Politically, their efforts to promote the cause of Poland further enhanced the positive image that most Americans held regarding their homeland.

The exiles of the November Uprising established the first permanent Polish presence in North America. Others soon arrived to join them. Throughout the three decades after the November Uprising there was a continuing movement of Poles out of their native land to neighboring states where some hoped to live in exile until their homeland was freed. Others actively plotted to bring about that freedom. Some viewed Switzerland as a pleasant haven from which to operate, and they established a Polish community, secure amid the mountains of this alpine land. Others turned to France as a natural ally against Russia, flocking to the Polish community in Paris to promote their cause along the banks of the Seine.

Some Poles, notably members of the Democratic Society, openly condemned those who chose to migrate to America, maintaining that such action would drain Polish manpower in Europe, thus having an adverse effect on the movement to free Poland. Bertold Wierciński, who returned to England, was bitter over his experience in America. He voiced the opinion of many who felt an obligation to return to Europe to further the cause of Poland when he wrote in *Kronika Emigracji* (Emigration Chronicle) that "every Pole going to the United States sins not only against himself but against his obligations to his fatherland."[7] Regardless, an increasing number of Poles sought to continue their lives in the New World. Some 600 voluntarily resettled in the United States between 1839 and 1847. About 50 of these arrived in New Orleans from France, preferring to settle in an area with familiar French culture and language.[8]

As fiercely dedicated to the cause of Poland as were the earlier exiles, those who came during the decade between 1835 and 1845 brought with them not only ambition but contacts. Many were associated with the various Polish organizations in Europe, particularly the *Zjednoczenie Emigracji Polskiej* (United Polish Emigration), led by historian Joachim Lelewel. In March 1842, 43 exiles with ties to Lelewel's group attempted to revive the increasingly dormant Polish National Committee founded in 1834. Adopting the motto "to die for Poland," the group established the new *Stowarzyszenie Polaków w Ameryce* (Association of Poles in America), a branch of the United Polish Emigration. In an effort to promote unity, the organization resolved that "every emigré Pole regardless of position and faith" could be a member.

Despite this attempt to reinvigorate a united Polish front in America, all was not harmonious. Władysław Lange led the committee in New York, with Henryk Kałussowski as secretary. Both men were radicals who espoused anti-monarchist ideals that conflicted with the aspirations of other factions in the emigré community. As a consequence, the aristocratic elements within the Polish exile community coalesced behind Prince Adam Czartoryski, and later Count Władysław Zamoyski, to organize the May Third Association. This factionalism within the Polish group in America mirrored the philosophical divisions then present in Europe. The radicals, who maintained close contacts with other groups of European political exiles, including Italians, Irish, Scandinavians, Jews, and liberal Germans, eventually emerged as the predominant group and proved somewhat successful in maintaining public support for Poland in the United States. The rift, however, was one of the first public manifestations of the factionalism that later came to mark the development of organized Polonia in the late nineteenth and early twentieth centuries.

Much of the credit for the success the organization enjoyed in raising the American consciousness about the "Polish question" was due Gaspard Tochman. A major in the November Uprising, Tochman arrived in 1836, quickly learned English and became a successful lawyer. A dynamic speaker, he proved remarkably successful in obtaining engagements in major cities and before state legislatures. In the four years between 1840 and 1844 he delivered more than 100 lectures on Poland to audiences said to total in excess of 250,000 people. His lecture "Poland, Russia, and the Policy of the Latter Towards the United States" was published in 1844 amid considerable public excitement. In 1846 he was instrumental in founding the Polish-Slavonian Literary Society, which numbered among its members Jared Sparks, Josiah Quincy, Albert Gallatin, William H. Seward, and various other "prominent politicians and intellectuals of the Eastern Establishment."[9]

In 1846 Polish hearts soared briefly with the news of a new revolutionary outbreak in Austrian Poland. The effort soon failed, however, as did an abortive revolt planned in Prussian-occupied Poland by Ludwik Mierosławski in the same year. These failures sent a new wave of exiles abroad. During the "Springtime of Nations" that followed the Polish outbreaks of 1846, the recent exiles, led by Henryk Kałussowski, appealed to all Polish exiles to assist Poland and to revive the Polish Committee in New York. Despite little support from the more conservative followers of Czartoryski, notable success occurred in St. Louis, New Orleans, Louisville, Pittsburgh, Cincinnati, and Boston.

The ultimate failure of the "Springtime of Nations" brought a myriad of political exiles to America. Between 1848 and 1851 some 300–500 Poles arrived in the United States, with many, about 200, settling in New York. Some 80 Poles led by Dr. Franciszek Lawrynowicz secured passage on the ship *Manchester* from Le Havre to New Orleans, paid for by a French government eager to rid itself of these troublemakers. Others came straight from the battlefields of Poland. The remainder included educated people motivated by patriotic zeal to continue working in America for the Polish cause. Much like the earlier exiles from the November Uprising, the post-1846 emigrés remained committed to Polish independence.[10]

The Beginning of Economic Migration

The "Springtime of Nations" did more than influence educated revolutionaries, it also had a dramatic impact on the poorer rural classes in agrarian Poland. Reforms meant to abolish the feudal system in Silesia, for example, resulted in increased economic obligations for the peasantry, many of whom found their socioeconomic situation actually deteriorating despite the improvement in their legal status. As early as 1848, members of the peasantry began moving out of rural Silesia, seeing new opportunities in the industrializing German cities or in nations farther west. Among these emigrants was a group of Silesian peasants led by Father Leopold Moczygęba, who began, however humbly, the mass economic movement that would bring hundreds of thousands of Poles to America later in the century.

Born in Upper Silesia in 1824, Moczygęba was a member of the Order of Franciscan Friars Minor Conventual, who journeyed to Texas as one of four Franciscans recruited by the bishop of Galveston as missionaries to work among German settlers in the remote regions of Texas. Arriving in Texas in September 1852, the Polish priest was impressed by the success of his German parishioners and, over the next two years, wrote letters to family and friends in Upper Silesia urging them to come to Texas to find success and good fortune. These letters eventually had the desired effect, serving as a catalyst for the movement of a group of Poles from Upper Silesia in 1854.

On December 3 the Silesian Poles arrived in Galveston, from where they moved inland to found a colony they named Panna Marya, after the Virgin Mary. Although life proved more difficult than they had imagined—they lived in sod huts and dugouts, a severe drought ruined crops and killed livestock, and inflation made the purchase of necessary supplies difficult—they succeeded in founding the first truly permanent Polish settlement in America, complete with family and religious life, ethnic organizations, and permanent elements of Polish culture.

About 100 families—some 800 individuals—settled in Panna Marya in 1854. Eventually, 1,500 others joined Moczygęba in Texas, lured by the promise of free arable land. The movement of these Silesians to Texas introduced a new element into the migration of Poles to America, presaging the mass economic movement later in the century. The change in origin of Polish immigrants was accompanied by a change in their socioeconomic background and an increase in the number of immigrants. When the federal census bureau began separating nationalities in 1860, it reported more than 7,200 Poles in the United States. But because Poland did not officially exist as an independent nation, many ethnic Poles were listed as Russian, Prussian, or Austrian, depending on the section of partitioned Poland from which they originated. Mieczysław Haiman, studying records in the Federal Bureau of Statistics but using the dubious technique of name recognition, concluded that a conservative estimate of the number of Poles—including those of Polish ancestry—in the United States in 1860 would be 30,000. By 1870 this rose to 50,000, with some 20 recognizably "Polish" settlements located primarily in Texas, Wisconsin, Illinois, Missouri, Pennsylvania, and New York. These colonies were significantly different in character from those of the earlier political exiles located primarily in the urban areas of the northeast.

The Civil War and the January Insurrection

The 1850s witnessed not only the first wave of economic immigrants from Poland but also an increase in activity and influence on the part of the older political emigrés. In 1853 about 150 of the more radical Polish emigrés founded in New York City the *Towarzystwo Demokratyczne Wygnańców Polskich w Ameryce* (Democratic Society of Polish Exiles in America), a branch of Stanisław Worcell's Centralization of Polish Democrats based in London. The constitution of the new organization declared that "every Pole, as long as he has the right to the name of an honest person and sincerely professes democratic principles, may become a member of our Society." There was a clear understanding that "everyone who was born on Polish soil regardless of his religious or political faith" was welcome, and the Poles made a particular effort to recruit members from among the large number of Jewish Americans residing in New York who were born on Polish soil. Membership lists show that several Jews did indeed play major roles in the society. One of these, Julian Allen, whose original name was probably Allensky, authored *Autocracy in Poland and Russia: or A Description of Russian Misrule in Poland, and an Account of the Surveillance of Russian Spies at Home and Abroad, including "The Experience of an Exile,"* published in New York by John Wiley in 1854. The society's primary successes outside New York City occurred in St. Louis, Charleston, Cleveland, Philadelphia, and Troy, but by 1855 membership included only about 15 percent of the Poles in America.

Despite the continuing concern for Poland, during the 1850s the Poles in America gradually grew apart from the exile centers and leaders in Europe. Some married Americans, and many became involved in American political and social life, particularly in the abolitionist movement.

The Civil War was arguably the most destructive and traumatic event in American history. The war tore friends and families apart, and Poles living in America were no exception. Most supported the North, many being in fact ardent abolitionists. To them, the crisis was a simple matter of slavery being incompatible with both the democratic principles articulated in the U.S. Constitution and similar ideals they brought with them from Poland. For Poles residing in the South, the choice was not so easy. Some favored the North, while others viewed the crisis as more analogous to the situation in their homeland, characterizing the North as an oppressor of the South's rights.

For Polish Americans, there was yet another dimension to the conflict. On January 22, 1863, a new Polish revolution began against Russia. Immediately, the emigré communities abroad were electrified into action. Only 10 days after the beginning of the January Insurrection, Polish exiles in London began publishing *Głos Wolny* (Free Voice) to publicize news of the insurrection and the efforts of Poles abroad to assist their homeland. The paper vigorously criticized Poles emigrating to America as traitors to the cause.

In America, news of the January Insurrection first appeared in the press on February 14, causing the exile community to leap into action. Polish leaders in New York quickly established a Central Polish Committee to serve as an umbrella organization for all Poles, and set about "arousing the sympathy of the public from among various nationalities without regard to religious and political principles." In an open letter dated April 10 and published in the American press, the committee's secretary, Romuald Jaworowski, wrote to "notify all the Poles residing there, regardless of their religious faith or past political shading, about the activities of the Central Committee and attempt to organize them into one body." The 13 members of the Central Committee did in fact represent various factions in the Polish political spectrum, including two representatives of the Jewish community. Jews were specifically targeted in a general appeal published by the Central Committee in the *New York Herald* and addressed "To the Poles of the Mosaic Persuasion in the United States of America."[11]

Polish Jews responded favorably, with a meeting at Pythagoras Hall on July 5 and another "mass rally" at the Cooper Institute on July 24, 1863. Strong support for the Polish cause also came from Irish Americans, who identified Poland's struggle against Russia with their own efforts to throw off British rule, and from other sympathetic ethnic groups, including Czech and Hungarian exiles and German liberals. Union generals Franz Sigel and Carl Schurz, leaders in the German American community, both spoke on behalf of the Polish cause, while Oswald Ottendorfer, editor of the influential *New-Yorker Staats-Zeitung*, lent his valuable support in reaching the German immigrant communities.

To reach its own compatriots more effectively, on June 1, 1863, the Central Committee began publishing the New York *Echo z Polski* (Echo of Poland), the first Polish-language newspaper to appear in America. Edited by Jaworowski, the newspaper was printed by P. L. Schriftgiesser, a Polish Jew who agreed to provide printing and distribution services in response to the Central Committee's call for assistance. *Echo z Polski* was primarily a political publication devoted to news and appeals focusing on the January Insurrection. Its content consisted mostly of reprints, with news of the uprising taken from emigré papers in Europe, and it rapidly became known among emigré circles as what Jerzy Lerski called "the official organ of the Polish government's delegation."[12]

The outbreak of the January Insurrection left many Poles in America in an ambiguous, if not outright awkward, position. Should they rush immediately to Europe to fight for the homeland, or was their presence in the United States more helpful to the cause through publicity and fund-raising? Some left the Union Army to return to their native land, but most chose to work for the Polish cause from America.

Although there was considerable sympathy for the Poles among other ethnic groups in America, and the Central Committee undertook publicity and fund-raising campaigns across the North, the political situation in 1863 was different from what it had been during the November Uprising. In the spring of 1863 the fate of the Union was not at all certain. Northern armies had been singularly unsuccessful in their campaigns to capture the Confederate capital in Richmond, suffering severe losses at Bull Run, in the Peninsula Campaign and the Shenandoah Valley, and at Fredericksburg. At the same time, England and France, while remaining nominally neutral, supplied the Confederacy with arms, equipment, provisions, ships, and other support for its war against the North. In this atmosphere of fear and isolation, the North sought allies in its fight to preserve the Union. Similarly, Czar Alexander II of Russia, his relations with the Western European nations decidedly negative since before the Crimean War, feared that England and France would intervene on the side of the Polish insurgents in 1863. Consequently, the czar sent his fleets on extended visits to New York and San Francisco both to curry favor in the North and to prevent them from being bottled up in their harbors in the event of war with England and France.[13]

Naturally, the North, desperately seeking a European ally to offset the potential threat from England and France, was only too happy to embrace the Russians as friends. Unfortunately for the Poles, the new friendship between the government of the czar and that of Lincoln meant that Northerners were no longer willing to give their unqualified moral and financial support to Poland. Indeed, American attitudes toward Poland underwent a considerable metamorphosis as the czar suddenly became a great friend of democracy. The infant *New York Times,* though devoting space to coverage of the January Insurrection, editorialized in favor of the czar. Commenting on the Russian abolition of serfdom, editor Henry J. Raymond stated that "Alexander steps out of his dreary traditions with his hands full of progress, and his heart full of sympathy." Similarly, William Cullen Bryant, who provided strong editorial support for Poland during the November Uprising of 1830–31, glorified the czar's act of emancipation, equating it with "the greatest liberal movements in history." As Joseph Wieczerzak noted, "Superficial analogies were made between [the czar's] emancipation of the peasant serfs and Lincoln's liberation of the Negro slaves. Similarly the so-called principle of non-intervention in 'domestic affairs' should not have been considered in case of a Russo-Polish conflict. Apprehensive of possible French and British support for the Confederacy, Union politicians sympathized with Russia's insistence that her handling of the Polish revolutionaries was no business of London, Paris and Vienna."[14]

With the North enraptured by the arrival of the Russian fleets, the cause of Poland naturally suffered. "From the practical viewpoint," Lerski observed, "the Insurrection substantially helped the international position of the North and adversely affected that of the South by diverting British and French attention from the Western Hemisphere to a possible confrontation with 'Eastern Powers' in Europe." Regardless, the traditional friendship between America and Poland suffered from the American preoccupation with Russia, with the result that Poles found in America little enthusiasm and less financial support for the January Insurrection. "The story of the Polish January Insurrection and Civil War America," wrote Lerski, "is a story of unfortunate circumstances making for a situation in which Poland's well-wishers in Europe, and occasionally on the American scene, were also the Union's foes, while Poland's enemies and oppressors were the Union's alleged friends."[15] It would not be the last time that the requirements of international politics conspired to deny Poland American support, as would become evident during World War II.

Abroad, there was an obvious feeling of disappointment on the part of Poles who counted on American support. On January 31, 1864, *Głos Wolny* severely rebuked those Poles who sought to migrate to America and join the Union Army. "What have the Federalists done for our cause in order that we should pay back with blood?" the newspaper asked. "Have they given us any proof of good will? Have they set up one committee to bring aid to Poland in her difficult battle with Moscow?" Similarly, *Ojczyzna* (Fatherland), published by Agaton Giller in Leipzig, Saxony, criticized the United States for its supposed alliance with Russia. On June 10, 1864, he wrote that "the imperial tendencies of the Federalists and hate of France and England leads them to maintain friendly relations with despotic Moscow and prohibits them from showing any friendliness towards Poland in her fight for freedom."[16] The Kraków-based publication *Czas* (Time) provided the following appraisal on August 19, 1863: "The behavior of Russia in regard to Poland is exactly like that of the Washington government in relation to the South. Their identical violent means are contrary to civilization and humanity. Their politics are the same. They hope to deny the rights of freedom and independence to other peoples. Russia does not want to encourage the end of the war in America, and the northern states do not want to intervene in Europe on Poland's behalf. Moscow liberates the peasants and oppresses the Poles. America gives freedom to Negroes and oppresses the Southerners."[17]

Surprisingly, *Echo z Polski,* which might have been expected to lament the lack of American support for its cause, completely separated the European and American situations. Adopting an unequivocally anti-slavery stance, it condemned the South and actually applauded the Russo-American alliance for helping to preserve the Union. It was unique among emigré newspapers in failing to equate the Civil War and slavery with the January Insurrection and serfdom. The eventual failure of the January Insurrection brought the bickering to an end, but it signaled a dramatic shift in U.S. policy and public opinion. While the United States would empathize with Poland now and again in the future, the infatuation of the antebellum era would never be rekindled.

Although largely a period of "individual" migration, the antebellum period witnessed the granting of land to Polish exiles by the U.S. Congress, the publication of the first Polish language newspaper (*Echo z Polski*) in America, and early attempts at organizing Polish immigrants into political societies to support the homeland in its struggle for independence. Indeed, the Polish search for political freedom was the predominant theme of the era, seen not only in the Poles' attempts to solicit help for their homeland but in their own willingness to follow the motto "For Your Freedom and Ours" in their support of the American and

French revolutions and the various movements of the "Springtime of Nations." These and their own rebellions against foreign rule in 1830, 1846, and 1863 resulted in the arrival of new political exiles in America. Many of these exiles took part in the abolitionist crusade, in the early movement toward women's rights, and in the Civil War that defined the future of America. Thus, while the early history of Polish America is primarily that of the migration of individuals and small groups, these early immigrants were generally successful in organizing themselves and exerting some influence on behalf of themselves and Poland. Although they were primarily male and did not develop the recognizably Polish communities that later immigrants founded, they did exhibit a keen interest in the homeland, found organizations to pursue their goals, lay the foundations for Polish churches, and begin, however tenuously, a Polish publishing tradition in America. As such, they were indeed the precursors of the mass migration to follow.

two

The Old World and the New, 1870–1900

B eginning in the late 1850s the Poles in Prussian-occupied Poland, particularly the gentry, suffered economic difficulties because of their support for the failed revolution in 1848. Bad harvests in 1848 and in 1853–56 greatly exacerbated the difficulties. Between 1846 and 1885 some 1,250,000 acres of land passed from Polish ownership to German hands in Poznania and West Prussia alone. As a result, an exodus began from the German section of the partitioned nation.[1]

When Germany united in the 1870s a spirit of Germanization swept the country. Naturally, this had a profound effect on the many minorities included within the new German nation, particularly the large numbers of Poles. Polish minorities in the German states were traditionally oppressed and exploited, but Bismarck's view of this large minority was if anything regressive. "Bismarck's attitude towards the Poles was essentially feudal," Thomas Michalski contends. "To him the Poles were simply non-German-speaking Prussians. . . . To Bismarck, the 'Polish problem' was essentially a problem generated by a few 'meddlesome priests' and disgruntled gentry. If only a few radical clergy could be muzzled, the problem would go away."[2] To Bismarck and the other German nationalists, all non-Germans were *Reichsfeinde* (enemies of the Reich).

As a consequence of this attitude, the German Constitution of 1871 contained no provisions safeguarding the rights of ethnic minorities. Further, Bismarck's government launched an overt attack on the Polish clergy, whom the "Iron Chancellor" viewed as the source of the troubling Polish ethnic consciousness. Bismarck began his assault in January 1872, with a drive to secularize education and replace the Polish clergy with Germans. The Germans warned the Polish clergy not to engage in politics and banned the Polish religious and patriotic hymn *Boże cos Polskę* (God, Protector of Poland). Priests who disobeyed were jailed, and Archbishop Mieczysław Ledóchowski of Poznań-Gniezno, himself only marginally nationalistic, was arrested when he could not control the Poles within his jurisdiction. Exiled to Rome when the Vatican interceded, his See remained unfilled for 12 years, leaving the Poles without strong leadership.[3]

In addition to the assault on the clergy, German nationalists also initiated a systematic attack on Polish culture. They discouraged use of the Polish language, launched a campaign to force Polish newspapers to print in both languages, and accused the clergy of polonizing Germanic names in an attempt to polonize the German population. The German mail system rejected letters if one wrote the Polish "Gdańsk" instead of the German "Danzig," or if "street" were rendered as the Polish *ulica* rather than the German *strasse*. By 1912, some 7,500 place names had been changed from Polish to German.[4]

Contrary to the what was intended, however, the massive German offensive backfired when the Poles became aroused over the persecution and arrest of their clergy. The twin pressures of economic decline and population increase in the rural areas of occupied Poland continued to push peasants toward the industrial cities in search of jobs, thus strengthening the Polish language and culture in those areas. The Germanization effort did, however, contribute to the beginning of emigration from the German sector to America, the beginning of a Polish migration that later grew to enormous proportions. The economic emigrants from the poorer rural areas moved first to the more industrialized areas of Western Germany and Western Europe, and then to the United States. In a detailed study of emigration from German-occupied Poland, Victor Greene concluded that the social and political repression of the German government was a contributory cause but that the single most important factor in the movement of people out of German-occupied Poland was economic dislocation.[5]

Polish immigrants during the 1870s came primarily from the German-occupied sector, with some 152,000 migrating from Poznania, East Prussia, West Prussia, and Silesia, compared with only 2,000 from Austrian Galicia. Emigration from the German-occupied areas peaked in the 1880s and declined somewhat thereafter owing to improving economic and social conditions in German Poland. Between 1840 and 1910 some 1,575,000 people migrated from German Poland to the United States, including 877,400 from Poznania, 628,110 from West Prussia, and 70,000 from Russian areas "proximate to Prussian Poland." This movement had a major influence on America, forming a majority of the early Polish population in New York, Chicago, and other urban settlements. The Poles from the German-occupied partition were at least somewhat urbanized, had some marketable skills, and tended to be young, energetic, and optimistic. Many had experience in European factories, mines, or foundries, while some were craftsmen, artisans, or entrepreneurs. Many opened businesses in the United States within a relatively short time.[6] Further, their experience in Germany made them reluctant to give up their language, culture, and religion, thus causing the formation of distinct communities that resisted acculturation and assimilation for generations.

In Russian Poland, the czar formally ended serfdom in 1864. By 1875 some 1 million acres of former landed estates were in peasant hands. The Russians also allowed some local self-government by instituting a *gmina*, a rural township whose ruling council consisted of landowners, including peasants. By 1870, however, a program of Russification sought to eliminate Polish as a language of instruction in schools and to limit the influence of the Polish clergy. At the same time, economic conditions deteriorated. In the southern textile center of Łódź wages for unskilled factory workers between 1880 and 1900 were approximately $.30 per day, one-quarter of the $1.15 paid in the United States during the same time.[7]

The northern sections of Russian Poland remained poor, economically depressed agricultural areas. It was these provinces—Suwałki, Łomza, and Płock—that accounted for most of the emigration from Russian Poland until 1904. As late as 1905, fully one-third of all the Russian Poles who migrated came from Suwalki. In that year, unrest in both Poland and Russia, economic problems caused by the Russo-Japanese War, and the political demands heightened by the war created near chaos. Thereafter, most of those who left the Russian section were industrial workers fleeing a declining economy. Thus, economic motivations again appear to be the strongest cause of migration from Russian Poland, with some 40,000 journeying to America in the 1880s and 134,000 in the 1890s.[8]

The third partition, Austrian-occupied Galicia, was a particularly poor agricultural area. Located adjacent to the Tatra Mountains, it had a short growing season and the emancipation of serfs came late owing to opposition by local Polish nobles. Politically, the Galicians fared considerably better than their German-dominated countryfolk. As early as the 1850s the Austrians instituted several liberal reforms including administrative and judicial changes and self-governing town councils. By 1861 Austria approved the establishment of the Galician Diet as a provincial parliament, with delegates from this diet attending the Vienna Parliament where they were known as the "Polish Club" because of their actions in behalf of their constituents. In 1890 a Polish peasant party was established under the leadership of Wincenty Witoś, and in 1907 the Austrian Empire declared universal male suffrage. Thus political and cultural motivations were probably less important in the migration of Poles from Galicia. The key factor appears to be the general economic situation that was both chaotic and depressed during the later nineteenth and early twentieth centuries. Victor Greene noted that the Austrian government purposely restrained economic development in order to retain large grain exports from Galicia to the rest of the Empire, particularly the highly industrialized areas in Bohemia and Silesia. It was not until 1910 that a special industrial bank was created to assist economic development in Galicia. Nevertheless, the farm population increased from 77 percent in 1890 to 90 percent by 1914, and Galicia had the smallest urban population of any of the three occupied zones.

It appears that once again economic considerations were the compelling factor in the beginning of mass migration from Galicia. Prior to emancipation, the rural economy of the Polish peasantry focused on barter. Money was seldom used or even available. After emancipation, money became important as a means to improve farms, buy or rent land and animals, and survive a poor harvest. Money was also increasingly important to pay for weddings, funerals, and other social events where family pride demanded as extensive an outlay as possible. The pressure to earn and accumulate cash led to the establishment of agrarian banks, cooperatives, collective purchasing, credit agencies, and loan associations devoted to serving peasant interests.[9]

Despite these efforts, conditions in Galicia remained poor. Homes and villages were devoid of amenities. Peasant dwellings generally contained two large rooms, one for the family and one for livestock, tools, fertilizer, and other supplies. An English visitor once noted that "Their cottages are hovels such as no English farmer would permit a laborer to inhabit." The average pay for agricultural workers was 40–50 percent lower than that of unskilled industrial workers, while the pay of the latter was about 50 percent lower than for similar positions in Western Europe. Similarly, male agrarian laborers in Poland earned 40–50 percent less for an entire season's work than those in Germany. This economic depression was exacerbated by decreasing landholdings and a rapid increase in the population. Farms were subdivided upon death so that by 1900, when the normal family required an estimated holding of 14 acres for its support, the average land holding in Galicia was less than six acres. With such small plots of land, peasants were extremely vulnerable to the vicissitudes of weather and market, with most having barely enough to feed their families. It was not a very good system, but property ownership was a symbol of family status, a sign of social superiority that could not easily be sacrificed for the common good. The result was that an estimated 50,000 per year died of starvation.[10]

A Galician peasant expressed the general sense of exasperation in a letter describing his feelings while watching the daily train pass his village: "This passing train . . . reminds us of our poverty here and tells us that somewhere else life is better, that the world is different, big, better, but not ours."[11] Gradually, the Galician peasants, like their kin in the other partitions, came to realize that there were alternatives to poverty. Though the Poles were firmly attached to the land, the pressure of economic necessity drove them to seek other ways of life.

For some, seasonal migrations were an opportunity to earn money in the German-occupied areas. By 1900 these movements were a significant source of income in Poland. A study of a single Galician village, for example, showed that in 1899 seasonal workers brought home an income exceeding the "total income from this village's local farming by 20 per cent."[12]

Another option open to Galician peasants was relocation to one of the growing European industrial centers. This allowed for both seasonal and permanent relocation, but regardless of which method was used, the result for the individual migrants was increased prosperity. Similarly, their Galician villages also prospered, and migrants, whether temporary or permanent, sent cash home to their families. By 1911, for example, the village noted above increased its annual income from migrants throughout the European continent by $18,000.[13] Between 1875 and 1914, it is estimated that some 9 million Poles migrated in one fashion or another.

A third option was to extend these migratory patterns across the Atlantic. In 1891 the average daily wage of $.90 for agricultural laborers in the United States was eight times that available in Galicia. At $1.48 per day, the average wage of an unskilled laborer in the United States was 12 times as high. The conclusion was obvious. As Polish peasant leader Władysław Orkan, a contemporary observer, explained, "For these minds, accustomed to the poor local wages, it was like a fantasy, like a dream pay!" As word of the great opportunities to be had in America spread, it became a very popular option in Galicia, with 82,000 migrating to the United States in the 1880s, increasing to 340,000 in the 1890s.[14]

Although Poles came to America from various circumstances throughout their partitioned homeland, some generalizations can be made. While Polish immigration to the United States in the antebellum years was generally political in nature, the mass movement of Poles between 1870 and 1914 occurred primarily for economic reasons. Yet, as Richard Zeitlin maintains, it was not exclusively "a movement of the 'huddled masses' or only of the 'tired and poor yearning to breathe free,' as Emma Lazarus' poem inscribed on the base of the Statue of Liberty would have it, but rather a movement of the young, the energetic, the confident, and the adventurous."[15]

PAROWCE LINII „RED STAR",

☞ SĄ MOCNE, SZYBKIE, PEWNE I WYGODNE. ☜

Z Antwerpii do New Yorku tylko $22.00

USŁUGA POLSKA POTRAWY ZDROWE.

Materace, poduszki, statki blaszane, noże, widelce daje kompanja dar Emigranci jedzą przy jadalnym stole. Po wszelki informacye zgłosić należy do *generalnego agenta,*

M.   M A K O W S K I E G O.

1132 Broadway.   —   —   BUFFALO, N. Y.

Advertisements like this one for Markowski's agency in Buffalo, New York, competed for the lucrative immigrant trade.

Most peasants migrated with the intention of finding jobs in higher paying industry so they could return in three to five years and purchase land, thereby resuming an agricultural life while at the same time bettering both their economic position and their status. This purpose can be seen in the pattern of settlement, with succeeding waves of immigrants selecting areas on the basis of information provided by relatives and friends who had migrated earlier or of press reports of economic opportunity, thus creating a "chain migration" pattern.[16]

An estimated 1.5 million ethnic Poles arrived in the United States between 1899 and 1913. Of these, about 47 percent were Galicians, 49 percent from Russian Poland, and only 4 percent from German Poland. As World War I approached, the percentage from the Russian areas increased, thus in 1913 66 percent came from Russian-occupied Poland, 32 percent from Galicia, and only 2 percent from German-occupied lands. The "typical" Pole who migrated between 1870 and 1900 was male, single, aged 14 to 44, and an agricultural laborer. Between 1899 and 1913 two-thirds of those who came were males, while even as late as 1913 55 percent were single. Most listed their occupations as unskilled workers and planned to return home with the money they earned to buy land and make a better life within their native country. Once established in America, however, most became sufficiently comfortable to remain so that only one in four actually returned to *Stary Kraj*—the Old Country.[17]

Although 64.5 percent of the immigrants had been engaged in agriculture in Poland, almost 90 percent settled in urban, industrial areas where they obtained jobs as unskilled laborers in factories. Others who resided outside the major urban centers often found positions in mining or the many small industries that covered New England and the Middle Atlantic states. Of those who chose to remain in agriculture, some located in the Connecticut Valley and upstate New York, but most settled in the midwestern states of Michigan, Wisconsin, Illinois and Indiana, where farmland was less expensive. "In comparative terms," Zeitlin noted, "Poles in agriculture proved to be the leading group of new immigrants in the rural areas of the United States and concentrated themselves overwhelmingly in the North-Central and Prairie states."[18]

How Many Came to America?

While much is known about the composition of Polish migration, one question still debated is the actual number of those who came. According to one estimate based on immigration and census records, between 1897 and 1913 U.S. officials counted some 2 million Poles coming into the United States, with the peak year being 1913, when 174,365 immigrants arrived from Poland. By 1918 the largest group of Polish Americans was concentrated in Chicago, with a population of some 400,000. Three of every four who journeyed across the Atlantic came to the United States, and in 1920, of the 1,335,957 Poles living abroad, fully two-thirds (820,595) lived in the United States. This represented 45 percent of the total Slavic immigration between 1899 and 1914.[19]

These numbers, however, are much in dispute. The U.S. census did not record national origin until 1820, and even then unnaturalized immigrants were not counted. Also, prior to 1885 the Bureau of Immigration did not list Poland as an option for "country of birth" since the nation did not "officially" exist. In practice, Poles entering the country were generally classified as Germans (or Prussians), Austrians, or Russians, and only rarely did a particularly insistent Pole manage to have himself recorded by his actual ethnicity.[20] This problem was further complicated by the fact that the Bureau of Immigration was not consistent over time, sometimes reporting all entrants together as a lump sum, sometimes reporting immigrants separately from visitors and other nonimmigrants, sometimes ignoring departures, and sometimes recording departures and even comparing them with original intent upon entry.[21]

Yet even when "Poland" was used as a "country of birth," the figures could be misleading. Poland contained many people who would not consider themselves Poles in the cultural sense. In 1897, for example, Russian Poland contained 64.6 percent Poles, 12.1 percent Jews, 6 percent Russians, 4 percent Germans, 3 percent Lithuanians, and varying numbers of Tatars, Bohemians, Rumanians, Estonians, Gypsies, and Hungarians. It was a truly multiethnic area, thus not everyone listing "Poland" was necessarily "Polish."[22]

The most comprehensive study of this question was published by Helena Lopata in 1976. Lopata made extensive use of the original immigration rolls that differentiate between "country of birth" and "race or people." She found that by using data from the "race or people" category, the highest number of Poles coming in a single year was 174,365 in 1913. Between 1899 and 1932, again based on "race or people," 1,443,473 Poles arrived and 294,824 returned to Poland for a net gain of 1,148,649. Lopata adds to this those listed by "country of birth" from 1885 to 1898 and from 1933 to 1972, when no separate list of "race or people" was maintained, a total of 641,502. By adding these, the maximum number of Poles arriving between 1885 and 1972 would be 1,780,151. In addition, there were 297,590 who arrived and later left, and 669,392 nonimmigrants and temporary residents identified as Poles.[23] Regardless of the specific number, Polish immigration was significant and was based primarily on economic causes.

The Polish American Community

The arrival of hundreds of thousands of Poles, most of whom settled in groups in the northeastern portion of the United States, created a distinct cultural presence. Most early scholars studying the Polish immigrant settlements in America concluded that the dramatic move from an agrarian, preindustrial society to a modern industrial setting involved a tremendous dislocation resulting in the destruction of traditional peasant culture and the assimilation of a new value system emphasizing "materialism, individualism, and progress." The Polish immigrants of the mass migration, Jerzy Jedlicki explained, "had not only jumped an ocean, they had also jumped a century—from a self-subsistent peasant economy to a capitalist job market—and for this they had to pay a high price of uncertainty, of lack of security, and of homesickness."[24]

The earliest comprehensive study of these Poles, which set the standard for describing Polonia for two generations, was the pioneering sociological work of William I. Thomas and Florian Znaniecki, *The Polish Peasant in Europe and America* (1927). After an extensive study of immigrant letters and other materials, Thomas and Znaniecki concluded that Polish communities in America suffered from "social disorganization," were in a state of decline, and would soon expire. Modern scholars, however, argue that this view of Polish American communities was inaccurate and failed to take into account the nature of the traditional Polish cultural elements that persisted in America.[25]

Polish peasant writer Władysław Orkan explained that "to outside observers the peasant mass appears as a solidly homogeneous class. Very little is known about the existence in this mass of hierarchical laminations similar to those occurring in the world of dresscoats and tuxedoes. The peasant society, meanwhile, like the urban one, possesses in its midst its own hereditary or monetary aristocracy, then a numerous class of moderately well-off yeomen and finally, scorned by both, the landless, often homeless and hungry mass, toiling away in sweat and misery."[26] In the same manner, those who first viewed the new Polish communities in America did not fully understand either the complexity of immigrant society or the degree to which its values and organization represented an ordered adaptation of Polish rural culture to the demands of an urban industrial society.

One of the most pervasive and important cultural values that Poles brought with them from *Stary Kraj* was a deeply held religious faith, a faith shaped by the adversity of national partition during which Catholicism became a symbol of resistance to the partitioning powers. The local parish was the central religious, social, and sometimes political institution in the lives of the Polish peasantry. Church attendance was not only a religious experience, it was a sign of patriotism and a means of acquiring status through participation. Aside from the obvious religious nature of the parish, it was a central social focus of village life. Both religious and national holidays were occasions for parish celebrations, the local priests provided a safe venue for the transmission of religious and national heritage, and the parish provided a central focus for village identity.[27] "The Catholic Church was the one institution common to all three partitions," observed William Galush, "and it served to differentiate Poles from their mostly non-Catholic conquerors. Priests in the German and Russian partitions promoted the Polish language and culture against hostile authorities, while under the more liberal regime of the Catholic Austrians the clergy inculcated a sense of Polishness, though not an overt Polish nationalism."[28]

In America, the early Polish settlers usually attended Irish and German parishes until they were able to form their own. This process generally began with the creation of a lay committee to raise funds and lobby with the bishop for the establishment of a Polish parish. When sufficient numbers and funds were present, the request was usually granted, a parish officially approved, and a priest appointed to lead the flock. The founding of the parish, in turn, led to the creation of additional societies to raise funds for church projects and to provide for the various needs of members. Chief among these were organizations providing financial insurance for illness and death, and fund-raising activities for the establishment of a parish school.[29]

The Poles brought with them from *Stary Kraj* a strong association between Polish nationalism and Catholicism. Thus, the role of the pastor as both religious and civic leader was often undisputed in the immigrant generation. "Not only was he generally better educated than the immigrant Polish peasant," Theresita Polzin explained, but he was also "the spokesman for God and had to be revered to the point of having his hand kissed in respect. Although the advantages of his office (such as better living accommodations) were sometimes resented, the priest was held in high esteem. The parish and the school were the core of the ethnic community, and, for the immigrant, the pastor's word was final in settling disputes and solving problems whether the persons involved were within the settlement or members of the outgroup."[30]

The parish was indeed the core of the Polish community in America, as it had been in Poland. It provided not only religious benefits but served as a focus for social activity, promoted Polish nationalism, and acted as an intermediary with the unfamiliar ways of American society. One of the chief means of transmitting both religious and cultural values was through the parish school. Polish immigrants generally viewed American public education with suspicion, considering it both anti-religious and anti-Polish. Consequently, Poles were willing to dig deep into their meager resources to support parish schools as guardians of their traditional values. Most early schools offered education only through the sixth or eighth grade, classes were generally taught in Polish, and the curriculum was heavily laced with religion and Polish history. English was taught as a foreign language. But the purpose of the parish school was *not* to speed assimilation; rather, its goal was to preserve religious and cultural traditions. In this, it proved to be the key factor in preserving Polish heritage, religious values, and social and family discipline.[31]

Once the parish, the school, and the religious societies were firmly established, Polish American communities inevitably developed a comprehensive system of secular organizations to address various community and individual needs. In some cases the development of secular societies resulted from feelings that the parish priest was too powerful, but most of the early secular organizations originated with the priest's blessing to meet real community needs.[32]

"Organizational participation," as Greenstone noted, "linked the immigrants and their children with their European traditions, and simultaneously meant

The Society of St. Kazimierz, gathered around Rev. Teofil Szadziński in Rochester, New York, was typical of early immigrant voluntary associations whose purpose it was to construct and support parish churches as centers of community religious and social life.

acquiring the organizational skills, attitudes, and perspectives and the interpretation of social reality necessary for acting collectively for long-term objectives." Ethnic organizations provided immigrants with opportunities for leadership roles and status within the ethnic community that they could not otherwise achieve among the dominant group, but in doing so they also retarded assimilation and social mobility within the general American community.[33]

In Poland, the rural peasantry identified closely with their village or region. In America, the same phenomenon can be observed in various forms. First, the loyalties from *Stary Kraj* were often transplanted to American soil. One trait that was transplanted was a status structure based on the partitioning of Poland. Poles from the German-occupied area enjoyed the highest prestige, partially because as a group they migrated the earliest and had initial control over most of the major organizations and parishes, and partially because they came from the most "westernized" part of Poland, which had a higher standard of living and education. Next were those from the Congress Kingdom (Russian Poland), followed by Galician (Austrian) Poles, who had the highest rate of illiteracy and the lowest income levels. Those from Galicia referred to their compatriots from the Russian and German sections by the derogatory terms *Moskali* and *Prusaki,* while they themselves were called *Galicjaki.*[34]

There were similar cleavages based on the regional subculture. The *Górale Podhalańscy,* the "Podhale mountaineers," for example, traditionally considered themselves quite different culturally and socially from other Poles. They took pride in their own distinctive cultural practices, physiognomy, economy, and dialect. They generally referred to other Poles with the derogatory appellation *ceper,* or "plainsman."[35]

Nor were these differences superficial; they were meaningful differentiations to people used to viewing anyone outside the local rural village as an outsider. There were cultural and linguistic variations from region to region, and in America those from one group tended to live with others from the same group in separate sections of urban areas, or within particular areas of a Polish neighborhood. Disagreements, often punctuated by violent outbursts, frequently broke out between the various groups, and social contacts were often limited by these cultural barriers. As a resident of Pittsburgh recalled, "One time I was going with a girl from Galicia. Her parents broke it up because we were from Congress." It was a frequent occurrence.[36]

One of the more important elements in the ethnic community, both in Poland and in America, was honor. William I. Thomas and Florian Znaniecki equated the important peasant concept of "honor" with the American concept of "social opinion." The worldview of the peasant seldom reached beyond the local community in rural Poland. Similarly, in America the unit of social identification, beyond the family, was the *okolica,* or neighborhood, the area where one's reputation was known. Community opinion was extremely important, and the force of public opinion was usually sufficient to contain any excesses. Public disapproval was a serious social penalty.[37]

The community or neighborhood was extremely important as a unit of identification. Polish American settlements were generally both segregated and decentralized. Poles were segregated in that they tended to live together in specific areas or wards of cities where they were found in large numbers. They were decentralized in that they were dispersed around larger cities in areas that were often not contiguous. Poles generally identified closely with their parish, telling those who inquired that they were from "Stanisławowo" (St. Stanislaus) or "Wojciechowo" (St. Adalbert). To say this implied not just a church but an entire neighborhood, an identifiable community within the anonymity of the urban center. More often than not, one's job, social activities, school, and virtually all other facets of life took place within the confines of the urban neighborhood. A report on Buffalo in 1910 concluded that the Poles "are in the Buffalo community, but they are not of it. They have their own churches, their own stores and business places, their own newspapers. They are content to live alone, and the rest of the population generally knows little about them and cares less."[38]

Research indicates that Polish Americans traditionally value "security, stability, order, and respectability" more than "progress." By developing their own self-sustaining ethnic communities they fulfilled these needs, while at the same time providing avenues for success and "progress" within the ethnic neighborhood in-group. In such a self-sustaining community they were protected from overt discrimination by non-Poles, while at the same time able to "achieve" in symbolic terms based on the rural culture of their origin—being active in the church and community, holding leadership positions in organizations, and owning their own home.[39]

The development of the self-sustaining ethnic community had another effect as well—it greatly retarded immigrant acculturation into American life. In fact, there was really no compelling reason to learn English unless one aspired to move beyond the ethnic community. As Adam Raczkowski wrote from New Britain, Connecticut, in 1906, "I find very little use for it [English]. My fellow workers are Polish, my landlord is Polish, I hear Mass on Sundays in Polish, I read the Polish newspaper and I even buy my food from a store owned by a fellow countryman."[40] Indeed, the Polish communities in Chicago, Buffalo, New York, and elsewhere came close to being complete, self-contained units.

Polish Family Life

Polish family life in America closely mirrored that in rural Poland. In the agrarian economy of *Stary Kraj,* the family was the basic economic and social unit. Poles lived in an extended family system with the eldest male the acknowledged leader of the family group. As an economic unit, there was a division of labor within the family based upon sex, age, and family status. Socially, the interdependence of individuals within the family led to the subordination of individual needs to those of the family group. Although each family member was entitled to personal respect, the individual was considered part of a unit, and success or failure was linked to family status. Thus, as Janice Kleeman noted, "The honor and status of the family were of the highest priority in the peasant value system."[41]

Social control occurred through peer pressure, the threat of gossip, and religious proscriptions enforced by the local parish priest. Separation and divorce were viewed as socially and religiously unacceptable, resulting in very stable family structures.[42] Within the family and the rural community there was an unquestioned "obedience to the church which not only provided norms for individual and social conduct, but also meaningfully integrated and rural economy through its liturgical cycles of recurring feasts and fasts; an inseparable linking of the ethnic with the religious (almost an identification) so that what was Polish was sacred—a major influence against mixed marriages, whether ethnic or religious."[43]

Early researchers, in keeping with the social disintegration theory of Thomas and Znaniecki, maintained that traditional Polish family life was not transplanted to America, leading to a deterioration of values and individual relationships. In fact, much of the essence of the close extended family structure *was* adapted to American needs, including the relationship between family and religious life. Various researchers, as well as the original U.S. census rolls, indicate that Polish families in America frequently contained aunts, uncles, grandparents, in-laws, and other relatives within a single household unit. In other cases, although portions of families resided in separate homes, they lived in proximity to one another and maintained traditional family ties. "If they were not pure extended families," Polzin explained, "it was generally only because of conditions, and not because of lack of interest or intent. Some members of the family stayed behind to tend the family lands in Poland. A shortage of money often curtailed the number of people from a family who could migrate. Once they arrived, many sent money back so that the rest of the family could come. Nevertheless, the modified extended family did exist."[44]

Although families were sometimes separated because of financial circumstances, further proof exists to show the permanence of the extended family bonds within Polish America. The oft-documented propensity of Polish Americans to write to relatives in Poland is indicative that extended ties were not broken by migration. In fact, over a period of years, as finances allowed, relatives and friends from *Stary Kraj* were gradually brought to America and the extended family reunited.

Another indication of these continuing effects is the financial tie between the New and Old Worlds, often made at great sacrifice to the immigrants. Between 1900 and 1906, Polish immigrants in America sent money orders to relatives and friends in the Congress Kingdom and Galicia alone totaling an astounding $69,041,227. This did not include money sent in cash or taken home by people returning to Europe to live or to visit. It is estimated that returning migrants brought to Galicia an average of $850 per person.[45]

The large families and high birth rates of the immigrant and second generation are also traceable to rural Polish origins, where numbers were an advantage on the land, large families tended to bring increased status, and religious teachings considered children to be a "blessing from God." In the rural agrarian economy of the Old Country, where most immigrants originated, large extended families were the basic economic unit and every member had specific functions to perform for the overall survival of the group. In America, this same tradition allowed Polish families to adapt to the demands of the factory system. Despite the surface changes, the family remained the central economic unit. Maintaining financial stability was a family affair. Men, women, and children all contributed in one form or another, pursuing what Ewa Morawska calls "penny capitalism," the accumulation of funds to meet family goals.[46]

The adult male family members were expected to work outside the family home. For some men who had been independent farmers, this was a serious change. Accustomed to being the authority figure in the family economic unit, to giving orders and making decisions, they now had to adjust to taking orders while being excluded from any decision-making role at work. This loss of status sometimes led to a loss of self-esteem and self-worth, an increase in alcoholism, and increased authoritarianism at home. Most men had to take jobs as unskilled workers. With wage scales for unskilled labor at very low levels, most families could not exist on the income of a single wage earner. Thus, women took on a new role in the immigrant household in America.

Polish women in America were expected to fulfill the traditional Old World roles of keeping house, sewing, cooking, and caring for children. Within the household, in fact, women generally wielded considerable influence. According to research by John Bodnar, "Women were simply preeminent at home and assumed a wide range of responsibilities including management of family finances."[47] Usually women were responsible for the family budget, serving as a fiscal manager to whom the father and children relinquished their pay. The female was also usually responsible for the family garden, using the produce to supplement the family diet or to sell or barter outside the home. Women also "made bread, butter, cheese and noodles, canned food for the winter, pickled and marinated, sewed and wove in order to minimize the costs of existence." Morawska estimates that this activity reduced family expenditures by $5–6 per month.[48] "Well," one immigrant explained, "if your wife was thrifty, she baked at home, kept chickens in the garden, sewed for the children—you did not spend too much then because everything was so cheap—if you had other people working in the family and if you did not drink in bars and saved your money, you could get somewhere like buy a house."[49]

In Poland, women were discouraged from working outside the home lest they acquire a negative "reputation." In America, however, the necessity of earning additional income forced an accommodation to this traditional prohibition. As soon as women began migrating in large numbers they were forced to seek employment outside the home as unskilled workers, domestics, factory operatives, and service workers to supplement the family income. In many cases Polish households in America began taking in boarders—first single relatives and then expanding to include nonrelatives. Though frowned on in Poland and generally not an option of choice in America, renting spare rooms to boarders could be lucrative. In fact, Poles had a higher percentage of households with boarders or lodgers than any other European ethnic group, some 48.4 percent as compared with an average of 32.9 percent.[50]

In some instances a spare room was rented out to a friend or newcomer to increase the family income. In extreme cases, where a family owned a large home, it was sometimes more financially desirable to rent space to several boarders. In these cases the female usually did not seek work outside the home but acted as a housekeeper, purchasing food, cooking meals, washing and mending clothes, and otherwise operating what amounted to a small hotel. Workers often paid $2.50 to $3.00 per week for boarding arrangements, which could greatly increase a family's income. In Johnstown, Pennsylvania, where more than half of the Polish American homes had boarders in 1900, the average number of boarders was five. This yielded a monthly income of $20–25, more than the wife could earn by working outside the home. The boarding system also provided security from the fluctuations of illness and seasonal lay-offs.[51]

In families where the wages of two working parents were often barely enough to support a subsistence level of existence, children were also called on to contribute to family finances. In rural Poland children were an economic asset, additional workers who could do household chores and contribute in the fields once they matured. In industrial America this tradition continued, with children expected to assist by caring for boarders, taking jobs in factories, or helping in the family store when a family was fortunate enough to own its own business. All too often economic necessity required that children leave school at an early age to earn money for the support of the family. Older children who worked were expected to turn their money over to the family, and were generally given an allowance of a few cents a week for candy or entertainment. Twelve-year-old Mary Yukenevich worked in a tailor shop, she said, "because I wanted to help my mother and father." Helen Hosey explained child work in terms of the traditional Polish family bonds: "You took care of one another. You never questioned it. In our family we never expected anything in return. It was the honor that we had. The trust—that's why we all felt so close to each other. There was no house divided here."[52] In Johnstown, Pennsylvania, 80 percent of Slavic children dropped out of school after the sixth grade. By age 15, nearly all male children were employed, earning $10–25 per month. Young females worked as maids or servants or in the mills earning $4–17 per month.[53] As a result, the sons and daughters of the immigrant generation generally obtained only a rudimentary education and followed their parents into the mills and mines that first lured their ancestors across the Atlantic. Education levels and social mobility were thus seriously inhibited in the second generation.

With this strategy of collective family action, Polish American families were successful in providing a better life for their members. Thus there is ample evidence that Polish rural family life was indeed transplanted to America, serving as a stabilizing factor in immigrant life and adaptation. This can be seen in the hierarchical family structures with the father as head, the maintenance of extended families, the expectation that children would contribute to the family finances, the close control of contact between sexes, the maintenance of close family relationships, and the recognition of the parish as the center of religious, community, and familial relationships.

Status, Property, and Other Cultural Values

There were also other examples of the transplantation of Polish cultural values to America. In peasant Poland, there was a direct relationship between status and land ownership. Although there was little opportunity or need to purchase large amounts of land in an urban industrial setting, the propensity of Poles to view ownership as a serious status symbol was also carried over into America. This can best be seen in the value of home ownership. In America, real property became a source of security and social prestige, replacing the ideal of land ownership in *Stary Kraj*. In 1930 a survey in Milwaukee revealed that 70 percent of Poles owned their own homes as compared with 63 percent of Czechs, 25 percent of Yugoslavs, and about 33 percent of English and Irish. A similar survey in Nanticoke, Pennsylvania, showed 57 percent of Poles owned their own homes compared with only 23 percent of native-born whites. In Cicero, Illinois, 67 percent of Poles were home owners compared with only 22 percent of native-born whites. Similar results were obtained in other areas.[54]

The transmission of values to America can also be seen in the focus on the dinner table. Polish peasants were accustomed to a restricted diet of cabbage, bread, noodles, and seasonal vegetables. To a large extent they measured their success in America by the amount and quality of the food on their tables. Although the staples of the Polish American diet remained as they were in rural Poland, the quantity and variety they enjoyed, even during the immigrant generation, led many to consider themselves lucky indeed. They often wrote home comparing their new situation with that of the *pan*, or gentry, in Poland. "Don't worry about me, 'cause I live here like a *pan*," wrote one immigrant to Galicia, while another explained that "In America . . . a pound of the fattest meat costs 3 and 4 cents, the leaner the more expensive, a pound of sausage 3 cents. I am a *pan* here."[55]

Finally, the transplanting of Polish rural values can be seen in the goal of migration. Poles migrated to the United States for a "better life." Wincenty Witoś, prime minister of the Polish Republic between the two World Wars, observed that in Poland a "better life" was measured in concrete terms. The "worth of a man was measured by the number of acres, horses and cows, by the quality of his land, his pastures and his family background. Very important [also were] prosperity, honors and ability. The *gospodarze* (yeomen) always had first and best pews in church, in the tavern and in the *gmina* (village council). The *zagrodnicy* (petty landowners) tried to keep close to them, the *komornicy* (landless) walked on their tiptoes and the *parobki* (farmhands) were total slaves."[56]

St. Josaphat's church dominates the skyline of this typical working-class Polish American neighborhood in Milwaukee, Wisconsin. The neighborhood was referred to affectionately by the residents as "Josafatowo," a term that referred not only to the church but to an identifiable ethnic community. *Milwaukee Journal* photo.

In America, these measures of worth were transformed: home ownership replaced land ownership, family affluence the number of cows, accomplishments such as organizational leadership roles the size and quality of farm buildings. The other criteria remained essentially the same in the urban industrial society. In Europe the Polish peasant defined his existence as part of a family, a community, a religious organization, and an organizational presence. In America it was the same.[57]

Far from being ambiguous masses, Polish American communities had a well-defined status structure. At the top were the ethnic merchants who assumed the role of the wealthy upper class in immigrant society. Next in rank order were the skilled workers and owners of small businesses whose income and job status ranked below the larger merchants, but well above the unskilled workers and others in society. The unskilled workers, miners, and day laborers ranked as the poor class in both economic and social terms. Aside from one's job, status within Polonia depended on the interplay of several factors, including length of residence in America, involvement in ethnic organizations, participation in church and public activities, economic standing, and education (defined by literacy and familiarity with Polish heritage).[58]

The average Polish American community of the immigrant generation was thus focused on Old World institutions, including the parishes and various mutual aid societies, around which developed ethnic organizations, newspapers, schools, clubs, and other associations. The ethnic communities were vigorous, structured societies providing for the needs of their members through means compatible with both their European heritage and the demands of the urban American environment. The lives of the immigrants were not easy—fraught with marginal economic existence, overcrowded housing, limited socioeconomic mobility, discrimination, and other ambiguities. Yet, as one immigrant wrote, "Although my standard of living . . . was at its lowest compared with the American standards, it was splendid compared with that in the old country."[59]

three

Unity and Disunity: The Organization of Polonia, 1880–1914

Both the political exiles of the antebellum period and the economic immigrants of the late nineteenth century discovered the need to obtain news from the homeland and other Polish American settlements and to organize to meet the demands of daily life. Initially, responses to both needs grew at the local level with the publication of newspapers and the organization of various local societies. Inevitably, some of these local initiatives led to regional and national efforts to communicate and organize. While some succeeded, differences over religious and political views just as often doomed such efforts.

The Polish Press in America

One of the most important features of the Polish American community was the development of a Polish-language press. "In those days regard for the printed word was great among peasants as it was not easy to arrive at this secret," explained Władysław Orkan.[1] The Polish press was thus viewed as an authority on virtually any subject and played an important and varied role within the Polish community. Its pages provided local news and information from Poland for people unable to speak English, carried organizational news, imparted information about American customs, laws, and naturalization procedures, and generally assisted in the adjustment of immigrants to their new environment. In this sense, the Polish press was an agent of education and of change.[2]

Polish newspapers began to flourish in the 1870s. In 1893 Henryk Nagiel surveyed the Polish press and found that 105 periodicals had appeared since *Echo z Polski* began publishing in 1863. Half were still being published in 1893. "Unlike the first publications of the political refugees who concentrated on Poland's survival and European politics," Jan Kowalik explained, "the immigrant press of the later period dealt with adaptation problems, served the community interests, and were determined to operate on a sound financial basis. In order to reach the farmer and factory worker, it had to lower the literary niveau [or standard] and tailor the content to its readers' needs and likings. Although most of the papers were typographically poorly outfitted and some lacked even the diacritical markings of the Polish alphabet, they did more than their share to educate the often illiterate immigrant masses and promote their ethnic and religious self-consciousness."[3]

Polonia contained a plethora of perspectives, and the Polish American press mirrored these various viewpoints. Among the most influential nineteenth century newspapers was Chicago's *Gazeta Polska* (Polish Gazette), whose editor, Władysław Dyniewicz, did much to popularize the press among early immigrants. The weeklies *Zgoda* (Harmony) and *Naród Polski* (Polish Nation) served as the house organs of the Polish National Alliance and the Polish Roman Catholic Union, respectively, with a combined circulation in excess of 100,000 copies. The Polish Women's Alliance published *Głos Polek* (Polish Women's Voice) beginning in 1910.[4]

Many of the early influential newspapers enjoyed religious backing. These included *Polak w Ameryce* (Pole in America), founded by Rev. Jan Pitass in Buffalo in 1887 and edited by Stanisław Ślisz; *Gazeta Katolicka* (Catholic Gazette), published by Ladislaus Smulski in Chicago beginning in 1880; and *Orzeł Polski* (Polish Eagle), edited by Rev. Aleksander Matuszek and Ignacy Wendziński in Missouri beginning in 1870. The latter lasted only two years, but was replaced by *Pielgrzym* (Pilgrim), published and edited by Jan Barzyński, which subsequently became the respected *Gazeta Polska Katolicka* (Polish Catholic Gazette) in Detroit.[5]

One of the leading liberal, anti-clerical publications was *Ameryka-Echo* (America-Echo), founded in Toledo by Antoni Paryski in 1889. Often referred to as the "Polish Hearst," Paryski was a talented individual who popularized folk literature while at the same time engaging in "yellow journalism." Paryski produced hundreds of thousands of copies of books, pamphlets, and other publications that his traveling agents sold throughout Polonia. Other anti-clerical publications included such journals as the weekly *Gwiazda Polarna* (Northern Star), the New York organ of the Polish Socialist Alliance in America, *Robotnik Polski* (Polish Worker), and the leftist *Dziennik Ludowy* (People's Daily), which later became *Głos Ludowy* (People's Voice), published by the Polish Bureau of the Communist Party of the United States.[6]

The first Polish daily in the United States was *Kuryer Polski* (Polish Courier), founded in Milwaukee in 1888 by Michał Kruszka. To counter the influence of *Ameryka-Echo* and *Kuryer Polski*, the Resurrectionists in Chicago founded *Dziennik Chicagoski* (Chicago Daily News) in 1890, one of the best and most popular of Polish papers. Another popular publication was Detroit's *Dziennik Polski* (Polish Daily News).[7]

The *Polish American Journal* was the first English-language Polish American newspaper with nationwide appeal. Gradually, as the second generation gave way to the third, many publications followed the lead of Kruszka's *Kuryer Polski*, which added an English-language supplement in 1939 to appeal to Polish Americans of the younger generations.[8]

The Polish press provided immigrants in America with valuable information, keeping them in touch with *Stary Kraj* and assisting them in their transition to American society. In addition, it served to educate Polonia, increasing ethnic self-awareness and informing public opinion.

The Role of the Fraternal

During the second half of the nineteenth century, an indigenous mutual aid movement swept Poland. Political leaders of the time referred to it as "organic work." According to Aleksander Świętochowski, a leader in the movement, "We want to extend work and learning in society to discover new resources, to utilize existing ones, and to concern ourselves with our own problems and not those of others."[9] This movement had its counterpart in America, where Polish immigrants found that collective action through the pooling of human and financial resources was effective in constructing churches, establishing schools, meeting unexpected expenses such as funerals, and providing for community needs. Thus, Polish American organizations, whether religious or secular in nature, were strongly imbued with mutual aid and benefit as their guiding principles.

The first mutual aid societies were usually formed to provide death benefit insurance, since the funeral expenses and loss of income attending a death could be devastating to an immigrant family living a marginal economic existence. Many of these were formed along regional lines by people originating in the same village or region in Poland. This provided the immigrants with the familiarity of an Old World organization, while at the same time offering an "opportunity to invest in their own future."[10]

Once established, these societies generally grew rapidly and expanded their activities to include provision of health insurance, community service, and fundraising for the parish or the homeland. Quite often a building and loan fund was established to assist members in the purchase of homes. Edward Kantowicz explained that in Chicago, "An association member made regular payments of fifty cents or a dollar per week for a number of years to build up a down payment, and the association supplemented this accumulation with a low interest loan when the member actually purchased his home. By 1900, Polish building and loan societies held assets approaching one million dollars."[11] Thus, the insurance fraternal eventually became, in the words of Frank Renkiewicz, the primary agency of "communal capitalism" and the foremost "institutional response of Poles to the challenge of an industrializing America."[12]

Polish American organizations provided social and economic support for people in their adaptation to American life. The initial Polish American organizations, whether religious or secular, focused on concern for the homeland and local issues of everyday life. There were attempts, beginning with the exiles from the November Uprising in the 1830s, to form a unified national organization, but none of these were permanently successful. By the mid-1860s Chicago was already the largest Polish settlement in America. Because of this, and the large concentration of Poles in a small geographic area, there were several movements to unify Chicago Poles into a single umbrella organization. These efforts were largely fruitless not only because the community was divided into myriad local societies but also because there was a deep division between nationalist and clerical factions.

Led by Władysław Dyniewicz, publisher of Chicago's first Polish newspaper and head of the *Gmina Polska* (Polish Commune) society, the nationalists were a secular group who believed that *all* Poles should be organized into a central association to work for the independence of the homeland. They also supported the creation of lay councils to oversee the operations of the local parishes. The clerical faction, led by Peter Kiołbassa, head of the St. Stanislaus Kostka Society, also favored independence for the homeland, but they equated the essence of what it meant to be a Pole—*Polskość*—with Catholicism and objected to the inclusion of socialists, Jews, schismatics, and nonbelievers.[13]

Bitter quarrels raged between the two groups as each attempted to gain control of Chicago Polonia. In the early years the nationalists predominated, but in 1871 the Resurrectionists, a Catholic religious order that included a strong Polish presence, negotiated an agreement with Bishop Thomas Foley to administer all nondiocesan Polish parishes for the succeeding 99 years. They became strong allies of Kiołbassa's clerical faction, providing it with the authority and resources to displace the nationalists as the more influential group. Under Rev. Wincenty Barzyński's leadership between 1874 and 1899, 19 Polish parishes were established in the Chicago area, with the Resurrectionists controlling each one. In further moves to consolidate the clerical position, Barzyński established a "Parish Bank" that held savings deposits and issued loans, and assisted in founding the influential *Dziennik Chicagoski* (Chicago Daily News) in 1889 to support the clerical and Resurrectionist position.[14]

The lack of any lay organizational structure beyond the parish level was a detriment to the solidification of religious influence over the immigrant community. To fill this void and to spread clerical influence even further, Rev. Theodore Gieryk founded in 1873 an organization designed to promote *Polskość* on the national level. Gieryk initially envisioned this organization, which adopted the name *Zjednoczenie Polskie Rzymsko-Katolickie* (Polish Roman Catholic Union; PRCU), as open to all. His primary supporters, Resurrectionist Father Wincenty Barzyński and his brother, Jan, lay editor of *Pielgrzym* (Pilgrim), insisted that membership be restricted to Poles loyal to Roman Catholicism. The Barzyńskis triumphed when the official constitution fused religion and nationalism, as emphasized in its motto, "Bóg i Ojczyzna" (God and Fatherland). The constitution called for maintenance of the faith, mutual aid, and cultural improvement, requiring members to be loyal to their priests and bishops.[15]

With its headquarters first in Detroit and later in Chicago, the PRCU was closely controlled by the Polish clergy, with its primary aim being the preservation of *Polskość* through maintenance of clerical control over immigrant communities.[16] The PRCU was closely tied not only to the clergy but to local parishes. In its early years it promoted the founding of parish schools, supervised the establishment of loan associations, and assisted with the founding of parish libraries. On the national level it funded a hospital, seminary, and convent and published a weekly Catholic newspaper, *Gazeta Katolicka* (Catholic Gazette).[17]

Initially, the debate between exclusivity and inclusiveness continued within the PRCU. In 1875, at its Third Congress, the PRCU formally voted to remain "Roman Catholic." With this, as Renkiewicz concluded, the PRCU was "dedicated first of all to the protection of the immigrant and the preservation of Roman Catholicism" and therefore lacked a truly national focus.[18]

As the dominance of the clerical element in Chicago spread under the influence of the Resurrectionists and the Polish Roman Catholic Union, the nationalist faction became increasingly determined to regain its former position of dominance in Chicago Polonia. In 1879 its leaders appealed to Agaton Giller, a prestigious Polish exile then residing in Switzerland, to use his influence to establish an umbrella organization for all Polonia. "In the spirit of organic work," Renkiewicz explained, "they concluded that the Polish nation would be best served through education, social and economic progress, unification, and integration into American political life of all immigrants. Presumably a prosperous and partially acculturated immigration would be the basis for national political revival when conditions justified direct action."[19]

Giller responded by publishing in the Polonia press "An Open Letter to the Poles in America," advocating a single, national, all-inclusive Polish American organization. Appealing to Polish patriotism, his letter read, in part, "Having become morally and patriotically uplifted by the fact that we have unified ourselves, the major task before a Polish organization must be to help our people attain a good standard of living in America. For, when the masses of Poles in America simply by their very presence in the country, reflect the good name of Poland to all whom they meet, they will be providing an enormously important service to Poland. In time this service to Poland will be even greater as Poles begin to exert influence upon the political life of the United States."[20]

Encouraged by Giller's initiative, and growing discontent with exclusive clerical control of the PRCU, nationalist leaders met at the home of Juliusz Andrzejkowicz in Philadelphia in 1880 and ultimately formed the *Związek Narodowy Polski* (Polish National Alliance, or PNA), a fraternal society organized along the lines of the Polish organic movement. The fundamental question that divided the PRCU and the PNA was the definition of *Polskość*. While the PRCU maintained that Polishness and Catholicism were inextricably linked, the PNA held, in the tradition of the old Polish-Lithuanian Commonwealth, that *anyone* born in Poland who supported the national cause should be admitted to membership. Consequently, it admitted all who sought membership, regardless of their religious or political views. Composed mostly of Roman Catholics, its membership included socialists, Jews, nonbelievers, and others whose beliefs were antithetical to the PRCU, as well as Lithuanians, Ukrainians, and other ethnic groups included in the geographic boundaries of the old commonwealth.[21]

These differences were best described by Edward Kantowicz, who explained that "The PNA was a nationalist organization, directed by political emigres from Poland who worked as a sort of Polish 'Zionist' force for the liberation of the motherland from the partitioning powers. PNA leaders considered the American Polish colonies to be a 'fourth province of Poland.' The Alliance's leaders were laymen, its policies at least mildly anti-clerical, and its membership open to Polish Jews, schismatics, and nonbelievers as well as Catholics. The PRCU, as its name implied, was a religious organization, open only to Catholics, dominated by the clergy, and dedicated primarily to the strengthening of Catholicism among the immigrant Poles."[22]

In short, the PRCU fought to preserve Roman Catholicism by resisting cultural assimilation into American society, while the primary goals of the PNA were to achieve the independence of the homeland and provide assistance to Polish immigrants in America. To achieve its goals, the PNA "sought to encourage at least some assimilation so as to gain influence in the United States in order to help Poland." Although the assimilating influence of each organization during this early period can be questioned, there is no doubt that the goals of the two organizations conflicted on several levels.[23]

Agaton Giller, a leading organizer among exiles in Europe, called on Poles in the United States to organize themselves to assist in the fight for Polish independence. His appeals led to the founding of the Polish National Alliance as an early umbrella group for local and regional Polish American organizations. Polish Institute of Arts and Sciences of America.

The administrative structure of the PNA was a prototype for other organizations to emulate. Ultimate authority rested in a diet, or *Sejm*, containing representatives from each individual lodge. As the name might indicate, the *Sejm* derived its general form and hierarchy of offices, with some modification, from the *Sejm* of the old Polish Republic. The officers included an elected president and an executive secretary charged with the daily functioning of the offices between meetings of the *Sejm* or the executive officers. Unique among the officers was a "censor" who presided at meetings of the *Sejm*. Renkiewicz described this position as "a kind of elected judge and constitutional monarch" who "headed a commission which judged the frequent disputes for power and representation, and saw to it that the Alliance and its publications remained true to their purposes." It was not an office designed to enforce "censorship" in the contemporary, restrictive connotation of that word.[24]

The PNA grew rapidly after its founding, incorporating as an insurance company in 1887 and moving its headquarters to Chicago in 1888. By 1894 the PNA included more than 200 lodges in 21 states. Largely because of its economic benefits, PNA membership increased quickly to more than 600 lodges in 25 states by 1905. By comparison, in the same year the PRCU numbered only 250 lodges in 18 states. The PNA continued to grow, reaching 1,670 lodges in 32 states by the early 1920s and 1,907 lodges by 1935. As its size grew, so did its assets. By 1900 the PNA commanded a net worth of $98,400, a figure that grew dramatically each decade thereafter: $1.1 million in 1910, $5.7 million in 1920, $20.3 million in 1930, $30.4 million in 1940, $56 million in 1950, and $170 million in 1980.[25]

The success of the PNA thwarted the aspirations of the PRCU to achieve hegemony over American Polonia. To counter the growing dominance of the PNA, the PRCU initiated in the 1880s a major structural reorganization, creating both a federation of local parish societies akin to the PNA lodges and an insurance option. Also mimicking its secular counterpart, the PRCU began publishing an official organ, *Wiara i Ojczyzna* (Faith and Fatherland) in 1887 and *Naród Polski* (Polish Nation) in 1897. After these changes the PRCU grew during the 1890s, but its financial base was hurt by the schism created when some parishes made a move for independence from the church in Rome, the depression of 1893–97, "ineffectual lay leadership, unrealistically low dues, and the practice of insuring wives through their husband members."[26] Thus, despite its willingness to adopt a new structure, the PRCU remained unable to overtake the PNA as the principal national Polish American organization.

The struggle for dominance between the PNA and PRCU in the 1880s and 1890s was a bitter one, punctuated by vicious editorials, legal actions, and sometimes violence. The clerical forces, led by Rev. Wincenty Barzyński of Chicago and Rev. Jan Pitass of Buffalo, attacked the PNA repeatedly over its inclusive definition of *Polskość*, labeling it a godless organization and at one time threatening excommunication to any Catholic who joined its ranks. The PNA struck back in kind, arguing in its weekly organ, ironically named *Zgoda* (Harmony), that the PRCU was not really interested in supporting the Polish national cause, only in promoting Catholicism.[27] In 1908 the PNA began publishing the daily *Dziennik Związkowy* (Alliance Daily News). The PRCU followed with the daily *Dziennik Zjednoczenia* (Union Daily News) in 1923.

The vicious attacks and counterattacks, coupled with the refusal of the PNA to exclude schismatics, atheists, Jews, anarchists, socialists, or masons, eventually led the moderate Catholic clergy, who hitherto supported the PNA, to withdraw their support as well. Led by Rev. Dominic Majer, the moderates founded the Polish National Union in 1889 as an alternative to the PNA and PRCU. This organization eventually split into the Polish Union of the United States, with headquarters in Wilkes-Barre, Pennsylvania, and the Polish Union of America, headquartered in Buffalo. Further defections occurred with the secession of the eastern Poles to form the Polish National Alliance of Brooklyn in 1903.[28]

The bitter rivalry between the PNA and PRCU prompted Erazmus Jerzmanowski, a wealthy New York businessman, to make a further attempt at forming a national umbrella organization in 1894. Viewed as an eastern challenge to the PNA, the movement failed, and most of its members joined the PNA of Brooklyn, the Association of the Sons of Poland in New Jersey, or other eastern organizations.[29]

"One for all—All for one" proclaims this banner of Polish Falcons Nest No. 37 in Lake, Illinois. The motto and its sentiments were popular among those who strived to organize Polonia into a unified ethnic community.

Although attempts to form a unified Polonia failed, a number of permanent national and regional organizations emerged to give Polonia structure and influence beyond the local ethnic community. In 1898 several women's groups in Chicago united into the *Związek Polek w Ameryce* (Polish Women's Alliance of America) under the leadership of Teofila Samolińska, Anna Newman, and Stefania Chmielińska. According to Renkiewicz, "They believed, first of all, that the emancipation, education, and protection of women would strengthen the nation and preserve Polishness through the influence of women upon the family and the rearing of children."[30] One result of this was that "within a decade of the founding of the Women's Alliance, the PNA and PRCU had revised their rules to admit women to full membership, elected women to their boards, and organized departments run by and for women."[31]

Another national organization to exert a permanent influence was the *Sokół Polski* (Polish Falcon) movement. The Union of Polish Falcons was founded in 1893 as an athletic and patriotic society not unlike the German *Turnverein* or the YMCA. Arguably the most patriotic and nationalistic of all Polish American fraternals, the Falcons were leaders in the movement to re-create an independent Poland, going so far as to introduce military training and advocate the formation of a separate Polish army to fight for Poland in Europe during World War I.[32]

Although a universal umbrella organization never materialized, and factionalism was often bitter between the contending groups, the fraternal movement was central to the health of Polonia. The best summary of the importance of the Polish American fraternal movement came from the pen of Frank Renkiewicz:

> The expansion of the fraternals was guided by some of Polonia's most talented men and women, individuals drawn largely at first from the small, progressive, educated middle classes who were born or reared in Poland. More interesting in the long run perhaps, the fraternals were often administered by persons with blue collar backgrounds or by women for whom such executive opportunities were not available in "American" society. They became schools in business management as well as channels to community leadership with important consequences for the future of Polonia's middle class. A recent study of top management in Chicago's major companies has documented the virtual absence of Polish Americans. They were less well represented even than the city's other major ethnic groups. Discrimination by the "establishment" was the natural explanation, but lack of interest within the ethnic group may have been equally or more important. The relative institutional completeness of Polonia, a fact for which the fraternals were heavily responsible, offered satisfying opportunities within the community. Ethnic communal capitalism was less a social trap than a trap door to improved status, and complaints in the 1970s of economic discrimination may reflect the ambitions of newer, more assimilated generations than they do the history of Poles in the United States.[33]

Religious Schisms

The most pervasive influence on the life of Polish immigrants in America during the period of mass migration was religion. In partitioned Poland, the Church transcended the boundaries of the three regions, providing both a unifying factor and a haven for the expression of Polish nationalism. In America, immigrants unfamiliar with the language or culture of their new environment relied on the familiarity of their deeply held religious convictions and institutions as a stabilizing element in their otherwise uncertain lives. In addition, in America, as in Poland, the local parish was central to the daily secular life of Poles, serving as a source of personal recognition and social interaction. The local parish priest functioned as spiritual father, temporal leader, priest, teacher, legal advisor, business advisor, and representative to the outside world of business, government, and society.[34]

In Poland there was a tradition of lay involvement in the founding of parishes. The *ius patronatus* was a long-established "right of patronage," under which a member of the gentry whose ancestors had endowed a parish "might nominate a pastor" to that parish. Although this right did not directly involve the parishioners, it was well known among Polish immigrants and established a precedent of lay involvement in parish affairs. As a result, most of the early Polish parishes in America were established by lay persons rather than by religious authorities. The normal scenario was for a lay committee to collect funds, purchase land, construct a building, and petition the local bishop for authorization to form a parish. A priest usually entered the picture some time after the first step.[35]

Once the lay committee received approval from the bishop, it was required to sign the title to the property and building over to the bishop. This the Poles usually did, "their desire for the re-creation of the primary homeland village institution usually triumphing over their sense of property rights."[36] The bishop then usually allowed several laymen to serve on a parish committee or board of trustees. Thus, most Polish parishes began with lay initiatives and continued to have lay involvement in the administration of parish affairs.

The Polish parish in America was a reflection of both Polish religious conviction and pride in collective accomplishment. The very extravagance of the buildings and furnishings of Polish American churches, standing as it did in sharp contrast to their spartan life, was a measure of the immigrants' joint success. Andrzej Brożek suggests that individual contributions to the local parish "became as important a source of prestige as land holdings had been in the Old Country."[37] By 1908 per capita church support among Poles in Chicago was $3.51, or $17.55 for a family of five. This was about one and a half weeks' wages for an unskilled worker, or about two months' rent in a tenement. The rate of Polish contributions was highest among the "new" immigrants. In fact, the proliferation of Polish parishes was evidence of the recent immigrants' importance in community life. In 1870 there were approximately 15 "Polish" parishes in America, a number that rose quickly to 75 in 1880, 170 in 1890, 330 in 1900, more than 500 by 1910, about 760 in 1920, and more than 800 in the 1930s.[38]

One difference between the Catholic Church in Poland and in America was that the latter was controlled by unsympathetic Irish and German bishops rather than conationalists, as in Poland. In fact, Polish Catholics generally received rather rude treatment from the American Catholic hierarchy and local priests, who displayed little understanding of the new arrivals, choosing instead to ignore them, or in some instances make them the focal point for derision and discrimination. As Polish immigration increased, however, the Catholic hierarchy quickly came to see that the Poles formed a large and growing percentage of Catholics in America, and as such some effort to retain their religious loyalty was in order. This became especially critical as the dispersal of Polish immigrants reduced the hold of Catholicism, while organized labor and other secular movements further eroded the influence of the Church. Rev. Wacław Kruszka estimated that through this "leakage" the Church lost as many as one-third of the immigrants.[39]

At the Third Plenary Council of Roman Catholic prelates in America in November 1884, Church authorities attempted to solidify their control over Catholics by decreeing that all American Catholics "should educate their children in parochial schools in order to protect them from Protestant and secular influences."[40] Bukowczyk noted that as a result of this decree the number of Polish American parochial schools increased between 1887 and 1914 from about 50 to almost 400, with student enrollments rising from 14,150 to 128,540. By the 1920s approximately two-thirds of all Polish American children were enrolled in parochial schools.[41]

In addition to mandating a parochial education for Catholic youth, Church leaders took other actions to maintain the loyalty of their Polish flock. In 1887 in Chicago, Victor Zaleski and Jan Radziejewski founded the aptly titled Roman Catholic newspaper *Wiara i Ojczyzna* (Faith and Fatherland), reflecting the basic assumption that the nature of *Polskość* inseparably linked Roman Catholicism and national identity.[42] Soon, other periodicals followed in most major immigrant communities.

Another policy adopted by the Church to maintain its influence over the ethnic communities was the creation of "national parishes." Under the general organizational structure in America, the Catholic hierarchy is arranged into parishes and diocese on a geographic basis. Thus, the national, or ethnic, parish was an exception. But it was an exception with some precedent. So-called "non-territorial" parishes were first sanctioned by the Fourth Lateran Council in the thirteenth century and later reaffirmed by the Council of Trent in the sixteenth century. Under this principle "parishes were organized not on the basis of numbers and locations but according to the particular character of the people or families requiring the service." In America, the "particular character" was usually indicated by language.[43]

By 1912 there were almost 1,600 "official" national parishes, including 346 German, 336 Polish, and 214 Italian. Bukowczyk, Kruszka, and others maintain that these numbers are vastly understated, with Kruszka citing a figure of 517 Polish parishes by 1900. Whatever the truth, from the perspective of the Catholic hierarchy the movement to establish national parishes was designed specifically to preserve the faith among immigrant communities. To the immigrants, however, the creation of the national parishes provided "a focus of group activity, preserved the group's ethnoreligious identity, and provided a means of passing on its language and culture to succeeding generations. The national parish was thus a compromise between the Church's interest in preventing the loss of adherents, and immigrants' concern with sustaining their religious and cultural heritage."[44]

Many Poles, however, were not satisfied with the largely symbolic nature of the national parish. In reality, Church authorities exerted strict control over the parishes, demanding title to all property, assigning priests, and otherwise denying any real lay participation in decision making. This seriously conflicted with the Poles' concept of lay involvement and the ideals of democracy and property ownership they equated with America. As their protests grew, Bishop Ignatius Horstmann of Cleveland asked: "Why is it that only the Poles cause trouble in this regard?" The answer lay in the "cultural baggage" that Poles brought from *Stary Kraj* and their concept of American democracy. Greenstone maintains that "the Poles were the most ethnically assertive among the Roman Catholic immigrant groups, since they found on arrival that 'their' church, in practical terms the most important Polish institution before 1918, was controlled in America by a foreign, particularly Irish, clergy and hierarchy."[45]

Most of the Poles' complaints involved their desire for democracy and equality in parish and Church governance. Since most parishes began through lay initiative, the Poles, relying for justification on both the Polish precedent of lay involvement and their view of American democracy, sought some control over parish finances, the right of parish councils to hold title to property purchased with the parishioners' money, and increased authority for the parish councils.[46]

The authoritarian rule of some priests, occasional charges of priestly financial mismanagement, and other local disputes often fueled the flames of dissent. In addition, Polish priests, often frustrated by lack of career mobility in the national parishes, voiced complaints over inequities in assignments and promotions. These grievances crystallized around the demand for appointment of Polish bishops. Not all of the Polish clergy supported this, but few, if any, opposed it.[47]

Rev. Wacław Kruszka led the fight for Polish equality within the Roman Catholic Church in America, arguing that a multinational church should provide sacraments and other services to parishioners in their native language.

In 1896 the first Polish Catholic Congress convened in Buffalo under the leadership of Rev. Jan Pitass to discuss concerns about the American Church. Deeply concerned about the continuing lack of recognition and sensitivity on the part of Church leaders in America, the meeting brought together religious and lay Polonians whose reaction ran the gamut from those who advocated schism to those who counseled patience and change within the Church.

Bishop Franciszek Hodur founded the Polish National Catholic Church as an alternative for Poles frustrated by the dominance of the Irish hierarchy in the Roman Catholic Church in America. Polish National Catholic Church Commission on History and Archives.

Although nothing concrete resulted from the meeting, the wheels of change were set in motion.

A second congress met in Buffalo in 1901, attended by representatives of several important Polish organizations, including both the Polish National Alliance and the Polish Roman Catholic Union. Chief among their concerns was the movement to appoint a Polish bishop to minister to the immigrants in

America. If there could be national parishes, they reasoned, why not a bishop to serve the needs of different cultural and linguistic groups?[48]

Perhaps acutely aware of their inferior status, the slogan was not *representacja* (representation) but *równouprawnienie* (equality). Rev. Wacław Kruszka, a strong voice for Polish rights within the Church, made an emotional appeal for "unity in diversity," a view of cultural pluralism within the American Catholic Church that was clearly ahead of its time. Largely through Kruszka's influence, the conference decided to send letters of appeal to the Apostolic Delegate, Archbishop Satolli, to Cardinal Gibbons, and to the American bishops. In the letters the Poles asked for the creation of Polish-speaking auxiliary bishops in 12 diocese whose population was 25–50 percent Polish American. If the requests remained unanswered, the congress determined to send a delegation to the Vatican to present the case.[49]

When their letters were ignored, the Poles proceeded with the second portion of the plan adopted at the Buffalo meeting, sending delegates to plead their case directly with the Vatican. Thus, Kruszka and Buffalo congressman Rowland B. Mahaney left for Rome in July 1903. There the Polish priest met with the Pope, whom he claimed promised that "something in the near future will be done according to your wishes." What the Pope did, after additional appeals, was to dispatch Archbishop Albin Symon, himself of Polish ancestry, to the United States in 1905 to investigate the situation. After an extensive review of conditions in America, Symon recommended the appointment of a Polish bishop in areas where Poles formed a large percentage of the Catholic population. As a result, Rev. Paul Rhode was appointed auxiliary bishop of Chicago in 1908, the first Polish American to attain this status.[50]

Despite Rhode's elevation, Kruszka and his supporters were clearly unhappy. They did not view the position of auxiliary bishop, with its limited influence and lack of real authority, as in any way fulfilling their desire for real equality. When no further action was forthcoming to redress their grievances, the sentiment for Polish independence increased dramatically.[51]

While most Poles attempted to work within the Roman Catholic Church to secure equality, by the mid-1890s a serious movement toward the establishment of "independent" parishes had already begun. The complaints of these local parishioners were emphatically articulated in *Kuryer Polski*: "The founders and benefactors of Polish churches in America are not priests nor American bishops. THE FOUNDERS AND BENEFACTORS OF POLISH CHURCHES IN AMERICA ARE THE POLISH PARISHIONERS. Polish parishioners give their hard-earned pennies for the founding and support of the churches. . . . But the priests and bishops are only the servants of the church. Therefore the bishops and priests should honor the founders and benefactors of the church, not tyrannize them. In the old country, the founders and benefactors had a voice not only in the running of church affairs, but in the selection of the pastor. Here in America, the founders and benefactors of the Polish churches, that is, the Polish people, should certainly have the same rights and privileges."[52]

Early dissent appeared in Chicago and Buffalo but soon spread to other communities as the issues of lay trusteeship for parishes and the appointment of Polish bishops became the focal issues representing equality and Polish nationalism. Roman Catholic authorities responded quickly and dramatically against the *niezależnicy* (independents), equating "lay rights" with heresy and labeling them pagans, heathens, atheists, revolutionaries, lawbreakers, and worse.[53] In a concerted effort to crush growing dissent, bishops used discipline and excommunication to enforce obedience from parishioners and priests alike.

Gradually, the independent movement crystallized around Rev. Franciszek Hodur, an educated, strongly nationalistic priest in Scranton, Pennsylvania. Serious trouble began when Hodur demanded that Church property in his parish be held by the laity and that the laity have a voice in the appointment of pastors—classic demands of those advocating "trusteeism." When Hodur refused to relent he was excommunicated, but even this drastic action failed to sway him. In 1897 he founded the newspaper *Straż* (The Guard) to disseminate his views, a move quickly countered by Roman Catholic publication of *Przegląd* (Review). As the bitter public debate continued, Hodur became the acknowledged leader of several independent parishes in central Pennsylvania.[54]

As support for Hodur increased he moved to consolidate support by organizing the independent parishes into the Polish National Catholic Church (PNCC). The new church's constitution, adopted in 1904, provided the following rationale for separatism: "Should we Poles renounce today our rights and our national character given to us by God? Should we disinherit our souls, and deprive ourselves of independence, in order that we might please the Pope and the Irish bishops? No, never! If our nation has any mission in humanity's reach for higher goals, then it must also have its own distinct, Polish faith, its National Church, as all creative peoples of the world have. Our Polish National Church in America is the first step in the work of forming an independent life in emigration, and, God grant, for the future of our entire people."[55]

Hodur's movement retained much of Roman Catholic tradition and belief, including the hierarchical church organization. The liturgical language changed from Latin to Polish, and the church calendar expanded to include many additional feast days commemorating events in Polish history. Hodur, elected bishop of the new church at its General Synod in 1904, characterized his church as "republican" in comparison with the "monarchical" Roman Catholics. This was a brilliant strategic move, for it at once branded the Roman Catholics with the stigma of the repressive foreign powers occupying Poland and aligned Hodur's church with the ideals of American democracy.[56]

PNCC membership rose steadily to between 60,000 and 85,000 in more than 50 parishes by 1926. By the time of Hodur's death in 1953 it numbered more than 130,000 members, but this was less than 5 percent of the membership of organized Polonia.[57] Although numerically small, the PNCC movement provided an outlet for Polish religious nationalism and eventually influenced the Roman Catholic Church to adopt a more conciliatory attitude toward its ethnic minorities in America.

four

Polonia in the Progressive Era, 1900–1920

T he years between 1900 and 1920 are usually referred to as the Progressive Era, a name taken from a coalition of political reform groups each advocating changes they thought would make America a better place to live. Some sought social changes such as prohibition, conservation, and woman suffrage, while others focused on industrial reform by supporting child labor laws, minimum wage legislation, food and drug regulation, worker compensation reform, anti-trust laws, and other controls. Still others concerned themselves with civic reform, concentrating their efforts on obtaining the direct election of U.S. senators, passage of corrupt practices acts, adoption of city-manager forms of government, public bids for government contracts, and other reforms designed to curb the economic and political excesses of city "bosses" as well as state and federal government. Some sought to treat the ills of the burgeoning urban areas by restricting immigration.

For Polonia, the Progressive Era brought dramatic increases in immigration until the beginning of World War I, the growth and development of Polish urban communities, and the further extension of Polonia's organizational infrastructure. Yet the major themes for Polonia during this period related to employment as the strongest magnet for Polish immigration, the independence of the homeland, and the growing nativist movement that strove to close America's shores to further immigration and that propagated the development of a Polish ethnic stereotype.

Employment

One of the most important factors in the life of immigrants of all nationalities during the Progressive Era was employment. Most immigrants during this period came to the United States for economic reasons. The job they occupied not only provided their livelihood, but enabled them to send money back to support family members in the Old Country, to bring relatives to America, and to achieve some status in the local community. Turn-of-the-century Polish immigrants were typically members of the working class who found jobs as unskilled laborers in foundries, mines, textile mills, refineries, stockyards, and a variety of other industries. By 1900 they were a major force in several industries. In 1912, for example, the United Mine Workers (UMW) began publishing the weekly

Górnik Polski (Polish Miner) to further communications with Polish workers. Similarly, the large percentage of Poles in the textile mills of New York and New England caused the United Textile Workers of America (UTWA) to employ Polish organizers and print union materials in Polish.[1]

The world the immigrants entered was not always pleasant. A Pole in Pittsburgh explained, "The only way you got a job [was] through somebody at work who got you in. I mean this application, that's a big joke. They just threw them away."[2] In other cases one had to ingratiate oneself with, or pay, a company official. Regardless of the exact nature of the system, personal relationships and obligations were important in the factories and mines, and a "connection" of one sort or another was often helpful in obtaining a job, and sometimes required if any promotion were sought.

Another problem was the cultural barrier. Since most Polish immigrants initially knew no English, and brought with them cultural values that differed from those of the Anglo-Saxon majority, they often encountered difficulties originating in cultural misunderstandings. These differences, coupled with competition for jobs, housing, and status, often led to serious ethnic differences that "reinforced economic divisions in the labor force to such a degree that the workers were unable to cooperate effectively to protect their common concerns."[3]

Once on the job, immigrants were at the mercy of the all-powerful foreman. As Renkiewicz explained, "Responsible for hiring and firing, paying wages, setting work rules, maintaining discipline and adjudicating disputes between workers, foremen exercised authority autocratically, arbitrarily and sometimes violently. Usually drawn from earlier waves of Anglo-Saxon or Irish immigration, they behaved like independent labor contractors, barely responsible to supervisors and department heads above them."[4] All too often foremen acted as arbitrary lords of the realm, every bit as powerful over the life of the worker as the landlords the Poles left behind in *Stary Kraj*. Foremen routinely used ethnic epithets, spat upon workers, and physically abused them. Wages were sometimes shorted, or foremen demanded payment for special favors. If a worker complained the foreman had the authority to fire the person on the spot.

Even when a job was obtained, wages were low and conditions difficult. The New York Mills Corporation, a textile manufacturing company in central New York, paid its weavers $6–9 per week for 56 hours of work. Weavers were fined up to 25 cents for every defective thread regardless of whether the fault lay with the worker or the machinery. Piece rate schedules were not posted, pay envelopes routinely held less than the workers expected, and labor agitators were fired on mere suspicion. Further, a "card system" required that an employee obtain the permission of his or her foreman before being employed in any other position, thus eliminating any economic mobility.[5]

Working conditions in the factories were also less than desirable. In Pittsburgh's steel industry between 1906 and 1910, the accident rate for non-English-speaking immigrants at the South Works was twice the average of the rest of the labor force. In a single year 127 Eastern Europeans were killed in Allegheny County, and nearly 25 percent of recent immigrants were killed or injured each year. In Lackawanna, New York, the Lackawanna Steel Company built a new factory complex and town at the turn of the century that was touted as a model. The company constructed a number of impressive structures for the Anglo-Saxon company officials and management personnel, but the living quarters built for the workers were spartan and unsanitary. According to one observer, "Open sewers emptied into the low swampy land and the houses were often surrounded by fetid water. Elevated boards served as walks and the streets were usually quagmires of mud." Lackawanna was crowded, congested, and plagued with disease; local physicians estimated in 1909 that "60 percent of the immigrants had some stage of tuberculosis."[6]

In 1902 unskilled laborers in Lackawanna were paid $1.50 per day, but when orders decreased wages were lowered to $1.38. In 1911 it was estimated that a family of five needed $560 per year for a subsistence living. The average family income for Lackawanna employees was $502 per annum, which required working 12 hours per day, 6 days per week, for a full year. Further, the work was dangerous and the accident rate high. Safety signs were printed only in English, with the result that accidents among non-English-speaking workers were twice as high as for English-speaking employees. None of the foremen spoke any foreign languages, but they frequently engaged in discrimination and ethnic slurs.

Life was little better in the textile industry. In the New York Mills Corporation noise in the weaving rooms from the constant clatter of thousands of shuttles was overwhelming. "The people who worked in the weave shop had their own language," explained Stanley Zima. "It was a hand or sign language. You learned lip reading." Some weavers scraped lint from the equipment to stuff in their ears, but one could generally tell a weaver anywhere because they were the people who were hard of hearing.[7]

Weavers were also exposed to dampness because of the need to keep the thread from drying out. The dampness, combined with dust and lint from the cotton fibers that swirled through the air, irritated throats and lungs, and contributed to chronic laryngitis and tuberculosis. In fact, in 1919 the U.S. Bureau of Labor Statistics reported that the likelihood of a textile worker between the ages of 15 and 44 dying of tuberculosis was "100 percent greater than among the general population." Further dangers came from the shuttles—heavy, 17-inch wooden instruments with metal tips that occasionally came loose to shoot across the room like a javelin, maiming those caught in their path. Those who were lucky escaped with cuts, bruises and scars. The less fortunate lost eyes, or even their lives.

Some scholars have theorized that Poles were well suited to the rugged demands of industrial America because of their cultural background. John R. Commons, a pioneer American labor historian, concluded that the Slavic worker was both too passive and too radical for organized labor. Each extreme, he commented, weakened unions. In general, he felt that the dull immigrants were much too ignorant to be organized, forming instead a leaderless mob that was so malleable it could be bent to the wishes of exploitive capitalists. Conversely, he noted that some Slavs, "once moved by the spirit of unionism . . . are the most dangerous and determined of unionists," but these were particularly dangerous because they could not be controlled by American leaders.[8] Thus, in Commons's view, immigrants who showed little enthusiasm for unions were unwitting pawns of big business, while those who did support unionism were dangerous radicals. Either way, they were a threat to American society.

Only recently have more sophisticated researchers attempted to find ties between Polish immigrant behavior and their Old World past. Ewa Morawska maintains that Polish peasant society contained both a "basic survival orientation" *and* "the image of and desire toward accomplishment as measured by the standards of the peasant-immigrant society—the 'positive wish.' In the ongoing interaction with the surrounding environment, the actions of peasants who left their villages and settled in American cities were motivated by both these elements."[9] The survival orientation of the rural peasant village taught Poles to live from day to day, making the best of every situation, while the desire for accomplishment manifested itself in a positive work ethic and the desire for home ownership.

John Bukowczyk found a similar cultural relationship to the ability of the Poles to endure and even thrive in the often difficult world of industrial America. According to Bukowczyk, "Peasant fatalism, reinforced by the dolorous worldview of Polish Roman Catholicism, helped inure Polish immigrant workers to these harsh conditions. But it was the purpose that many Poles had in mind when they emigrated which actually encouraged them to endure industrial hardship. Many young Galicians and Russian Poles left behind families in Poland who struggled to hold on to undersized parcels of land. Less immigrant than migrant, these Poles considered their sojourn in American factories a temporary expedient. They fully intended to return to Poland and use their American wages to buy land or to bail out debt-ridden rural households."[10]

The desire to succeed, whether to return to Poland or to better one's life in America, combined with a cultural socialization to hard work, no doubt provided Poles with a psychological makeup that was compatible with the industrial system. Indeed, it appears that the Poles behaved, as Renkiewicz concluded, in a "culture-specific" manner that reflected neither the Protestant nor the market capitalist ethic. One of the problems with this was that the American labor union had no obvious counterpart in the experience of immigrants from rural Poland, thus the immigrant was left to piece together a coping mechanism from past experiences that often had little in common with industrial America.[11]

One of the first to dispute the negative image of Slavic workers was David Brody, who found that unskilled immigrant workers, including Poles, were engaged in organizing activities before 1910 and were a well-defined and active force by 1920.[12] This conclusion was supported by Donald Cole's study of the textile center of Lawrence, Massachusetts, as well as by Victor Greene's work focusing on the Pennsylvania anthracite industry. Among the discoveries by these and other historians was the fact that despite the general anti-union sentiment among the public and state and federal government agencies between 1880 and World War I, there was widespread support for unionism and collective action among Polish and other Slavic workers. This tendency was seen, for example, in the Cleveland Rolling Mill Company strikes of 1882 and 1885, in the large strikes at McKees Rocks, Pennsylvania, in 1909, in Lawrence, Massachusetts, in 1912, in Paterson, New Jersey, in 1913, in Akron, Ohio, in 1913, and in the bitter steel strike of 1919. Poles were also active as leaders in labor activities in the Pennsylvania anthracite region in 1887–88, 1899, 1900, and 1902, making important gains in advancing the union cause.[13] "The significant part of this record," Bukowczyk correctly observed, "is the striker's identity. They were not the same native-born tradesmen who had acquired a reputation for protest in the later 19th century, but unskilled immigrants. These men and women who so dramatically reshaped the American working class during the mass-production years had often remained outside the American labor movement. But as their attitudes hardened and their numbers grew, immigrant workers now posed the first serious challenge to America's industrial capitalist order since the great labor upheaval of the 1890s."[14]

Another sign that Poles responded well to calls for collective action was the changing attitude of some sectors of organized labor during this same period. In 1897 the United Mine Workers abandoned its anti-immigrant stance and openly appealed to Poles and others to organize and join its ranks, hiring Polish organizers to recruit members from among the large numbers of Polish American miners. By 1902 this effort had increased the union's strength to the point where it was able to mount a strike that achieved some of its aims; all previous efforts had ended in failure. Similarly, the United Textile Workers of America hired Polish organizers and printed union materials in Polish and other languages. Its efforts were rewarded with successful strikes by Polish workers in Auburn, Little Falls, and New York Mills, New York, as well as several other locations around the country. The Amalgamated Meat Cutters and Butcher Workmen in Chicago appealed directly to Poles by hiring interpreters, with success similar to the UMW and the UTWA.[15]

The organization of Polish workers was not easy, not because of unwillingness on their part but because of language and cultural differences. Among the most important and effective strategies unions employed in the decade before World War I were the employment of Polish-speaking organizers and translators, the printing of Polish language materials, and the attempt to cooperate with local immigrant church leaders. Union officials soon came to realize the importance, both symbolic and financial, of renting immigrant-owned halls for labor meetings and advertising in the local Polish language press.

The struggle of Polish workers was not easy. On May 4–5, 1886, a labor dispute in Milwaukee resulted in a "riot" in which five people were killed—all Poles. As similar tragedies occurred elsewhere, the *Nation* led the American press in characterizing Poles as "bomb throwing" radicals "roving around with red flags." It further opined that "The riots in Cleveland, Chicago and Milwaukee are producing a rapid change of sentiment in regard to the partition of Poland. It has hitherto been considered by the bulk of American people as a monstrous crime on the part of the three powers which took part in it. But the events of the last few weeks are leading many to condemn the powers for not having partitioned the individual Poles as well as Poland."[16]

One of the most notorious cases of brutality occurred in 1897 during a strike by Slavic coal miners in northeastern Pennsylvania. On September 10 of that year a peaceful march by 400 in Lattimer encountered the county sheriff and 86 deputies, who halted the marchers and commanded them to disperse. While the sheriff confronted the march leaders, some of the deputies, without any physical provocation or warning, fired into the crowd, killing 19 and wounding 38. The "Lattimer massacre" has been characterized as "the most serious act of labor violence in Pennsylvania's history and nationally one of the most devastating, in which public authorities were responsible for attacking, wounding, and killing American laborers."[17] In a detailed analysis of the Lattimer tragedy, George Turner explained, "Those feeling the sting of the Lattimer bullets were members of the Eastern European immigrant society. Living in a strange new country, they felt the despair of being isolated, the frustration of being powerless, and the pain of exploitation. Attracted to a nation that inspired hope, they suddenly faced a situation in which members of their own group were, in their

Striking miners on their way to the Lattimer Mines on September 10, 1897, shortly before sheriff's deputies opened fire, killing and wounding many in one of the worst episodes of violence against Slavic workers in America. Division of Archives and Manuscripts, Pennsylvania History Museum Commission.

Ze Strajku w N. Y. Mills. Strajk rozpocz. 18 Lipca 1916. Czysty dochód na straj-kierów.

View of the N. Y. Mills Strike. Started July 18th 1916. Benefit for the poor Strikers

By S. Kaczowka

Polish strikers of Local 753, United Textile Workers of America, stand along the road beside their belongings after being evicted from company housing during a successful strike against the A. D. Juilliard Company in New York Mills, New York, in 1916. The strikers printed postcards like this one to raise money to support those out of work and to gain sympathy in the community. Despite stereotypes to the contrary, Polish workers were early and avid supporters of unionism.

eyes, mercilessly killed and injured by a sheriff's posse without any justification. Underscoring this sense of injustice was a report in which a mine foreman, who knew the Italian, Hungarian, and Polish workers, expressed the opinion that if the strikers in the Hazleton region were of the English-speaking class there would have been no bloodshed."[18]

Far from cowing the immigrant workers, Lattimer became a symbol of their determination, a case of mass martyrdom that inspired others to take up the union cause. Rev. Francis Pribyl commented at the time that "the slaughtering of them in cold blood is the most high-handed piece of butchery that has ever been perpetrated upon a peaceable people and a sad commentary upon the boasted freedom of fair Columbia, whose extended arms we are taught to believe are continually outstretched to the down trodden and oppressed people of other lands."[19] Making use of the symbolism of their adopted land, the editors of *Straż* paraphrased Lincoln's Gettysburg Address: "May their death not be in vain, may they become the patron saints of the working people in America."[20] Lattimer not only aroused renewed union spirit in America, it also led to strained international relations and a formal diplomatic protest from the Austro-Hungarian Empire, the European government from whose territories most of the slaughtered miners migrated.

Not all of the strikes Poles participated in resulted in international consequences or national concern; nevertheless, there were many of great importance to their local communities and to the general cause of unionism. By 1900 Poles predominated in the refinery industry in Bayonne, New Jersey. In July 1915 about 1,000 employees went out on strike in protest of poor working conditions and ill-treatment. The strike spread rapidly, but the Standard Oil Company retaliated by engaging Italian strike-breakers and calling in the Bayonne police. The latter was possible because the city's mayor was also employed as a counsel for Standard Oil. On July 20 a riot broke out, following which organizers arrived from the rival American Federation of Labor (AFL) and the Industrial Workers of the World (IWW). To meet this threat, the mayor advised the company to employ guards from a private detective agency. "Get me two hundred and fifty husky men who can swing clubs," an oil company executive commanded. "If they're not enough, get a thousand or two thousand. I want them to march up East Twenty-second Street [Bayonne] through the guts of Polacks."[21]

The result is best described by Bukowczyk: "For the next four days . . . [the] private army of so-called 'nobles' terrorized the strikers by sniping at pickets and launching armed sorties into the assembled crowds. No fewer than five strikers died and several more sustained gunshot wounds before the corporate reign of terror at the hands of . . . 'armed thugs' finally subsided. In the end, force—and persuasion—applied from another quarter finally restored order to the city of Bayonne. Hudson County Sheriff . . . broke up the strikers' organization, beat up their young socialist leader Jeremiah Baly, dispersed . . . [the private company] forces, arrested IWW organizer [Frank] Tannenbaum and banned the sale of the radical newspaper the *New York Call*."[22] The 1915 strike ended with the workers winning a salary increase, but little else. In 1916, however, they again walked off the job, forcing Standard Oil to increase wages and adopt a policy of "welfare capitalism," including benefits such as "accident, sickness, and death provisions."[23]

A similar strike occurred in the textile industry in Little Falls, New York, when the owners of the Phoenix and Gilbert Knitting Mills reduced salary levels. From October 1912 to January 1913, more than 1,300 workers, most of whom were Polish, Slovak, and Italian, struck in a dispute whose physical and emotional bitterness more than matched that of the inclement weather of a brutal winter.[24]

The Little Falls strikers were also faced with a company that had won over local law enforcement officials. Labor activists, and even the socialist mayor of Schenectady, were refused permission by the city police to address the workers in a mass meeting, the county sheriff commenting to the local press that "Socialist speeches at this time would tend to 'rioting' among the strikers, a thing we intend to prevent if we have to call out every regiment of the national guard in the state."[25]

The city police chief explained further, "We have a strike on our hands and a foreign element to deal with. We have in the past kept them in subjugation and we mean to continue to hold them where they belong." To overcome this attitude, and the restrictions placed upon them, the workers turned for support to the IWW, which adopted a strategy of insisting upon the constitutional right to free speech, while provoking mass arrests to overcrowd the local penal system and draw attention to the violation of legal rights and due process by local law enforcement officials. Eventually this strategy proved effective, as Governor John A. Dix "cautioned" Little Falls officials, "Your attention is invited to the fact that the Constitution of the State of New York guarantees the right of free speech and the right of people peacefully to assemble and discuss public questions. The people of the State of New York wish to see that these rights are not unnecessarily curtailed, but are respected in spirit as well as in letter, within your jurisdiction."[26]

On October 30, when pickets failed to move quickly enough in clearing a path for scabs to enter the mills, mounted police attacked with clubs, beating some strikers into unconsciousness. When the strikers fled, police pursued them across the Mohawk River into the immigrant section of town, where the officers attacked the strike headquarters in Slovak Hall. The police threw women bodily from the steps, broke down the doors, destroyed the musical instruments of the Slovak Society Band, smashed the framed IWW charter, confiscated several cases of beer and liquor, and arrested the entire strike committee and other supporters. Despite the denial of basic constitutional rights and the brutality of the police, the Poles and their Slovak and Italian brethren continued the strike to a successful conclusion, winning an agreement to reemploy all strikers without prejudice, an increase in salary, and other concessions.

A final example, and perhaps the most successful, were the two strikes waged by Polish workers against the New York Mills Corporation in 1912 and 1916. In this instance, Poles suffering under poor working conditions, maltreatment, and economic deprivation organized Local 753 of the United Textile Workers of America. In 1912, their overtures to company officials rebuffed, the Poles went on strike. Company officials retaliated by recruiting strike-breakers, swearing in foremen and other company officials as deputy sheriffs, and calling in the New York National Guard to protect their property. The deputized company officials provoked fights with strikers, ran horses through picket lines, and engaged in other provocative activities.

The strikers, however, maintained a strict discipline and called upon fellow unionists for support. In the end, through the intervention of New York State officials, a compromise settlement was reached wherein the workers received a pay increase and assurances of better treatment. No sooner had the ink on the agreement dried, however, than company officials began firing union organizers, cutting salaries, and otherwise violating the strike settlement.

In 1916 Local 753 began another strike, this time attempting to encourage Italian, Syro-Lebanese, and other workers to join them. The company once again retaliated by hiring private detectives, deputizing company officials, hiring strike-breakers, and provoking violence. They also attempted to drive wedges between the various ethnic groups and eventually evicted workers from company housing despite epidemics of infantile paralysis and influenza. When these tactics failed to defeat the strikers, company officials filed legal actions against union officials for lost profits and also began a smear campaign, claiming that strike leaders were profiting from collections intended for the strikers.

The Polish union members reacted with considerable thought, sending representatives to other Polish communities to raise funds, forming alliances with English-speaking unionists in the local area, and raising funds by selling picture postcards of those evicted from their homes. In the end, after four grueling months, the Poles won a complete victory, gaining every concession they sought. In fact, John Golden, president of the national United Textile Workers of America, proclaimed it one of the most successful strikes ever waged.[27]

The conclusion to be drawn from the above strikes, which represent only a few of the hundreds of labor actions in which Polish Americans played leading or supportive parts between 1880 and 1920, is that far from being the passive pawns of corporate capitalism, Poles were quite interested in and supportive of organized labor as a means of obtaining equal treatment, a better life for themselves, and a better future for their children.

The Fatherland

One of the constants in the life of Poles in America was their concern for their *Ojczyzna*, their "fatherland." By the time most Poles migrated to America between 1880 and 1914, their nation had been dismembered and occupied for a century. Unsuccessful revolts in 1830, 1846, 1848, and 1863 sent political exiles abroad, where they established communities and organizations that continued to advocate and plan for eventual Polish independence. Although the Poles of the mass economic immigration were not as politically and intellectually involved as the earlier exiles, they nevertheless maintained an intense emotional tie to the fatherland, if only because they retained their traditional bonds to family still in *Stary Kraj*. This interest in the fate of Poland manifested itself in America frequently during the nineteenth century, and by the early years of the twentieth century was institutionalized in many communities through the activities of the Polish National Alliance, the Polish Roman Catholic Union, the Falcons, and other organizations.

The prospect of eventual independence was viewed with increasing optimism after the unrest in Russia in 1905. As part of this heightened interest, several Polish American leaders and editors renewed their advocacy of an umbrella organization to unify Polonia into a single political and economic voice in support of Polish independence. The most successful of these efforts began in December 1912, when the prospect of war between Russia and Austria led the Falcons to call a meeting in Pittsburgh to plan for the political future of Poland. The meeting brought together representatives of various groups, resulting in the founding of the *Komitet Obrony Narodowej* (National Defense Committee, or KON). Conceived as an American affiliate of the Polish Provisional Commission of Federated Independence Parties, an Austrian-based movement centered on Józef Piłsudski and known by the Polish initials KTSSN, the KON was more a coalition of groups than a true organization. Given its affiliation to the Piłsudski movement in Europe, it was pro-Austrian and modestly socialist in outlook.[28] As such, it drew to its ranks many of the anti-clerical, politically leftist, sometimes socialist-oriented laymen who held editorial positions on many Polish-language newspapers in America. Similarly, since its organizational basis was patriotic rather than religious, it also drew considerable interest and support from among the ranks of the Polish National Catholic Church and other independents, Jews, recent arrivals from Poland, and East Coast Poles who saw the KON as an alternative to the preeminent leadership of Chicago's Polonia.

Given its orientation and inclusiveness, the KON soon came under serious attack from the Polish Roman Catholic Union. Roman Catholic leaders pressed for hegemony in the organization, while Polish National Catholic priests fought just as vigorously for equality. When a vote on whether to seat the PNCC representatives ended in a tie, a compromise solution called for the elimination of special influence by *both* the National Catholics and the Roman Catholic Alliance of Polish Priests. The rift between the KON and the PRCU rapidly escalated into a full-fledged battle for the allegiance of Polonia. Although the KON enjoyed initial success because of its popular appeal for support of the fatherland, its credibility was seriously eroded when, after only six months, Bishop Paul Rhode led the PRCU out of KON and established the rival *Polska Rada Narodowa* (Polish National Council), a group that allied itself with the pro-Russian elements in Poland. As the invective between the two groups increased, and the KON took an increasingly leftist partisan position, further defections occurred. Thus, on the eve of World War I Polonia presented not a unified, strong position but a fragmented and quarreling factionalism.

As the situation in Europe became increasingly dangerous, many elements in Polonia began preparing for the eventual struggle to liberate the fatherland. In 1913 the Falcons consciously shifted emphasis from gymnastics to military training. In fact, when it appeared in 1914 that the United States might become involved in a war with Mexico, the Falcons offered President Wilson 1,000 trained volunteers to serve alongside the U.S. Army. The War Department declined.

The outbreak of World War I in August 1914 brought a renewed sense of concern and urgency to Polish Americans. Although the United States was neutral, Poland became a battleground on which the armies of the kaiser met those of the czar in tremendously destructive combat that ruined crops, destroyed villages, and killed innocent civilians with impunity. For Poles it was also a civil war, with the contending empires drafting their Polish subjects to fight against friends and family in each other's service. Under these circumstances, the choice of sides among Polish Americans was not always easy. Those with relatives in the Russian section of Poland tended to favor the czar's cause, while those with relatives in Germany or the Austro-Hungarian Empire sided with those powers.

As a Catholic nation that traditionally accorded better treatment to subject Poles than the other partitioners, Austria was in the best position to capitalize on Polish support. Prior to the outbreak of hostilities, the Austrian government allowed the formation of Polish riflemen's societies that were quickly incorporated into the Austrian Army in 1914 as a Polish Legion under Piłsudski. Further, in the same year Falcon president Dr. Teofil Starzyński went to Kraków in Austrian-occupied Poland to develop plans to unite Falcons worldwide to place an army in the field. Many plans were considered, but nothing ever came of the initiative.

Realizing the importance of Polish support, both in Europe and America, the Central Powers issued in November 1916 the Two-Emperor Manifesto promising an autonomous Polish state upon the successful conclusion of the war. This appeal for support did not go unnoticed by the Allied powers. On Christmas Day 1916 the czar retaliated by declaring that a free Poland would be created, composed of all the partitioned sections. To convince the Poles of their sincerity, each side established Polish political bodies and began raising armed forces.

Many Polish Americans welcomed the Two-Emperor Manifesto, particularly those tracing their roots to areas then controlled by Germany and Austria-Hungary. To overcome these divisions, and the increasingly socialist tone of the KON, the influential PNA and Falcons withdrew their support for KON in favor of a new nonpartisan, nonpolitical Polish Central Relief Committee. With Poland as a major battleground in the fighting between Germany and Russia, the committee, known by its Polish initials PCKR, was organized by five major groups previously aligned with KON. Its stated purpose was to aid war victims.

Though ostensibly seeking to unify Polonia behind the cause of Polish relief, regardless of political affiliation, the formation of the PCKR only intensified the domestic struggle for the allegiance of Polonia waged against the KON. Although neither group was able to extinguish the other, the clear success of the PCKR in gaining hegemony over the vast majority of Polonia can be viewed as a victory for the "establishment" over its rivals. As M. B. Biskupski explained, the success of the PCKR was, in effect, the reassertion of an older, organizationally mature, midwestern Polonia, built largely on a late nineteenth century German Polish base, turning back the challenge from a more recent and more radical group led by a variety of eastern Poles tracing their origins to the Austrian and Russian sections of partitioned Poland. By the end of 1915 the KON actually represented only about 15 percent of Polonia, but what it lacked in size it compensated for with what Joseph T. Hapak termed its "strident, personal attacks on people it blamed for its declining influence. Jan Smulski, the Chicago banker, and Teofil Starzynski, the Falcon president, were favorite targets of the organization's leaders."[29]

Despite continued internal factionalism, the PCKR proved successful in rallying support for Polish relief. As the war in Europe became more ferocious, Polonia's leaders increasingly called for direct involvement to ensure eventual Polish independence. The Polish press in America led the way with a vigorous campaign calling for the rebirth of Poland. "Their pages were filled with emotional appeals for assistance to the 'Fatherland,'" Jan Kowalik noted, "and interest in Poland's fate became the single most important issue drawing the readers to the Polish-language newspaper."[30]

Without doubt, the most effective and influential figure in rallying Polonia, and the sympathies of the American population in general, to the Polish cause was the world-famous pianist Ignacy Jan Paderewski. Living in Switzerland when the war erupted, he immediately joined Nobel laureate Henryk Sienkiewicz in forming a committee to assist war victims in Poland. By early 1915 Sienkiewicz and Paderewski determined to form branches of the committee throughout Western Europe and America. Since the large Polish American community was viewed as an important source of potential resources, Paderewski journeyed to the United States in March 1915. There, over the course of the next year, he organized relief efforts and performed at a series of concerts richly infused with pleas for support of the Polish cause.[31]

Paderewski's efforts proved tremendously successful. Both Polonia and the American public responded positively, yet even his tremendously popular persona was not immune from attack. Since he supported the Allies, he came under attack from the KON, which opposed Russia and advocated cooperation with the Central Powers. Paderewski's stature, however, was such that the KON's cries were quickly drowned amid the praise and support of the general public. By late 1915 he met with President Wilson's personal advisor, Col. Edward M. House, to lobby on behalf of the Polish cause. When he met Wilson, the two got along well, with Paderewski continually lobbying for American support of an independent Poland.

By the beginning of 1916 the political situation in the United States was at once dangerous and full of opportunity. On the one hand, government officials were quite uneasy about support among Polish Americans for the Central Powers. On the other, the presidential election of 1916 promised some opportunity for political support as candidates reached out for votes among the various ethnic communities. In fact, it appeared that the election might bring support for the Polish cause when President Woodrow Wilson proclaimed January 1 as Polish Relief Day, an occasion on which every Polish American was supposed to donate one day's wages to the Red Cross to be used to aid victims in Poland. Despite this and professions of support for Poland, little substantial was promised during the campaign.

As America moved closer to becoming involved in the war, Polonia became increasingly supportive of direct military action. Given America's official proclamations of neutrality, military training by the Falcons continued in secret under the guise of picnics and weekend outings. On one occasion local authorities in Poughkeepsie, New York, arrested all the Poles at one such gathering and threw them in jail.[32] Nevertheless, efforts continued, and contacts with the Canadian government increased.

On January 22, 1917, President Wilson delivered his famous "Peace without Victory" speech, in which he stated "Polish independence would be a just result of the conflict." Paderewski received nearly universal credit for influencing the president's support for Poland. Further, this statement, coupled with the entry of the United States into the war and the imprisoning of Piłsudski by the Central Powers in the same year, caused Polish American sympathies to shift dramatically toward the Allied cause. At the same time, the Polish cause became increasingly popular among the Allies. In June France agreed to sponsor a Polish Army to fight on the Western Front, and President Poincaré signed a decree creating a Polish Legion. A recruiting mission sent to the United States met with enthusiastic support from Polish Americans, while the U.S. War Department agreed to allow recruiting on American soil for a Polish Army, provided that

Internationally renowned piano virtuoso Ignacy Jan Paderewski helped rally Polonia to the cause of Polish independence and influenced President Woodrow Wilson's decision to specify Polish independence as one of his famous "Fourteen Points" during World War I.

Polish Americans who were citizens and subject to the draft, or heads of families, were not enrolled.

In 1918 Paderewski successfully negotiated American recognition of the Paris-based Polish National Committee (*Komitet Narodowy Polski*, or KNP), led by Roman Dmowski, as the official representative of Polish interests. "As leader of American Polonia," Biskupski concluded, "Paderewski was simply irreplaceable." Due in large part to his charismatic presence, the cause of Poland became popular in America and the Polish American community became a major factor on the American political scene. Jan Smulski, then leader of Polonia, commented that "no one could resist him . . . they saw in him the truly providential man."[33]

"It was Paderewski," Biskupski maintains, "who made Polonia something significant in America." The pianist and his colleagues were so successful in mobilizing Polonia that it became known as the "Fourth Province" of Poland.[34] By 1916 efforts progressed beyond the stage of relief work and emotional rhetoric. Paderewski, Roman Dmowski, and other Polish leaders convinced the PCKR to establish the *Wydział Narodowy* (National Department) as a political arm to coordinate relief efforts and promote Polish independence. With this, William Galush observed, "Parishes were the local centers, and the cause of liberated Poland took on the character of a crusade." At the same time, the Falcons concluded a secret agreement with the Canadian War Office under which Canadian military personnel trained Polish Americans for military service.[35]

Aside from fund raising and moral support, Poland's "Fourth Province" was also willing to place its blood where its rhetoric led. At the annual Falcon convention in 1917, which convened prior to American entry into the war, a serious proposal was made to recruit an army of 100,000 men to fight for Polish independence. Raising such an army, however, involved sensitive international diplomacy. Since the United States was not at war, and had proclaimed its neutrality in the conflict, Polonia could not appear overtly aggressive lest it violate American laws. Consequently, Poles sought a sponsor overseas. England indicated no interest in "foreign legions." Similarly, the French rejected sponsorship, citing their desire not to offend Washington. Thus rebuffed, the Falcons began secret negotiations with the Canadian War Office in December 1916. In fact, the first small band of volunteers crossed the border into Canada on New Year's Eve that year and proceeded to the University of Toronto campus, where they trained before the United States entered the war in April 1917.[36]

At the same time, the French officially recognized the Polish National Committee in Paris as the representative of Polish interests and began serious negotiations for the creation of a Polish Army to fight against the Central Powers in France. In the United States, the National Department launched a vigorous recruitment campaign. Dinners, speeches, sermons from the pulpit, parades, fund raising, and other activities designed to rally support for the new Polish Army met with enthusiasm in Polish American communities throughout the country.

As popular support increased, organizers developed methods to bring considerable pressure to bear on those eligible to volunteer. Some communities listed the names of potential "volunteers" on church vestibules or hall entrances, while one Polish newspaper in Chicago published lists of "*Tchórze*" (cowards, skunks), including "slackers" who did not volunteer for service. In cases where eligible men moved out of town, "Wanted" notices appeared.

"It took much love of country to join this Polish Army," Stanley Pliska explained. "Privates received their uniforms, three meals a day, a canvas cot, and five cents per day (twenty-five cents at the front). To this was added a French government overseas bonus of $150 annually (always in arrears). There were no servicemen's insurance policies as no Polish organization was financially capable of cooperating with the American Red Cross in defraying the premiums for such insurance. Certainly the men could not afford it. As a result, some 100 widows and orphans were thrown on local charity after the war."[37]

Polish Army recruits trained at Alliance College in Cambridge Springs, Pennsylvania, at Fort Niagara in western New York, and at Niagara-on-the-Lake, Ontario. A cadet school opened at Alliance College to train volunteers as non-commissioned officers, but the cost of this training was generally borne by the volunteers. As Pliska explained, "Each cadet paid $14.00 per month for room and board, he purchased his own uniform, and he paid transportation costs to and from camp. The overall outlay for a three-month training course in many instances amounted to $150—this in days when a steel worker was earning the grand total of $3.00 per day! Yet, the school never lacked applicants. Its promising graduates were selected for additional training as officer candidates and sent to Canada. Of the 389 graduates produced by the school during its existence, almost one-half qualified for officer training. In the summer of 1917 this NCO school was moved to Camp Quinton, Cotes du Nord, Canada, the official training site for the future Polish Army."[38]

Buoyed by the enthusiasm of volunteers willing to contribute their own money to fight for Poland, supported by the efforts of Count Michał Potocki's League for the Care of Polish Soldiers, Madame Helena Paderewski's Polish White Cross, and other groups to raise funds and medical supplies, the movement to create a Polish Army moved forward rapidly. This effort received a tremendous boost on January 8, 1918, when Woodrow Wilson delivered a statement of American war aims to a joint session of both houses of Congress. His famous "Fourteen Points" vigorously endorsed the principle of national self-determination, including the "Thirteenth Point," which called specifically for the creation of an independent Poland comprising all territories with an ethnic Polish population and with free and open access to the sea.[39]

Wilson's firm statement on behalf of Poland, coming as it did as an "official" war aim of the American government, spurred enthusiasm throughout Polish communities all over the nation. Recognizing the potential of ethnic communities, the American government moved to focus this emotional outpouring to support the U.S. war effort. Ethnic-oriented posters appeared, and advertisements in Polish-language newspapers urged Poles to volunteer for service, purchase war bonds, increase industrial production, and conserve food, fuel, and other resources. "Are You 100 Percent American? Prove It!" challenged one poster, while another invoked the memory of Kościuszko and Pułaski to urge Polonia to contribute to relief efforts. "Kościuszko and Pułaski fought for liberty in America," it read. "Will you help America fight for liberty in Poland?"[40]

Encouraged both by the possibility of working for Polish independence and the opportunity to support their adopted land, Polish Americans volunteered for service in the U.S. Army in tremendous numbers, some scholars estimating that in excess of 40 percent of the first 100,000 volunteers were Polish Americans. By the end of the war, approximately 215,000 Polish Americans served in the U.S.

armed forces, far beyond their relative proportion in the population. Those who did not serve in uniform also contributed generously. Jan Smulski, president of the National Department, later reported that Polonia contributed more than $50 million to the cause of Polish independence and relief efforts. At the same time these committed immigrants, most of whom held low-paying, unskilled jobs, purchased an astounding $67 million in American Liberty Bonds, with another $1.5 million raised specifically for the support of the Polish Army in France.[41]

Recruits for the new Polish Army consolidated at Niagara-on-the-Lake in the fall of 1917. Originally constructed as a summer camp to hold 1,200 campers, the site accommodated more than 4,300 volunteers by the end of November. Never prepared for occupation in cold weather, the lack of heat and sanitary facilities caused great hardship and overcrowding became so severe by the end of the year that new arrivals were housed in a nearby cannery, hotels, and private homes in the Polish areas of nearby Buffalo, New York. In January 1918 the American government opened Fort Niagara, an old outpost at the mouth of the Niagara River dating from the French and Indian Wars, for use in accommodating the increasing number of recruits.[42]

Gradually, as the recruits completed training, they began to leave for Europe to join Polish forces consolidating under the command of General Józef Haller. In June 1918 the First Polish Regiment went into combat to relieve the American 81st Division. By the end of the war the Polish Army numbered some 108,000 volunteers. Polonia had contributed about 40,000, of whom 30,000 completed training before the armistice, and 24,260 went overseas. Employed only in the final months of the conflict, Haller's Army suffered 206 killed in action and 862 wounded. Among the dead were 106 Polish Americans.[43]

With the end of the war on November 11, 1918, the status of Polish Americans in Haller's Army became uncertain. Recruiting for the army ended in February 1919, but when the Bolsheviks invaded Poland, Haller's forces were transferred to their ancestral land in April to join Józef Piłsudski's army defending Warsaw. Ill-supplied and generally ignored by Piłsudski and the new Polish government, many Polish Americans applied for discharge by the end of the summer. Lacking supplies and funds, some 19,000 finally returned to the United States when Congressman John Kleczka and Senator James Wadsworth, chair of the Senate Committee on Military Affairs, orchestrated passage of a bill to permit the Atlantic Transport Fleet to retrieve them. About 5,000 chose to remain in Poland, but many of these became disillusioned and were repatriated to the United States after 1922 with the aid of the Polish government.[44]

Polonia contributed substantially to Polish independence, and to the American war effort, through its financial support, volunteers for military service, and moral and political support. With the end of the war, Polonia rejoiced doubly, celebrating not only the Allied victory but the prospect of a reconstituted, independent homeland. To guarantee the latter, the substantial political apparatus developed to support Polish independence turned to the task of lobbying on Poland's behalf, both in the United States and in Europe. At the Paris Peace Conference three of the victorious "Big Four" powers were concerned primarily with protecting their own interests and destroying the capacity of Germany to ever wage aggressive warfare again. Only Woodrow Wilson came with the idea of creating a lasting peace through a just settlement rather than through force. "For the first time in history," wrote Jan Ciechanowski, "a President of the United

States came to Europe to inspire the Old World with new, American, hitherto untried concepts of statesmanship, to persuade its statesmen to adopt a new code of morality in international relations, a code conforming with the principles of Christian civilization, and to apply this new code to a peace settlement that would preclude future armed conflict and make the world 'safe for democracy.'"[45]

Although its boundaries remained somewhat ambiguous, a new, independent Polish state came into existence as a result of the peace negotiations. In the United States, Polonia scarcely rejoiced less than those in Poland about the resurrection of their ancestral land. In fact, as Robert Szymczak eloquently illustrated, "when a Polish consulate opened in New York after World War I, pilgrimages from all over America began to make their way there, merely to see the Polish flag and the White Eagle over the building. It reached such a point that the New York Police had to close the street to traffic, since it was always crowded with Pilgrims, sometimes kneeling to pray and weep."[46]

Yet beyond the euphoria of Polish independence, serious problems existed in wartorn Eastern Europe. As Szymczak observed, "when the celebrations subsided, the world was shown an old and battered nation reconstituted as a democratic republic without secure, guaranteed borders and suffering from a severely depleted agricultural system which was unable to feed its war-weary citizens. The problem of malnutrition was so severe that the very future of the country appeared to hang in the balance. Immediate relief measures were necessary, especially to save Polish children from starvation."[47] Typhus, smallpox, cholera, dysentery, and tuberculosis spread rampantly through Poland, adding to the starvation, destruction, and displacement of war—first the World War and then the Bolshevik invasion.

Stories of suffering and privation gradually found their way westward, causing a tremendous revival in sympathy for the destitute Polish nation. Indeed, the cause of Polish relief soon became the new cause célèbre in Polonia, and briefly revived throughout America an empathetic outpouring. Herbert Hoover, who took part in the subsequent relief efforts, later wrote in his memoirs that "many hundreds of thousands had died of starvation. The homes of millions had been destroyed and the people in those areas were living in hovels. Their agricultural implements were depleted, their animals had been taken by armies, their crops had been only partly planted and then only partly harvested. . . . The cities were almost without food; typhus and diseases raged over whole provinces. Rats, lice, famine, pestilence—yet they were determined to build a nation."[48]

Given this picture of desolation, Americans of all denominations and political persuasions joined the effort to assist the Polish people. The American Red Cross, the Federal Council of Churches of Christ in America, the Joint Jewish Distribution Committee, the Knights of Columbus, the National Catholic Welfare Congress, the Young Men's Christian Association, and many other organizations collected funds, clothing, medical supplies, books, and other items for shipment to Poland.[49]

The American Relief Administration (ARA), headed by Herbert Hoover, created a committee to distribute relief material from the United States. The ARA sent money and food, provided transportation for supplies and specialists, and assigned personnel to assist in the collection and distribution of aid. The first American food shipments arrived in early January 1919 and increased thereafter to a total of some 751,135 tons. The United States also donated used military clothing, medical supplies, 60 million pounds of raw cotton, and $176,541,079 in credit and charity. In January 1920 alone, the ARA's Children's Fund distributed 700,000 sets of children's clothing and fed 1.2 million children. It did so without regard to race, religion, politics, or ability to pay.[50]

In one of the more unique relief efforts, the Young Women's Christian Association recruited bilingual Polish American girls and trained them as nurses for work in Poland. Ninety young women were selected and sent to New York City for a six-month training program, during which they underwent "welfare training in the slums of the city, attended lectures at the New York School of Philanthropy, and were given Red Cross courses in cooking, health, and hygiene." They underwent further training in business principles and arts and crafts at Columbia University, as well as attending YWCA lectures on social manners. Seventy-five graduated, receiving badges and grey uniforms, from which they took their name—Grey Samaritans—and reciting the following pledge: "I, _____, in accepting the Polish Grey Samaritan uniform, pledge myself to uphold the highest ideals of womanhood in every action of my life; To be faithful in the fulfillment of the duties of a Polish Grey Samaritan; To be obedient to the orders of my Superiors; To serve the cause of Poland; To allay suffering and bind up the wounds of those by the wayside; Believing that in so doing I serve the cause of humanity."[51]

The first group of 20 Grey Samaritans sailed for Europe in July 1919 aboard the SS *Rochambeau*. They were assigned to hospitals as nurses' aides and also sent out as social workers to make home visits and distribute food and clothing. Amy Pryor Tapping of Utica, New York, assigned to oversee the Grey Samaritans in Poland, recalled that Madame Paderewski "calls them *szary kotki,* little grey kittens. For so do they look in their blue-grey uniforms. And . . . they are my job, these Polish American girls; I wish that you might know them in their youth and enthusiasm. They are Poles and to be a Pole is to be a patriot. They have been in America and America has given them something to bring back to their newly reconstructed country. And here they are, ready to serve, my basket of *szary kotki*."[52]

The Grey Samaritans treated wounded soldiers from the Russo-Polish War in a hospital that Josephine Tarkowska of Cleveland described as "a death trap" where the wounded had no sheets or blankets, subsisted on black bread and bitter coffee, and lay about for weeks without proper medical treatment. Despite the disease and privation, the Grey Samaritans served in Poland almost three years. A YWCA report concluded that "their work was an act of devotion to the land of their ancestors," while APA director and future President Herbert Hoover asserted that "the hardships they have undergone, the courage and resource they have shown in sheer human service is a beautiful monument to American womanhood."[53]

The re-creation of an independent Poland was a major emotional victory for Polonia, a development that at once removed a traditional rallying cry and provided the impetus for new relationships with *Stary Kraj*.

Nativism and the Creation of an Ethnic Stereotype

The first two decades of the twentieth century marked a period of unprecedented growth in immigration. As immigration increased, fears of crime, slums, and labor unrest caused the dominant group to become more hostile toward newcomers.

Anna Badura of Rochester, New York, was one of the Grey Samaritans who took part in Polonia's efforts to provide the destitute in Poland with relief in the aftermath of World War I.

This was reflected, for example, in a renewed emphasis among nativist writers on the natural superiority of the so-called Anglo-Saxon race and in calls for the use of a literacy test to establish whether people could read and write as a means of limiting immigration.[54] Another result was the adoption by many in the Progressive movement of the demand for an end to unrestricted immigration, which it blamed for the growth of slums and bossism, the twin pariahs of urban America. The Progressives were joined in their crusade by Samuel Gompers, president of the American Federation of Labor, who in 1902 commented, "Both the intelligence and the prosperity of our working people are endangered by the present immigration. Cheap labor, ignorant labor, takes our jobs and cuts our wages."[55] His sentiments were echoed by his constituents when the AFL convention that year endorsed the literacy test by an overwhelming vote of 1,858 to 352.

Lobbyists for the Immigration Restriction League and the American Federation of Labor renewed their efforts for a literacy test in 1906. The author of the new bill, North Carolina Senator F. M. Simmons, appealed to Congress to preserve America's Anglo-Saxon civilization from a new class of immigrants whom he described as "nothing more than the degenerate progeny of the Asiatic hoards [sic] which, long centuries ago, overran the shores of the Mediterranean."[56] This position was increasingly propagated in the press, espoused by such notables as Ellwood Cubberly, "the father of school administration in the United States," who wrote in 1909 that "these Southern and Eastern Europeans are of a very different type from the Northern Europeans who preceded them. Illiterate, docile, lacking in self-reliance and initiative and not possessing the Anglo-Teutonic conceptions of law, order, and government, their coming has served to dilute tremendously our national stock, and to corrupt our civic life."[57]

Opponents of the 1906 literacy test hoped to postpone or prevent its passage by calling for the establishment of a commission to study the entire immigration question. Thus was born the U.S. Immigration Commission. The commission employed a staff of more than 300 people for more than three years, spent better than a million dollars, and accumulated a mass of data and conclusions that it published in 42 volumes. The commission's findings supported the proponents of restriction, officially declaring for the first time that there was a distinct difference between what it labeled the "new" immigration and the previous groups from Northwestern Europe, which it termed the "old" immigration. Restriction of the former, it concluded, was "demanded by economic, moral, and social conditions."[58]

Although based on faulty research and reasoning, these reports extended federal sanction to the stereotyping of millions of Americans. The reports appeared to "legitimize" calls for restriction. The effects can be seen in T. J. Woofter's survey of popular literature between 1900 and 1930. Woofter found that during 1907–14, "there occurred a marked change in public sentiment toward immigration" and concluded that the old restrictionist arguments based on economics were giving way to a rationale based on "the undesirability of certain racial elements."[59]

This new rationale became a favorite of writers such as Madison Grant, whose *The Passing of the Great Race,* published in 1916, argued that the pure, superior American racial stock was being diluted by the influx of "new" immigrants from the Mediterranean, the Balkans, and the Polish ghettos. Thinly cast in the guise of scientific theory, Grant's racist diatribe gained wide popularity among the American public and greatly influenced federal immigration legislation.

Bills for a literacy test passed Congress, only to be vetoed by William Howard Taft in 1913 and Woodrow Wilson in 1915. When the measure passed again in 1917, Wilson vetoed it a second time, noting that, in addition to reversing traditional American policy on immigration, the test would reflect opportunity rather than character. Congress remained unimpressed and overrode Wilson's veto. Thus the stage was set for further restriction. The result of this renewed agitation became clear once the Republicans gained control of Congress in March 1919. Albert Johnson issued a call for immigration restriction, backing up his words with the introduction of a measure designed to restrict total immigration by allotting quotas based on national origin. The influence of the Immigration Commission was evident throughout the hearings on the measure from 1919 to 1921.[60]

A new restriction bill passed Congress, only to expire through Wilson's pocket veto. Shortly afterward Warren G. Harding took the oath of office as the new president and summoned a special session of Congress to consider the immigration act. The measure cleared both houses of Congress in a matter of hours, and on May 19, 1921, the president signed the first law in American history designed specifically to restrict European immigration.

The First Quota Act of 1921 imposed a maximum of 357,803 as the number of immigrants that could enter the country from outside the Western Hemisphere in any year. The number was considerably less than the average of 625,629 who entered annually between 1901 and 1920. In addition, each nationality group was given a separate quota based on 3 percent of the number of people from that group residing in the United States in 1910. This provision discriminated directly against Southern and Eastern Europeans. The quota system reversed a trend in prewar years that saw Southern and Eastern Europeans outnumbering Northwestern Europeans by four to one. It is clear that the law was designed specifically to limit, in a discriminatory fashion, immigration from Southern and Eastern Europe. A quota board was responsible for determining the precise proportions of the population to be assigned to each nationality. Poland's first quota of 25,827 was increased to 31,146 in 1922, and then cut to 30,977 in 1923.

The National Origins Act of 1924 reduced the total number of immigrants per year from 357,803 to 164,667. To ensure the predominance of the "old" immigration, the quota percentage of each nationality was reduced from 3 percent to 2 percent, while the base year was moved from 1910 to 1890. This was a clear attempt to lessen the impact, and therefore the quota, of immigrants from Southern and Eastern Europe who entered en masse after 1890. For Poland, this resulted in an annual reduction from 30,977 to 5,982, a loss of 80.69 percent. The final quota established in 1927 recognized Poles as the fifth largest group in the United States behind Germany, Great Britain, Ireland, and Italy, and assigned them a quota of 6,524.

While the limitation on Polish immigration deprived Polonia's communities of immigrants from Poland, the report of the Immigration Commission, which was based on faulty scholarship that resulted in invalid conclusions, led to far graver consequences by "legitimizing" a derogatory ethnic stereotype of Polish

Americans. As Janice Kleeman explained, "Mainstream America's reluctance to embrace the Poles was rooted in three discriminatory stances: *religious prejudice* (Protestant America eschewing Catholicism), *racism* (Anglo-Saxon/Teutonic America depreciating the Slavic Poles), and *general resentment of immigrants* as alien and as competitors in the job market."[61]

Although the Progressive Era is known as a period of great political, economic, and social reform, for Polish Americans the era also brought condemnation by the U.S. Immigration Commission, a restriction of Polish immigration, and the development of a pervasive stereotype that characterized them as submissive, yet explosive; fatalistic, yet irascible; docile, yet undisciplined; of limited mental capacity; satisfied with poor housing, clothing, and food; and prone to excessive use of alcohol and criminality. In time this image, reinforced in literature and film, gradually developed into the stereotypical "hard-hatted, beer-bellied Joe Sixpacks" of the 1960s.[62]

Aside from the ugly stereotyping and the restrictions imposed by the Immigration Commission and Congress, Polish Americans during the Progressive Era witnessed the realization of a dream they had held for more than a century, the re-creation of an independent homeland. In addition, they made serious inroads into organized labor, waged successful strikes aimed at bettering their economic status, and developed both family and organizational means of accommodating their needs to the demands of urban, industrial America. By the end of the Progressive Era Polonia was poised to begin serious integration into mainstream America.

five

Emergence of the Second Generation, 1920–1940

T he 20 years between the end of the "war to end wars" and the beginning of the next world conflagration were dominated in the United States by economic themes—the cultural and recreational explosion that came with the prosperity of the 1920s and the unemployment and deprivation that accompanied the Depression.

For Polish Americans, the interwar period was also one in which socioeconomic issues played an important role. The period witnessed the beginnings of the movement of Polish Americans out of the lower socioeconomic class. During the 1920s, for the first time a majority of Polish Americans were employed outside the confines of the urban Polonia communities, or at least in non-Polish businesses. By 1920, many were becoming small business operators in the ethnic communities, an intermediary step to becoming part of the general American middle class.

The decades during which most of second-generation Polonia grew to maturity were dominated by several major themes, including the end to mass migration, the response of Polonia to an independent Poland, further development of organized Polonia, changes within the parish community, increased political awareness, and fundamental changes and challenges within Polonia itself as the mantel of leadership passed from the immigrant to the second generation.[1]

The End of Mass Migration

One of the events that exerted an immediate influence on Polonia was the implementation of immigration restriction. The effect of the nationality quotas imposed by Congress in 1921 and 1924 was to sharply reduce the influx of nearly 100,000 Poles per year to a fraction of that number—30,977 under the 1921 law and a mere 5,982 after 1924.

Following passage of the quota acts, the flood of Polish immigrants diverted to France and to a lesser extent Belgium. The result was that fewer Poles came to the United States during the period between 1921 and 1940 than came in any single year between 1900 and 1914.[2] The exact number, of course, depends on how you defined a "Pole." Helena Lopata compared the arrivals and departures listed by the U.S. Bureau of Immigration by "race or people" and found that between 1920 and 1932 there was a net exodus of 33,618 Poles from the United States. Yet when she used the figures for "country of birth" there was an increase of 107,476. The discrepancy, which led to some confusion and contradiction among historians of the Polish experience in America, occurred because of the multinational nature of the Polish republic between the two world wars. Because of this, many who, in conformity with U.S. immigration policies, listed their "country of birth" as Poland were in reality members of other ethnic groups. A review of Polish sources by Edward Kolodziej shows that of those who left Poland for America during this period, 34.2 percent were ethnic Poles, 6.4 percent Ukrainians and White Russians, 1.0 percent Germans, 56.9 percent Jews, and 1.4 percent were of other or undeclared heritages. Of these, 41.0 percent were farmers, 0.1 percent miners, 18.8 percent industrial workers, 6.9 percent trade workers, 0.3 percent transport workers, 2.7 percent engaged in the learned professions, 3.9 percent provided household service, 8.4 percent were members of unspecified professions, and 17.9 percent were unknown.

With the rebirth of Polish independence after World War I, many Poles in the United States elected to return to their homeland. Lopata found that 5,227 Poles arrived in the United States in 1920, while 19,024 left for a net loss of 13,797. In 1921 the outflow continued with a loss of 19,039, and in 1922 the loss increased to 26,075. In 1923, however, the immediate postwar departure thinned and immigrants thereafter outnumbered those returning to their ancestral land. Relying on Polish sources, Kolodziej calculated that between 1918 and 1938 approximately 273,161 Poles migrated to the United States, while 106,793 returned to Poland—a net gain to America of 166,368.

Polish historian Adam Walaszek identified four primary motivations for reemigration: some returned because of failure in the United States, some because they succeeded in earning enough money to return to a better life, some to retire, and some for political reasons. American sources indicate that 96,832 ethnic Poles returned to Poland between 1918 and 1923. Many of those who returned to Poland reported feeling "different." They had changed. Their experience in America made them different. Some had been away from their homeland for 5 years, and some for 35. In the intervening years they became accustomed to life in the Polish American urban ethnic enclave. Although few realized it, they had already begun the process of assimilation. Their recollection of Poland was an idealized, even romanticized vision shaped by the forces of time. Upon their return some complained of the low standard of living and poverty in their rural homeland. Some were treated with respect by the Poles, but others were envied by their new neighbors or ridiculed because of the Americanisms in their speech and their unfamiliarity with contemporary Poland. Many, having been Americanized more than they realized, no longer fit into Polish society, and an estimated 20,000 once again made the voyage to America after 1924.[3]

The 1930 U.S. Census counted 1,268,583 people born in Poland and 2,073,615 with one or both parents born in Poland. The effect of the quotas can be seen as natural attrition began to take its toll on the immigrant generation in the 1930s. By 1940, the U.S. Census reported only 993,479 who were actually born in Poland and 1,912,380 with one or both parents born in Poland. Both figures represented decreases from 1930.

The drastic reduction in Polish immigration not only cut off the external source of immigrants used to perpetuate the urban ethnic communities but also cut off direct access to cultural renewal from Poland. Even before the effects of these acts became apparent, Father Bójnowski warned that "in a few decades, unless immigration from Poland is upheld, Polish American life will disappear, and we shall be like a branch cut off from its trunk."[4] As a consequence, Polonia had to rely on limited cultural contacts with *Stary Kraj* to nurture continuing ethnic awareness and development. In this, Poland was only too willing to help.

Relations with Independent Poland

One of the most significant results of World War I was the re-creation of an independent Poland. Lost in the general euphoria over the realization of a century of Polish dreams was the fact that independence of the homeland meant a fundamental change in the fabric of Polish America. During the entire period since Kościuszko and Pułaski first came to fight in the American Revolution, the cause of Polish freedom and independence was on the minds of Polish immigrants to America. It was in many respects a unifying factor among Poles. Although they might disagree on the best methods for aiding Poland, their nationalism and patriotism were pervasive influences in their lives.

Now Poland was free and independent. The unity that could be mustered by an appeal to patriotism would not be the same. One of the immediate difficulties that arose concerned the relationship of Polonia to the homeland. Many veterans of Haller's Army returned from Poland disillusioned, as did a large number of those who reemigrated with such enthusiasm in the immediate postwar years. For those who chose to invest in Polish business enterprises, an alarming number of such ventures either ended in failure or did not fulfill their initial high expectations. Then, too, the political situation in Poland posed another problem as many immigrants objected to the dictatorship of Józef Piłsudski. Given the disenchantment of people arriving back in America, the less-than bullish Polish economy and the debate over Piłsudski's policies, the interest of Polish Americans in interwar Poland tended more toward the cultural than toward any significant political or economic ties.[5]

From the standpoint of Polish authorities, cultural relations with Poles living abroad was an important issue. Given the serious domestic and international difficulties the reborn nation faced, the Polish government looked on Polonia as a source of financial and political support. As such, it tended to view Polonia as an extension of the homeland, to assume a moral responsibility for the cultural condition of Poles living abroad, and to treat Polonia in a rather paternalistic manner. Given this perspective, the obvious beginnings of assimilation clearly evident among Polish Americans were of great concern to Polish authorities. The Americanization of immigrants abroad even became a serious subject for debate in the Polish *Sejm,* where the general consensus held that assimilation was "incompatible with the interests of the Polish nation and state."[6]

To arrest the process of Americanization, the Polish government inaugurated a number of cultural and educational programs focusing on Polonia with the intent of forming ties between it and the homeland. The government in Warsaw, however, did not grasp the complicated political divisions within Polonia. This lack of understanding, combined with Warsaw's penchant for treating Polonia as a national minority at a time when it was beginning to think of itself as a distinct entity, led to suspicion, distrust, and a failure of the Polish attempts to court Polonia back into the fold.

In 1922 the journal of the Polish Emigration Society advised its readers that the assimilation of Poles in America was a natural and irreversible process and that they could no longer be expected to owe allegiance to Poland. Its president, Wojciech Szukiewicz, argued that Poland should emphasize cultural activities if it hoped to have any influence at all over Polonia. The Polish government accepted this view, adopting a new policy of avoiding overt criticism of Americanization while at the same time encouraging the development of organizations that might forge cultural ties with Polonia. Within a few years, more than 25 organizations of various descriptions arose in Poland to promote Polish history, literature, folklore, handicrafts and other cultural activities, funded with covert government subsidies, for the Poles abroad.

As late as 1924, Warsaw instructed the Polish legation in Washington "to conduct an official inquiry into the feasibility of altering the Americanization process for the benefit of Polish interests in the United States." The legation sent a questionnaire to Polish consuls throughout the United States, seeking their advice on how best to conduct a cultural initiative for the benefit of Poland without alienating either Polonia or American government officials. The result was disappointing. According to the Polish minister in Washington, Władysław Wróblewski, "We should scrap any illusion that a cultural action among the Polish emigrants in America could give us political leverage in the United States, such activity could only be of moral value."[7]

Nevertheless, the issue continued to be debated in the Polish *Sejm*, receiving a strong and emotional endorsement. According to Dr. Tadeusz Brzeziński, an official with the Polish Foreign Ministry, "Poles living outside Poland represent our country abroad; their presence may either be beneficial or detrimental to Polish relations with other states or nations. . . . Cultural care over Poles abroad is to be understood as an action designed to maintain and develop Polish language, traditions, and national sentiment as well as cultural unity with the mother country. It is necessary that the Poles abroad sustain a certain extraterritoriality of the spirit in order to remain a part of our nation. In such a way, they will be able to promote the interests of the nation at home through reemigration and serve the nation abroad in the area of cultural and economic expansion."[8]

Brzeziński's plan was to inform the general public in Poland of the need to maintain close cultural contacts with Polonia, to send Polish teachers abroad to assist Polish American organizations with their cultural and educational programs, and to "work towards the establishment of a spiritual bridge between the nation at home and the nation living abroad by the promotion of mutual contacts between Polish and Polonia organizations and the direct exchange of students, artists, and educators."[9] What the Polish government still failed to understand was that any attempt at overt interference in the affairs of Polonia, even by an erstwhile private Polish organization, was sure to stir at least resentment of this "meddling" and quite possibly outright hostility. Further, the increasingly patronizing attitude of Warsaw toward Polonia provoked much animosity.

Despite limited results, Warsaw did not concede. In 1927 the Polish government sent Józef Stemmler, "a renowned Polish educator," to the United States to report on the condition of Polish education within Polonia. Stemmler concluded that the most effective means to influence Polonia was through the existing parochial elementary and secondary school system. At the same time, however, he was especially critical of teaching methods, professional competence, educational standards, and the "scandalously simplistic and outdated textbooks." Nevertheless, he felt that with curricular reforms, the shipment of modern textbooks from Poland, and the upgrading of teachers, the parochial school system could be an effective means of propagating Polish culture among the younger generations of Polonia.[10]

The Polish government accepted Stemmler's recommendations and determined to send Poles to the United States to assist in improving Polish schools "instilling a strong sense of Polish cultural pride in Polonia youth." Once in America, however, the Polish teachers found themselves in the midst of the conflict between the PNA and PRCU. The former was then sponsoring "supplementary schools"—what generally came to be known as "Saturday schools"—to promote the teaching of Polish history and culture, while the latter feared the competition of the PNA efforts on parochial schools. In 1932 one teacher reported to Warsaw that "if the instructor cooperates with one faction he is automatically spurned by the opposition. Personal animosities and ambitions prevent any form of constructive cooperation between the feuding sides."[11]

To bolster its attempts at making inroads into Polonia, Warsaw hosted the First World Congress of Poles Abroad in 1929. Originally scheduled to be held two years earlier, the meeting was delayed primarily because of the factionalism within Polonia. Delegates to the congress were apportioned on the basis of the estimated Polish population of various nations, with the United States receiving 38 of 134 delegates. When it came to filling these slots a serious disagreement broke out between the Polish National Alliance and the Polish Roman Catholic Union over their respective shares of the representatives. Further, when the Polish National Catholic Church was allotted two delegates the PRCU refused to participate at all. August Cardinal Hlond, the primate of Poland, attempted to intervene, but even this proved ineffective. Finally, the congress went on without the Roman Catholic representatives, but their absence was an embarrassment to Warsaw. The marshal of the Polish Senate commented dryly that it showed "a lack of religious tolerance" among Polish Americans.[12]

Ostensibly to discuss the problems of Poles abroad, the congress actually sought means by which those abroad could be brought into closer alliance with the homeland. One result was the formation of the Council of the Organization of Poles from Abroad, through which Warsaw hoped to establish a permanent link with Poles throughout the world. Once the council became a reality, Warsaw began to look more hopefully toward its educational and cultural policy to open inroads into Polonia. The teachers sent to assist Polonia reported glowingly toward the end of 1933 that more than 22,000 students attended 274 Saturday schools, a 12-fold increase since their arrival in 1928. The two educators also organized regional teachers' associations and held two educational conventions. During the same period, the Polish government sent more than 10,000 new textbooks and 8 "mini-libraries" for the Saturday schools.[13]

This record, thought impressive belied the true effect of the Polish policy. There were at that time about 400,000 Polish students enrolled in schools, only

In an effort to mobilize Polonia to support newly independent Poland, the Polish government sponsored teaching missions to America and cultural meetings as occasions for Poles living abroad to visit the homeland. Here members of the Polish American Harcerstwo (scouts) visit Częstochowa in the 1930s. Eugene and Michael Dziedzic.

23,200 of whom were in Saturday schools directly related to Warsaw's cultural efforts. There were about 171,000 children in Polish American organizations, of whom only about 6,000 could be influenced by Warsaw's policy.

The Depression, by forcing many Polish Americans into public schools for economic reasons, led to increased assimilation and greatly eroded the effectiveness of the Polish effort. Thus, plans were made to offer financial support for Polish American students to study in Poland, for refresher courses for Polish American priests in Poland, for exchanges of visits and instructors between Polonia scouting organizations and Polish scouts, and for sending English-speaking Polish instructors to work with Polish American clubs and organizations.[14]

Encouraged by the First Congress, Warsaw planned a Second Congress for 1934 to further reinvigorate its efforts to woo Polonia. By that time, nearly 8 million Poles lived abroad, approximately 22 percent of all those with one or both parents born in Poland. This represented an enormous source of financial and political support if it could be harnessed for the good of Poland. The Polish effort was clearly no longer philanthropic but political and economic in motivation. Thus, a major purpose of this Second Congress was to establish a more effective organization to deal with Poles abroad. The council established by the First Congress was redesigned into the World Alliance of Poles Living Abroad. The Polish architects of this alliance were greatly discouraged when it was suggested that the delegates swear allegiance to the new Alliance and the delegation from the United States refused. To do so, the Americans explained, would place Polonia under the control of an agency of the Polish government. This would be inappropriate because Polonia was "neither a Polish colony nor a national minority but a component part of the great American nation, proud, however, of its Polish extraction and careful to make the young generation love everything that is Polish."[15] With this, it was obvious to all that the Polish attempt to influence Polonia would never yield substantial dividends. By the 1930s, Polonia was no longer Polish, it was American.

Organized Polonia in the Second Generation

The tremendous successes of World War I that led to the reestablishment of an independent Poland eliminated a strong unifying factor within Polonia. The result, according to Renkiewicz, was the immediate "collapse of Polonia's unity and an overwhelming preoccupation with the internal development of the ethnic community." The National Department succeeded in fostering a sense of unity within Polonia by appealing to the "higher purpose" of Polish independence. With this dream realized, the National Department quickly lost its influence, disbanding in 1923. It was replaced by the Council of Polish Organizations in America, but this attempt to establish a formal link between the major fraternals proved weak and soon succumbed. Similarly, the Polish Interorganizational Council formed under the leadership of Francis Swiętlik in 1936 enjoyed no great success until the invasion of Poland in 1939 brought forth a renewed interest in the fate of the homeland. Renamed the Polish American Council, the organization raised over $20 million to aid Polish refugees in Europe.[16]

While the independence of Poland triggered a general demise in the unity of Polonia, individual Polish American organizations nevertheless enjoyed a renaissance during the interwar years. Returning veterans of both Haller's Army and the U.S. Army eagerly formed veterans organizations, ostensibly to maintain their support for Poland but in actuality to provide a social outlet for their members within the ethnic community. Nor was growth limited to new organizations. By 1924 total membership in Polish American fraternal organizations grew to 350,000, about 15 percent of the Polish American population. By 1935 membership nearly doubled to 650,000. Between 1920 and 1935, membership in the Polish Women's Alliance doubled about every four years and its assets rose to a total of $4.5 million. The assets of the Polish National Alliance doubled approximately every five years, reaching more than $24,000,000 by 1935.[17]

The success enjoyed by organized Polonia during the interwar period was due largely to a reorientation away from European affairs to a more domestic focus on issues of concern to Poles in America. Following World War I the vast majority of Polish immigrants decided to stay in America. Once they made this conscious decision, they became much more involved in ethnic organizations and community life. They continued to send donations to their home villages, but in other respects acted like the permanent residents they were. Ethnic communities grew in economic fervor as Polish business and professional enterprises flourished and a genuine Polish middle class developed in virtually every ethnic community of any size. While readership of Polish language newspapers continued to rise, the contents of those papers focused increasingly on American issues rather than

European, and the formats changed to include typically "American" features such as comic strips, crossword puzzles, and sports sections.[18]

Another factor in the growth of organized Polonia was a change in the orientation of the major fraternals that matched the new focus of Polonia. By the late 1920s, most of the major organizations became increasingly concerned with the domestic issues of urban life. The rapid increase in real income for workers between 1915 and 1929 greatly increased the buying power of Polish Americans and their ability to purchase insurance and make other investments. As income increased, many fraternals wisely invested funds in real estate and provided mortgages for members, thus appealing to the tendency of Poles to place a high value on home ownership. This policy, while perhaps returning less profit to the organization than more speculative ventures, had the added advantage of contributing to the "valued goal of geographic and communal stability."[19]

Polish American fraternals became so successful at providing insurance that by the 1930s commercial companies increasingly objected to their practice of insuring people who were not active members, including children. Nevertheless, the fraternals continued to offer this service to members and the community at large and to be successful in developing special activities of interest to the younger generation, including "scouting, camps, family recreation, language classes, cultural programs, and popular education suited to the social background and aspirations of a Polish American community."[20] The result was a strong financial base and growing membership that continued to increase even in the depths of the Great Depression.

Another focus of organized Polonia was a growing emphasis during the interwar period in preserving Polish cultural heritage. A renewed interest in this can be seen in such events as the founding of the first Polish Arts Club in Chicago in 1926, the establishment of the Joseph Conrad Literary Club in Buffalo, the founding in 1935 of the Polish Museum of America in Chicago, and the inauguration of the first Pułaski Day Parade on Fifth Avenue in New York City in October 1937. Yet while all of these activities spoke to a renewed interest in Polish cultural heritage, they also reflected signs of assimilation. The Joseph Conrad Literary Club used English as its official language, the Polish Museum focused on collecting materials relevant to the Polish experience *in America,* and Pułaski, the hero to be celebrated in an annual parade, played his most significant role in American—not Polish—history.[21]

The most important cultural development of the interwar period was the founding of the Kościuszko Foundation in New York City in 1925. Established under the leadership of Stephen Mizwa, the initial charter members were unique in that they included "six white Anglo-Saxon Protestant Americans": Samuel F. Vauclain, Willis H. Booth, Cedric E. Fauntleroy, Robert Howard Lord, Paul Monroe, and Henry Noble MacCracken. Because its board was predominantly non-Polish and non-Catholic, its early growth was hampered by a lack of support within the Polish American community. Nevertheless, it embarked on an ambitious program of providing scholarships for Polish students to study in the United States and for American students to study in Poland. One of its early successes was a grant that made possible publication of *The Trumpeter of Kraków* by Eric Kelly, which won the Newberry Medal as the outstanding American literary work for children in 1928. During World War II it offered assistance to

As a means of stimulating Polish American pride, this group of fraternal leaders organized the first Pułaski Day parade in New York City in 1937.

refugee Polish scholars, and in 1945 it purchased a townhouse on East 65th Street as a permanent home.[22]

Once ensconced in its new location, the Kościuszko Foundation was able to increase its assistance to scholars, host frequent meetings and lectures, initiate a program of artistic and cultural events and encourage the publication of books dealing with Polish and Polish American history and culture. In 1978 its net worth was estimated in excess of $5 million in assets and irrevocable trusts. Today the foundation maintains a strong scholarship and publication program, as well as supporting other cultural events and scholarly research.

The Parish

A major factor in the rise of Polish ethnic identity and cohesion in the interwar period was the work of the Polish American clergy. While the fraternals provided social and economic motivations for membership, it was the parish that provided the legitimacy of underlying ethnic values and their early socialization into the psychological makeup of Polish youth in the second and third generations. It was, Blejwas and Biskupski pointed out, a fundamental duty of the Polish American clergy "to transmit a Polish identity to an increasingly Americanized and secularized Polonia."[23] In this, they were faced not only with encroaching secularization and Protestant appeals, but with a Catholic hierarchy still dominated by Irish and German bishops who sought Americanization of the immigrants as a means of maintaining their religious loyalty.

The decade of the 1920s was particularly pivotal as a new generation of Polish American clergy grew to maturity. The younger clergy were born and raised in America. "At the heart of their commitment as Christian pastors," noted Daniel Buczek, "was *salus animarum suprema lex* [the salvation of souls is the highest law]. Parishes on the fringes of the Polish neighborhoods began to receive non-Polish communicants, thus the necessity of introducing English-language sermons." This represented a definitive stage in the development from Polish immigrant parishes, to Polish American parishes, to parishes of Polish ancestry.[24]

Further, the Polish American clergy had to face the conflict in philosophy between the authority of the priest and the democratic principles of America. As Buczek explained, the Catholicism of the Polish peasant village was complete. In America, the dominant society was Protestant and the Church controlled by Irish and Germans. This difference was significant because during the interwar period the Roman Catholic hierarchy vigorously pursued its belief that "to Catholicize America we must Americanize the immigrants." Between the wars many states adopted laws requiring that instruction be in the English language, thus supporting the Americanization of Polish parochial schools.[25] In the face of these forces, the task of the Polish American clergy was indeed daunting.

That Poles remained religious during this period can be seen in the fact that the number of official "national" parishes within the Roman Catholic Church continued to increase and the enrollment at Orchard Lake Seminary, an institution designed to produce priests to minister to Polish parishes, continued to rise until it peaked at 540 in 1929. Also, more Polish National Catholic parishes came into existence in the decade ending in 1926 than at any time in history. Based as it was on an appeal to Polish ethnicity, the rise in the latter is especially indicative of the desire among Polish Americans to preserve their heritage through religious affiliation.[26]

Chief among the forces acting to maintain *Polskość* were the Polish parochial schools and their complement of teaching nuns. By 1927 there were more than 500 Polish Roman Catholic grade schools. According to Thaddeus Radzilowski, the various sisterhoods made a tremendous contribution to "defining Polish American identity through their schools and textbooks, in shaping its institutions, channeling its human resources and surplus capital into educational and charitable endeavors, tying together its neighborhoods and educating its youth."[27]

Much has been written about the Polish parochial school, and there is still a debate among historians and sociologists about the effects of the system on second- and third-generation Polonians. As early as the 1920s there was disagreement over the effectiveness of this form of education, with the Polish-language press frequently lamenting the failure of these schools to teach in the English language. A study of the problem by Polish historian Józef Miąso concluded that while the parochial system may have "saved the young Polish generation not only from denationalization, but above all from illiteracy," the education itself was adequate only for living within the restricted environment of the Polish ethnic community. In comparison with the public school system, or for that matter the non-Polish parochial schools, "the majority of these [Polish] schools remained for a long time . . . far behind in both their educational level and in their teaching methods."[28] Thus, the argument goes, the Polish parochial

Religious education was fundamental to the maintenance of ethnic and community life among Polish Americans. Here Rev. Alexander Fijałkowski poses for the camera with a first-communion class at St. Mary Our Lady of Częstochowa Parish in New York Mills, New York, during the 1930s.

schools and parishes may have been a significant deterrent to entry into the mainstream of American socioeconomic life.

The opposite point of view was taken by Daniel Buczek, who argued that "the Polish ethnic parish was, in the 1920s and 1930s, an intelligent transition from the Polish immigrant parish-community before World War I to the American community of Polish ancestry after World War II."[29] The truth probably lies somewhere between these two extremes. It seems likely that the Polish parochial school was a significant factor in assisting in the transition from Poland to America and in preserving Polish history and culture. It also seems likely that by the end of the second generation the low academic standards and focus on Polish issues did not prepare students adequately to compete in mainstream America.

Cementing a National Political Allegiance

The political development of Polish America during the interwar period continued along the lines set earlier in the century. Poles continued to be concerned about issues that affected their everyday life—employment, immigration restriction, discrimination, lack of equal status and opportunity, prohibition, and citizenship. Although Kantowicz maintained that Polish Americans were predisposed toward the "Democratic" party because the term held more meaning for them than the moniker "Republican," it is safe to say that for Polish Americans it was the issues that were important, not some abstract ideology. While most

Poles identified with the Democratic party, this resulted from their attempts to procure social and economic equality for themselves and their children. During the period that most Poles arrived, between 1880 and 1914, the Republicans tended to control the national government and to represent the more affluent interests of business and commerce. Excluded from equal participation in the dominant party, Poles gravitated toward the other available alternatives.[30]

In addition to support for the Democrats, Poles lent their votes to other parties that addressed their basic needs. A small but vocal number of Poles under the nominal leadership of Leo Krzycki attached themselves to the Socialist party, which advocated a strong prolabor policy. Strongest in Detroit where they published their own daily, *Głos Ludowy* (People's Voice), the Socialists gave their wholehearted support to Franklin Roosevelt and continued to be an active force into the 1960s.[31]

To a large extent the Poles who settled in urban centers became involved in the "machine" politics of the era. They became part of a system of political "brokerism" in which the politician provided services and patronage in return for votes. This was not a one-sided relationship, but a reciprocal one in which both sides obtained something they sought. The party "bosses" obtained ethnic votes, and the Poles received political patronage, jobs, and a sense of influence over their own neighborhood.[32]

Although urban ethnic politics provided short-term gains and access to at least the illusion of power, Poles were generally unsuccessful in obtaining real control over major cities. In Chicago, for example, most Poles supported the Democratic party but were in the peculiar position, as Kantowicz explained, "of possessing the largest new immigrant group in Chicago yet falling short of a numerical majority in the city." He maintains that by stressing group solidarity, the Poles in Chicago were looked upon as a threat by other groups who, when combined, possessed larger voting power. Successful politicians in ethnically divided Chicago were able to build bridges to other "hyphenated" groups. The Poles, Kantowicz argues, "used the hyphen as a bludgeon rather than a bridge and Polonia's capital remained in the stage of hyphenated politics far too long."[33]

A similar pattern emerged in most of the other major metropolitan areas as Poles were successful in electing their own on the local level, but generally unsuccessful in electing mayors or other citywide officers. In Milwaukee, Donald Pienkos found that the limited success of Polish Americans in local politics was due to a combination of the dominance of German Americans and internal conflicts within Polonia. In Detroit, Radzilowski found that Poles enjoyed only limited success on the citywide level because of an "at large" election system and the fact that the Polish stronghold of Hamtramck, though geographically within the boundaries of Detroit, was governed as a separate city, thus diluting the Polish vote in the larger city.[34]

An exception to the general portrait of Polish urban political limitations can be seen in Buffalo, where Poles maintained a strong political presence, electing mayors, state representatives, judges, and other city and county officials. Walter A. Borowiec attributed this success not only to the size of Buffalo's Polish community but to its willingness to cross party lines to vote as a bloc for ethnic candidates. In 1936, for example, angered by the restrictive control of the Democratic party machinery by the Anglo-Saxon, German, and Irish politicians,

Poles organized the EC POLE (Erie County Pole) Party. Although they did not elect any of their candidates, they deprived the Democrats of Polish support, with the result that the Republicans achieved a plurality. The long-term result was to make both parties more sensitive to Polish concerns, thus increasing Polish influence in the two established parties.[35]

The difference between the general success Poles had in obtaining political influence in Buffalo and their relative failure in other large cities rests, according to Borowiec, with the Buffalo Poles' propensity for voting for their own regardless of party affiliation. Indeed, his studies indicate that "of all the ethnic groups, Poles rank first in supporting their own."[36]

On the national level, the support of Poles for the Democratic party during the interwar period began to crystallize in 1928, when Alfred E. Smith, a Catholic, proved popular as the Democratic standard bearer. Before Smith, the "Polish vote" might have been very real at the local level, but there was little evidence that it was solidified at the national level. Smith's background, coupled with his advocacy of policies favorable to the working class and his opposition to Prohibition, won a clear and significant majority of Polish votes. In a sense, Smith's candidacy presaged the urban/ethnic/working-class/black coalition that later provided the basis for Franklin Roosevelt's ascendancy. In Chicago, for example, Kantowicz found that 79.95 percent of the Polish vote went to Smith.[37]

Thus, during the interwar period Polonia became strongly identified with the Democratic party, an identification that has persisted into the 1990s.

Changes and Challenges

As the second generation grew to maturity in the interwar period signs of assimilation were unmistakable. By the late 1930s church societies still functioned much as usual, controlled by the clergy and emphasizing religious and cultural preservation, but some other aspects of Polonia began to change. Athletic teams grew in number and popularity, and Polish-language newspapers began to lament the lack of Polish awareness among the young. Polish radio programs began playing fox-trots, tangos, and other non-Polish music. Traditional religious songs were usually reserved for holidays, and folk songs and dances were rarely performed except by special folklore groups as curiosities of the past. Clubs became more politically aware, aiding labor strikes and supporting candidates for office. A sign of the increase in assimilation can be seen in the constitution of the Pułaski Democratic Club of New Britain, Connecticut, which stated that the organization would "aim toward advancement of our interests in political undertaking, inculcating the principles of Jefferson into our young generation" and "preparing our youth for political positions." The allusions were to Jefferson and American political interests, not to Polish history or issues.[38]

Between the wars, the activities of second-generation Poles in some ways mirrored those of the original immigrants, and in other ways were quite distinct. The original immigrants were greatly influenced by the transoceanic migration and the foreign environment of urban America, focusing much of their attention on means by which to survive in their new surroundings. The second generation often became immigrants of a sort as well, leaving the farms and smaller manufacturing villages in New England and the Midwest and the coal mines of Pennsylvania and West Virginia to relocate in the larger industrial

An example of the growing Americanization of Polonia during the 1930s can be seen in this drum and bugle corps sponsored by Local 2066 of the Polish National Alliance. Eugene and Michael Dziedzic.

cities along the Great Lakes. In fact, the continued existence of many Polish communities in these areas results from this relocation during the 1920s and 1930s. Similarly, some of the early Polish farming and mining communities ceased to be Polish or ceased to exist entirely because of this movement to the industrial centers.[39]

The original immigrants of the mass migration founded the institutions that shaped Polonia's character and patterns of adjustment. The second generation, as it matured and gradually inherited the leadership roles in these organizations, began adapting them as well as founding new organizations to meet the expanding needs brought on by gradual assimilation. Athletic teams, social clubs, business and professional organizations, neighborhood groups, and youth clubs supplemented, or in some cases eclipsed, the organizations founded during the immigrant generation.[40]

The second generation also faced the forging crucible of the Great Depression. Jobs and home ownership were two of the most important factors in the stable Polish American communities. The Depression threatened the security of both, presenting a major challenge to Polonia as it did to all of America. "The insecurity, anger and militance that resulted," Radzilowski observed,

marked henceforth the culture and psychology of second generation Polish Americans. Their major response was to join the battle for unions and even to lead it. Between 1936 and 1938, 500,000 to

600,000 Polish Americans joined the new CIO unions with the most militance being shown by the native born generation. They became in the words of Homer Martin, the first president of the UAW, "the most militant and progressive workers" in America. The CIO victory is one of the major Polish American contributions to American history. At the time when the descendants of the founding fathers sought to limit civil and political rights and to prevent participation of workers in setting the terms and conditions of their employment, Polish Americans through their resistance helped to widen the meaning of justice and democracy. Polish American institutions were often the agencies through which the unions were created and they provided them a secure base in the face of hostility, intimidation and violence from state and employer. The class and ethnic militance that the thirties created were changed and overlaid by the experience of World War II, which, paradoxically, both reawakened ties to Poland and subjected an entire generation drawn into military service or war work to an intense nationalizing, patriotic pressure.[41]

As Polonia began to "Americanize" in the second and third generations, it also underwent internal conflict, frequently displaying the classic symptoms of the "marginal man." The "marginal man" concept argues that people who attempt to fulfill the expectations of two cultures live in a world of ambiguity that often leads to tension, despair, and psychological doubt. On the one hand they may suffer feelings of guilt for leaving their original culture, while on the other they may suffer rejection as an "outsider" attempting to enter a new cultural group. Since a person in this "marginal" area between cultural groups lacks a strong group identification and support system, the individual may have difficulty coping in various situations. Data gathered in Buffalo as early as the 1920s clearly reflects adjustments by Polish Americans seeking to maintain Polish traditions while at the same time adopting American customs. Indeed, this experience was characteristic of the second generation. "Rejecting the Old World meanings of being . . . Polish," Eugene Obidinski emphasized, "individuals barely tolerated the traditions of their parents while moving out of the ethnic ghettos and often Anglicizing their names. In psychological terms, the most distressing instance of this kind of situation is when individuals attempt to deny entirely any identification as a minority group member, in the face of a society that simply refuses to let people forget 'who they are.'"[42]

Conflict between generations increased steadily as the traditions and perspectives of the parents—that is, the immigrants—were reshaped or discarded entirely under the powerful pull of Americanization. This phenomenon was familiar to most immigrant groups during the 1920s and 1930s, leading "to the condition of *anomie*, which may be defined as loss of perspective, rootlessness, aimlessness, cultural deprivation." Rev. Michał Wenta used this argument in *Nowiny Polskie* (Polish News) in 1925, after being castigated as a traitor to *Polskość* by *Kuryer Polski* (Polish Courier) for instituting an English-language Mass.[43]

"Ironically," Theresita Polzin noted, "the old immigrants, in attempting to retard or prevent assimilation, gradually adulterated their own culture in many ways by becoming marginal men and straddling the Polish and the American culture at the same time." One obvious place where this can be seen is in the

Patrz Kościuszko, Jak Się Bawią Niektórzy Nasi Rodacy?

Symbolic of the conflicts between the immigrant and second generations, this cartoon that appeared in the newspaper *Słowo Polski* in Utica, New York, in 1926 depicts a concerned Tadeusz Kościuszko, representing Polish historical traditions, looking down upon the Americanized second generation. To the left, an "Old Sport" leans against a pole while holding a bottle of "Moonshine," and to the right a "Polish flapper" asks a "Polish sheik" who Kościuszko was. The incorrect reply, illustrating the younger generation's lack of concern for its heritage, is that he was an actor. The caption at the top reads "Look, Kościuszko, look at the way some of our countrymen are carrying on."

development of Polish American speech patterns. Even where Polish remained the predominant language of conversation, as the years went by English words were increasingly adapted by affixing Polish endings. Thus, for example, the Polish word *ulica* was replaced by *sztreta,* a corruption of the English word "street," spelled phonetically with a Polish ending. "The Polish vernacular in the United States," Franciszek Lyra noted, "can be regarded as the Polish language in the same way as an inadequate knowledge of English by a foreigner who started to learn the English language can be considered as English." While many adopted this pattern, the older immigrants and the Polish press tended to bemoan the loss of "purity," and Polish Americans who traveled to Poland were generally regarded as barely literate by Poles who had difficulty understanding the corrupted Americanisms of Polonian speech.[44]

The dilemma of this marginalism, Radzilowski explained, required "negotiating between identities, with all of the attendant pain and alienation that brought. Because they were Americans, because their identities were less secure than those of their parents, because they could not avoid intimate contact with American society as successfully as their parents could and because they were drawn to American culture, they felt more acutely and painfully the insults of nativism and prejudice and the sting of exclusion. Their struggles, negotiations and compromises, as a result, are much more responsible for the shaping of the modern Polish American identity than are the experiences of the immigrants. They created the context within which succeeding generations discovered what it meant to be a Polish American."[45]

six

World War II, 1939–1945

The sudden invasion of their ancestral homeland stunned Polish Americans. In Rochester, New York, the local newspaper carried an emotional photograph of a man in the Polish section of that city reading the early news of the invasion with tears streaming down his cheeks. Throughout America, shock and grief soon gave way to anger and cries for revenge against the invader. Not since the movement for Polish independence prior to World War I was the Polish American community so united in both word and action.

Hanging on every news report, Polonia swung into action. The Polish National Alliance, the Polish Roman Catholic Union, the Falcons, and the other national organizations called on their members for financial support while also exploring the creation of national coordinating committees to oversee relief activities. In cities and villages throughout the United States Polish American communities rallied behind the leadership of established organizations or quickly formed special committees to solicit contributions for the relief of their beleaguered homeland. Parishes and fraternal organizations conducted special collections of money, food, clothing, and medical supplies, while communitywide committees were formed in many areas to bring together representatives of all the various factions to work for Polish relief.

Day after day newspaper and radio reports brought increasingly distressing news as the Nazi blitzkrieg flashed across Poland. Faced with the onslaught of an enemy vastly superior in both manpower and equipment, the Poles fought desperately in hopes of holding back the German tide until help arrived. Bound by treaty to come to the assistance of Poland if it were attacked, Great Britain and France reluctantly issued formal declarations of war; but other than deploring the German invasion and calling up reservists, they did little to honor the spirit of their commitment. While Poland fought and bled, England's Royal Air Force dropped leaflets on German cities and the French broadcast propaganda over loudspeakers from the safety of their fortified Maginot Line.

Deprived of any meaningful support from its western allies, Poland suffered a fatal blow on September 17, when Soviet troops entered the country from the east. Although many Poles at first welcomed their Slavic neighbors as agents of salvation from the German peril, it soon became apparent that the Soviets came not as allies but as conquerors eager to occupy the portion of Poland reserved for them by the secret protocols of the Molotov-Ribbentrop pact, which had publicly announced a Nazi-Soviet agreement on nonaggression only the month before. Faced with invasions on two fronts, the Poles found themselves in an impossible position. Within five weeks major organized resistance collapsed and the German army stood at the gates of Warsaw. The formal surrender came on October 7, 1939, but thousands of Polish military personnel escaped south across the Carpathian Mountains into neutral Romania, from whence they made their way to France to continue the fight. Polish submarines fled to England, and other naval vessels already at sea made their way into Allied ports to bolster the forces that would once again face Hitler's wrath the following spring. A government-in-exile established its headquarters in Paris, transferring to London with the fall of France in the summer of 1940, and Poland continued to be numbered among the Allied nations, contributing more than 100,000 infantry, armored troops, skilled naval personnel, and aviators to the Allied cause.

Within the Polish American community the shock of the initial invasion was more than matched by the despair that accompanied the defeat of Poland's armed forces in the fall of 1939. Throughout the United States families worried about relatives and friends caught in the war-torn nation, while the Polish American press began to mirror the acrimony and finger pointing characteristic of Polish factions in Europe seeking to place blame for the stunning defeat.

Polonia and the Sikorski Government

With the outbreak of war in Europe, the debate between isolationists and interventionists intensified within the United States. The former, concerned lest the country become involved in another European war, as it had in 1917, rallied behind the slogan "America First" to lobby for strict neutrality and the avoidance of any activity that might involve the United States in hostilities. Polish Americans overwhelmingly opposed the isolationists, supporting instead lend-lease, cash and carry, and the other programs that Franklin Roosevelt designed to assist England and its allies.

Polish Americans viewed the successful defense of England and its continued resistance to Nazi aggression as their only hope for an eventual resurrection of the freedom and independence of Poland. In this context, the large and politically important Polish American community formed a potentially significant voting bloc for the Democratic incumbent in 1940. "It must be remembered," explained George H. Janczewski, "that the feelings of the Americans of Polish extraction toward Poland were a most personal issue, as almost each Polish-American family had close relatives living in Poland and their concern for their own people was far more tangible than many a politician had realized."[1] Indeed, in 1940 Polish Americans were motivated by a sincere and emotional attachment to friends and relatives in Poland suffering daily atrocities at the hands of the Nazi occupiers. They were prepared to give their votes to the party that promised relief efforts and support for those engaged in the fight against fascism. Although some Polish American immigrants were not yet citizens in 1940, political strategists of both major parties regarded the group's potential political clout as significant. According to the 1940 census, Poles constituted "the third largest group of foreign-born European-Americans" at 6–7 million. This population was concentrated in the important northeastern states of New York, Illinois, Michigan, Pennsylvania,

New Jersey, and Massachusetts, which together accounted for a crucial bloc of electoral votes. Further, the Poles, with their infrastructure of religious, fraternal, and social groups, were regarded as well organized and already counted several representatives in Congress.[2]

To harvest this crop of votes Anthony Biddle, Jr., well regarded within Polonia because of his service as U.S. ambassador to Poland between 1937 and 1940, traveled across the nation during the summer and fall of 1940, speaking eloquently to ethnic audiences on behalf of Roosevelt's candidacy for a third term. Given the circumstances, Polish Americans, who unequivocally approved of FDR's assistance to Great Britain, rewarded Biddle's efforts with enthusiastic support and firm promises of votes for Democratic candidates in the fall elections. Further support for Roosevelt's policies, and thus also his reelection campaign, came from Francis Swiętlik, dean of the law school at Marquette University, who was extremely influential in Chicago's Polish American community. Swiętlik served as grand censor of the Polish National Alliance and as president of the Chicago-based Polish-American Council, an umbrella organization for that city's Polish fraternals. Bolstered by the status derived from these important positions, he claimed authority to speak on behalf of Chicago's massive Polish American community—and he remained firmly behind Franklin Roosevelt. Swiętlik took the lead in asking all Polish organizations, not only in Chicago but throughout the United States, to deluge the president with a flood of telegrams supporting his bid for a third term. With this, and a similar outpouring of support from the Polish American press, Roosevelt won an overwhelming majority of Polish American votes in 1940 as he easily beat back the challenge of Republican contender Wendell Willkie.

Roosevelt's successful appeal to Polonia during the election campaign of 1940 no doubt convinced him of the benefit of befriending this large ethnic group, to win not only votes but public support for his efforts to aid Britain. In March 1941 FDR met with Jan Ciechanowski, ambassador of the London-based Polish government-in-exile, to voice his support for the Polish cause. As the president explained, "I want you to know that personally I have a deep feeling for the Americans of Polish descent, not merely because they voted for me so overwhelmingly in the last three elections, [but] because they are very good citizens, conscious of their duties and always loyal Americans."[3] Roosevelt stressed to the Polish ambassador his fear that communist agents were attempting to slow American war production and asked Ciechanowski to undertake a speaking tour through the Polish American communities to underscore the importance of increasing the production of war materials as a means of aiding their ancestral land in its time of need.

When the popular Polish premier, Władysław Sikorski, visited the United States in April 1941, Roosevelt used the occasion to urge him to undertake the same mission as Ciechanowski. Roosevelt was particularly concerned about the adverse effects of a strike being waged by the United Auto Workers in Milwaukee involving large numbers of Polish workers. By using Sikorski's popularity as a symbol of the Poles' homeland, the president hoped to bring an end to the strike and to counter the growing clamor of isolationists and what he termed "communist influences inspired from abroad."[4] Sikorski agreed, with results deemed highly successful by the American administration.

Whatever the extent of this influence, other forces soon came into play to silence the isolationist challenge and unite virtually all Americans behind the

Polish National Alliance leader Francis Swiętlik (right) dines with Polish Prime Minister Władysław Sikorski in Chicago in April 1941. Polish National Alliance.

need to boost industrial production for national defense. The Japanese attack on Pearl Harbor effectively silenced domestic opposition to American involvement in the war, while the subsequent Nazi declaration of war on the United States brought renewed hope to Polish Americans that Poland might someday be freed from the yoke of its oppressors. Although the second generation of Polish Americans did not directly support the Polish armed forces, as their ancestors had in World War I—in fact, attempts to recruit Poles living in the United States for the Polish armed forces proved a dismal failure—Polish Americans wholeheartedly supported the American war effort, enlisting in the U.S. armed forces in large numbers, working in defense-related industries, and purchasing government bonds in record numbers.

Because of Sikorski's successful speaking tour during his visit to America the previous year, FDR was eager to have the Polish premier repeat his earlier triumph. Sikorski obliged, meeting with Roosevelt on March 24 and 26, 1942. By March 1942, however, the international political situation was considerably different from what it had been the previous year. In June 1941 Nazi Germany unleashed a massive invasion of the Soviet Union. With this, the USSR became a de facto ally of England. As such, Roosevelt immediately sought ways to assist Moscow in its fight against the forces of fascism. This placed the United States in league with the USSR—a participant in the 1939 partition of Poland—putting Sikorski in a very difficult position.

Openly critical when the Soviets participated in the dismemberment of Poland, many American newspapers now rushed to publish accounts favorable to the Soviet Union as the latest victim of Hitler's treachery. The adoption of the Soviet Union as a new ally placed American support for Poland, and in particular the government-in-exile in London, in a new and ambiguous light. The London government resented the Soviet Union's invasion of Poland in 1939 and rejected Soviet claims to territory in eastern Poland, citing the Treaty of Riga in 1921, which established Poland's eastern border following the Russo-Polish War of 1919–20. Soviet leader Joseph Stalin argued that those territories were rightfully part of the Soviet Union. In an effort to foster Allied unity following the Nazi invasion of the Soviet Union, the Poles came under increasing pressure to compromise on the politically and emotionally important border issue. This delicate matter was addressed, if only temporarily, with the signing of the Sikorski-Maisky Pact on July 30, 1941. Under the terms of this agreement, which Sikorski signed as a compromise to promote unity, the Soviet Union agreed to renounce the secret protocols of the Molotov-Ribbentrop pact that dealt with Poland, but the delicate border issue remained unresolved. Although U.S. Undersecretary of State Sumner Welles quickly reassured Ambassador Ciechanowski that the official American policy remained "non-recognition of territory taken by conquest," a position also adopted by the British government, Poles remained uneasy regarding Soviet intentions.

The question of relations with the Soviet Union caused a serious schism in the Polish leadership. Sikorski, acting as both premier and commander-in-chief of the Polish armed forces, took a moderate stance, seeking compromise for the good of the Allied war effort. Opposition leaders pleaded for caution based on the past experience of Soviet invasions in 1919 and 1939, while a few of the more aggressively inclined called for a joint Allied war effort against *both* Hitler and Stalin. As a result of this discord in the Polish ranks, three members of the Polish cabinet in London resigned.

Despite Sikorski's moderate stance, by the time he and Roosevelt met again in March 1942 the American president harbored some doubt about the premier's "reliability" on the question of friendship with the Soviet Union. In an effort to avoid controversy, Sikorski purposely distanced himself from anti-Soviet leaders among both Poles and Polish Americans. His refusal to make a firm statement in support of Poland's eastern borders, a very emotional question among Polish Americans, led many leaders of the ethnic community to label him "tepid" in his defense of Poland.[5]

Following Sikorski's visit, cracks began to appear in the generally united front put forth by Polonia. Within a month of Sikorski's meeting with Roosevelt, 2,500 representatives from various organizations founded the American Slav Congress at a meeting in Detroit. Although Poles were heavily represented among its early membership, the leftist leadership of socialist labor activist Leo Krzycki, the organization's president, soon caused most to withdraw from what they viewed as a pro-Soviet movement.

A more serious challenge to the supporters of Sikorski arose in June 1942, when Frank Januszewski, publisher of Detroit's influential *Dziennik Polski,* called a meeting in New York City to form the *Komitet Narodowy Amerykanów Pochodzenia Polskiego* (National Committee of Americans of Polish Descent). Known by its Polish initials (KNAPP), the organization, led by Maximilian Węgrzynek, consisted primarily of "ultranationalistic Piłsudskiites" who "lobbied vigorously for the reestablishment of prewar Polish borders and a 'Russophobic' foreign policy."[6] Although the movement's activists were only about 2,000 strong, they were extremely vocal. Węgrzynek's New York daily *Nowy Świąt* (New World) forcefully denounced Sikorski and his moderate policies, while also voicing criticism of Roosevelt for his failure to take a strong stance against Soviet demands on Poland. Similar attacks, particularly on Sikorski, appeared in the anti-communist *KNAPP Biuletun* (KNAPP Bulletin) founded as a press organ for the new organization.

In addition to its attack on Sikorski, KNAPP launched an even more vicious verbal assault on the Soviet Union. Emphasizing the duplicitous record of past Soviet behavior, Węgrzynek vigorously lobbied the State Department to refuse recognition of Stalin's claims to eastern Poland. In a letter to Secretary of State Cordell Hull dated March 3, 1943, he labeled the Soviet Union a "wanton aggressor" that "cynically distorted the lofty principles of the Atlantic Charter."[7] The U.S. government in turn considered KNAPP a "fanatical" group and monitored its activities closely.

The anti-Sikorski forces enjoyed their strongest support in New York and Michigan; thus they not only split Polonia on the question of support for the Polish Premier's moderate policies toward the Soviet Union but also revived fears on the part of Polish leadership in Chicago of an "eastern" challenge for the national leadership of Polish Americans. These fears appeared confirmed when Stanisław Gutowski, an attorney and KNAPP loyalist from Newark, New Jersey, launched a bitter attack on Świętlik over his support of Sikorski. The long-term result of this conflict, according to author Charles Sadler, was "to increase political self-consciousness among all Polish-Americans, moving them away from the largely nonpolitical activities of the Polish National Alliance and Polish-American Council."[8]

In an effort to counter growing pressure from KNAPP, in September 1942 Świętlik issued an invitation to Sikorski to speak in Chicago. The premier, realizing the political potential of such an appearance, indicated to Roosevelt's advisors that he could use the occasion to rally support for Democratic candidates in the upcoming congressional elections. By the fall of 1942, however, the international political situation was extremely delicate and the president was reluctant to have Sikorski visit lest a controversy develop between his supporters and anti-Soviet elements within Polonia. Further, by 1942 Roosevelt felt confident that Polish Americans were safely within the Democratic fold. "The President does not require speeches from Sikorski to obtain Polish-American support," Sumner Welles stated flatly, while Cordell Hull, with somewhat more diplomacy, explained that "trouble-making persons" could misrepresent anything that Sikorski might say. In the end, Biddle, acting on behalf of Roosevelt, made it clear to Sikorski that he would be welcome only *after* the fall elections.[9]

Sikorski's inability to accept Świętlik's invitation was a blow to his efforts to rally support for Poland's wartime aims; it denied him direct access to the American public and thus the opportunity to explain his position and answer his critics. Beyond this, the premier's absence was a great disappointment to Chicago's Polish community, many of whom vented their frustration on Świętlik, who lost considerable prestige, and on Roosevelt, whose protests of support for Poland were openly questioned in some quarters.

Despite Roosevelt's confidence that the Democrats could count on Polish votes, some disaffection began to occur beyond that caused by Świętlik's failure to secure a visit by Sikorski. Despite several requests from Polish American leaders, the president failed to support Red Cross relief for the thousands of Poles deported to Siberia by Soviet authorities. Roosevelt's failure to act on behalf of the captive Poles caused great consternation throughout Polonia, as did his refusal to reply to two public letters addressed to him by a "Republican who voted for the President." As a result, a memorandum prepared by the Democratic National Committee prior to the 1942 election campaign warned that the party could no longer take the Polish vote for granted.[10]

True to the memorandum's predictions, the Republicans made substantial gains in the congressional elections held in the fall of 1942. Although political analysts could not agree on the cause of the Republican resurgence, most Democratic planners, looking ahead to the crucial presidential election of 1944, agreed that "one key to victory lay in retaining the strong loyalties of certain ethnic groups, especially Polish-Americans."[11] Thus, when Sikorski finally arrived in the United States on December 1, en route to meet with the president, Roosevelt was already thinking of the political implications of the Pole's visit on his next election campaign.

But politics were also on the premier's mind. Indeed, Sikorski found himself in a particularly sensitive position, especially when Swiętlik renewed his invitation to the Pole to visit Chicago. On the one hand, Sikorski felt compelled to avoid alienating Roosevelt with any denunciation of Soviet expansionism in eastern Poland, while on the other he was keenly aware of the risk of being labeled an appeaser by vocal anti-Soviet elements in both the Polish and Polish American communities. After much soul searching, Sikorski attempted to head off any showdown over the Soviet question when, prior to his public visit to Chicago on December 17, he issued a statement declaring that the purpose of the war was "not about frontiers," a stance that placed him in line with Roosevelt's previous pronouncements. Sikorski went on to explain that while he was personally alarmed by Soviet territorial claims in Poland, he was determined to work with Stalin in an effort to present a common front to a mutual enemy. He was, he said, willing "to overlook past wrongs . . . and work for friendly relations."[12]

Sikorski's position on the issue of Poland's eastern border met with severe criticism from KNAPP and other anti-Sikorski groups in the United States. In fact, it not only increased criticism of the Polish premier but also caused a continued decline in the leadership status of Swiętlik, who continued to support Sikorski's approach. The latter was important because Swiętlik, by virtue of his status as a leader of the Polish American community in Chicago, the largest in the United States, was uniquely situated to unite Polonia under a single umbrella organization to lobby for Polish American concerns. His loss of prestige through close association with what opponents viewed as Sikorski's "appeasement" policy meant that both Swiętlik and by extension Chicago's Poles lost their preeminent claim to the leadership of Polonia.

The Katyn Controversy

The beginnings of Polish American voter defection from the Democratic fold, clearly visible in the 1942 elections, coupled with the growing criticism of Polish and Polish American leaders advocating compromise with the Soviets for the good of the wartime alliance, also had an effect on Roosevelt's approach to Polish issues. Within a few months the divisive border issue took on new dimensions when the Germans announced on April 13, 1943, the discovery of the mass graves of nearly 5,000 Poles in the Katyn Forest about ten miles from Smolensk. When the Red Army invaded Poland in 1939, some 250,000 Polish combatants were taken prisoner. The Sikorski-Maisky Pact provided for the release of these prisoners of war and their organization into a Polish Army to fight alongside the Red Army against the Nazis. For months the Polish commanding officer, General Władysław Anders, inquired into the whereabouts of 15,000 men who could not be found, including approximately 8,000 officers. The missing men, it appeared, had been held in Soviet prison camps at Kozelsk, Ostashkov, and Starobelsk until the spring of 1940, when letters to relatives in Poland ceased after the prisoners were transferred to unknown locations. During the months following the Sikorski-Maisky Pact, the Polish premier addressed to Soviet officials more than 50 inquiries on the whereabouts of these men. The Soviets steadfastly claimed to have no knowledge of them.[13]

Now the awful truth began to unfold. The German radio, as might be expected, maintained that the victims were murdered by the Soviets prior to the German occupation of the area. The Soviets countered that the men were captured by Nazi troops during the German invasion in the summer of 1941 and murdered by the Fascists shortly thereafter. Shocked by the loss of some 45 percent of the entire prewar officer corps, the Sikorski government demanded that the Red Cross be authorized to investigate and fix blame for the crime. When these demands were pressed Polish-Soviet relations deteriorated rapidly, until Stalin unilaterally broke diplomatic relations with the London government-in-exile.

The American press generally accepted the Soviet explanation of Katyn, preferring to believe that such a heinous crime had been committed by the enemy. The *Nation* told its readers that "the German report of the alleged atrocity . . . has all the earmarks of a phony," while *Newsweek* focused on the incident's potential damage to Allied relations, noting that "One of the most tragic disputes to haunt the relations between the United Nations has arisen from the mass graves of . . . Polish officers." Indeed, the *Newsweek* editorial appeared to set the tone for response by the influential American press. In his analysis of this phenomenon, David Januszewski correctly concluded that to the American press, "it was the dispute, not the massacre which was viewed as a tragedy."[14] In this light, *Newsweek* castigated the Poles for requesting the Red Cross investigation, because to do so implied that the German charges were true. While some publications informed readers that both powers were capable of committing the atrocity, and *Life* magazine in particular noted that "Russians as well as Germans have shot plenty of Poles," most placed their trust in Soviet denials and ascribed blame to the Germans.

The Katyn controversy led to a decided shift in the attitude of American politicians, newspaper editors, and the general public away from the legitimate Polish government headed by Sikorski. Ironically, although it was the Soviets who broke diplomatic relations, the American press generally blamed the Poles for instigating the crisis with their appeal to the Red Cross. In the opinion of the press, the Polish request was, as *Newsweek* maintained, a "tactical mistake." Only the *Saturday Evening Post* supported the Poles, blaming both the diplomatic crisis and the break in relations on the Soviet Union. Nevertheless, American opinion, previously sympathetic to the plight of the Poles, turned dramatically against Sikorski and his colleagues in London. "While this desire for Allied unity was certainly reasonable," concluded Januszewski, "it had harmful ramifications for the Polish government-in-exile. As soon as the issue became the diplomacy instead of the atrocity, the Polish government itself became a vulnerable target of criticism in the debate over the Katyn incident."[15]

As the Polish cause deteriorated in the international arena, divisions also began to appear in Polish American ranks. KNAPP, already a vehemently anti-communist organization under the leadership of Ignacy Matuszewski and Wacław Jędrzejewicz, took the lead in placing blame for both the atrocity and the diplomatic flap directly on the Soviet Union. Within weeks it was circulating a detailed pamphlet titled "Death at Katyn," presenting strong evidence that the Soviet Union was guilty of the crime. Nor was it only KNAPP that protested. While the pamphlet made its way through Polonia and into the American main-stream, nine Polish American congressmen, led by John Lesiński of Michigan, Thaddeus Wasielewski of Wisconsin and Joseph Mruk of New York, sought to examine documents on the crime collected by the U.S. War Department. The request was denied by War Department officials, who maintained that the documents in question were "classified information."[16]

Faced with the Katyn revelations, the continuing border issue, and Stalin's increasing hostility toward the London-based government-in-exile, Stanisław Mikołajczyk, who succeeded Sikorski as premier when the latter was killed in a mysterious plane crash in July 1943, demanded that FDR, Churchill, and Stalin include him in any and all negotiations involving Polish interests. To lend weight to his demand in the United States, he linked it with a threat to appeal to the New York–based National Committee, a much more militant group than the Chicago-based Świętlik faction, should the legitimate Polish representatives be ignored. U.S. Ambassador Biddle took the threat seriously, as did FDR's closest advisor, Harry Hopkins, who cautioned that the Polish question could be "political dynamite" in the 1944 elections. Roosevelt also regarded this development as serious, and, as Charles Sadler noted, it had "a profound impact on the Roosevelt administration."[17]

The Teheran Agreement

The Katyn affair also sent shock waves through Polonia, animating and mobilizing it as much as the initial invasion of Poland in 1939. With growing distrust of Soviet intentions, Polish Americans were especially interested in the results of Roosevelt's meeting with Churchill and Stalin at Teheran in November 1943. There, Churchill began the discussion on Poland by proposing the acceptance of the Curzon Line—the line established by the Allied powers following the Treaty of Versailles in 1919 to define the Polish-Lithuanian border—as Poland's eastern border, a suggestion that meant de facto recognition of Soviet claims to eastern Poland. Despite his assurances of support to both the London government-in-exile and Polish American leaders, Roosevelt interposed no objection, tacitly agreeing to Soviet predominance in postwar Eastern Europe and to Stalin's annexation of eastern Poland. In doing so, however, Roosevelt made it clear to the Soviet dictator that these agreements must be kept secret, for "he could not participate in any public discussion on Poland for at least a year, lest he antagonize the six to seven million Polish Americans living in the United States."[18]

Thus, at Teheran, in a single sweeping move, Winston Churchill and Franklin Roosevelt effectively repudiated the noble aims of the Atlantic Charter, innumerable commitments made to allies who were even then fighting and dying for the common cause, and a whole generation of political rhetoric stretching back as far as Woodrow Wilson's Fourteen Points, with its emphasis on open covenants openly negotiated. The "Polish question" was decided in secret, much like the move to dismember Czechoslovakia at Munich in 1938, without the participation or knowledge of the victim. The issue was settled, historian J. R. Thackrah noted, "without previous consultation with the duly elected representatives of the Polish nation." It was a pattern of action that would repeat itself all too often in the months and years to come.[19]

Anxious to determine what, if any, agreements were reached at Teheran, both Polish and Polish American representatives called on the White House for some clarification of the outcome of the meeting. When no substantive reassurances were forthcoming from Washington, a sense of apprehension set in as Poles the world over, fearing the worst, intensified efforts on behalf of their homeland. On January 8, 1944, the *New York Times* carried a letter from several major Polish organizations that reflected the emotional depth of their concern and their view of the gravity of the situation. It stated, prophetically:

> If no circumstances are visualized under which we can fight for Poland, our ally, it is more doubtful that we should be willing to fight for the borders of Lithuania, Latvia, Estonia, not our allies. Obviously, we shall not fight in defense of Rumania, Hungary and Bulgaria, with whom we are at war, or Turkey and Persia, neutral but within the Russian sphere of influence. Therefore the people of Europe can come to only one conclusion: that the United States has resolved to resign forever from the realization of the principles of the Atlantic Charter in that part of Europe that is within reach of the military power of the Soviet Union. If this should prove to be the case, then the Atlantic Charter is nothing but a miserable propaganda trick to induce those peoples to continue their resistance against Germany on the basis of false pledges.[20]

Three days later Secretary of State Cordell Hull received a letter from Rev. Alphonse Skoniecki, executive secretary of the Coordinating Committee of American Polish Associations in the East, requesting that the United States "use its political and economic power to persuade Russia to support Washington's policy of self-determination for Poland."[21] Pressure was also brought to bear on Roosevelt by several congressmen, including Buffalo's Joseph Mruk, who warned that if the Red Army were allowed to remain in postwar Eastern Europe the war would be lost "idealistically and morally." Roosevelt replied with vague reassurances that he would "seek a just and enduring peace based on the sovereign equality of all peace-loving states, large and small."[22] When Mruk, obviously unsatisfied, asked the president point-blank whether any agreements on Poland were made at Teheran, Roosevelt replied reassuringly—and deceptively—that "there were no secret commitments made by me at Teheran and I am quite sure that other members of my party made none either."[23]

As resentment against the Soviet Union increased throughout Polonia, Stalin moved in March 1944 to sway Polish American opinion by inviting two pro–Soviet Polonians—Rev. Stanisław Orlemański of Springfield, Massachusetts, and Oskar

Lange of the University of Chicago—to Moscow. Founders, along with labor leader Leo Krzycki, of the pro-Soviet Kościuszko Polish Patriotic League, the two undertook their journey with Roosevelt's permission, but they represented only a small minority of American Poles, most of whom repudiated the two as traitors. The leaders of organized Polonia, however, were quick to bring pressure on their elected representatives, pressure that was strong enough to elicit from Washington a statement that the priest and the professor had no official function and acted only as private citizens. If anything, Stalin's attempt to sway Polish American opinion only increased efforts to lobby on behalf of the Mikołajczyk government.

The Election of 1944

While Stalin pursued his abortive attempt to influence Polish American opinion, serious political changes unfolded within Polonia that shaped the collective Polish American voice for the duration of the war and decades beyond. By the end of 1943 there was growing rejection among Polish Americans of Świętlik's moderate leadership. Opposition within Chicago's Polish American community crystallized around Charles Rozmarek, who, though previously a supporter of Świętlik, became increasingly concerned about Soviet intentions and the wisdom of Świętlik's approach. One of the major differences between the two was Rozmarek's support for seeking a rapprochement with Polish Americans on the East Coast to promote the creation of a national organization. In this struggle Świętlik lost and was replaced as president of the influential Polish National Alliance by Rozmarek in early 1944.

Once Rozmarek assumed leadership in Chicago, he immediately began working to mend fences with the eastern Poles and create a unified national organization. To this end, eastern leader Maximilian Węgrzynek journeyed to Chicago to meet with Rozmarek and Honorata Wołowska, president of the Polish Women's Alliance, to conduct preliminary negotiations regarding the formation of an umbrella political organization to coordinate lobbying on Polish concerns. The three agreed in principle, and soon Rozmarek and Detroit publisher Frank Januszewski issued a call for a meeting in Buffalo, New York, to form a single organization that would unite some 6 million Polish Americans.

Such a massive political effort did not go unnoticed by the Democratic administration, which dispatched Roosevelt aide David Niles to Detroit to meet with Rozmarek and Januszewski. Niles later reported that the Poles had "a terrific resentment against the Administration, which will eventually crystalize in some unfriendly form. The main aim of this Congress is to save Poland from a new partition."[24]

Faced with this potential political backlash, the administration directed the Foreign Nationalities Branch of the Office of Strategic Services to investigate the implications of the proposed Polish gathering. The OSS had already been employed in August 1943 to prepare and distribute a questionnaire to Polish Americans in Chicago, Detroit, Buffalo, Cleveland, and New York. The survey questioned whether the respondent believed that the Polish government in London represented the Polish people and contained other questions asking for knowledge or opinions on world events, particularly as they related to Poland

and the Soviet Union. Many familiar with the survey—even including the U.S. State Department staff—felt that the questionnaire was both unfair and anti-Polish. It angered Polish American leaders, who charged that it served no other purpose than to determine how Polish Americans would vote in 1944. Dewitt Poole, Foreign Nationalities branch officer of the OSS, defended the questionnaire as an attempt to assess the effect of Polish and Soviet propaganda in the United States. Poles everywhere, however, sided with the Polish Roman Catholic Union's Joseph Olejniczak, who criticized the pro-Soviet bias and labeled the questionnaire "highly improper and un-American."[25]

With this controversy fresh in mind, the OSS maintained a low profile as it carried out its assignment to investigate the proposed gathering of Polish American leaders. The opinion of the OSS was that the numerical strength of Polonia could very well make the Polish-Soviet issue, including the suppressed Katyn affair, an important ingredient in the 1944 election. On April 1 the Foreign Nationalities Branch further warned that the ultranationalists of KNAPP might gain control of the congress and "bring to full flood tide the Polish nationalist sentiment in the United States."[26] Clearly more interested in the potential effect of a unified Polish American voting bloc than in the merits of the Polish cause, one Roosevelt advisor cautioned openly that "the Polish-Americans may be able to start enough of a rumpus to swing over other groups before November."[27]

As the move to create an organized Polonia gathered momentum, political aides of the Roosevelt administration became increasingly concerned about its potential effects on the "Polish vote." The significance of the Polish vote lay not only in its force of number but in its concentration in the northeastern urban centers and in states with large shares of electoral votes. Also important was the fact that Poles constituted a large and hitherto reliable voting bloc within the Democratic party as well as a vocal minority within two other traditional groups of the Democratic coalition: the Catholic Church and organized labor. Clearly, any development with the potential to upset this political coalition would be viewed with concern by Democratic strategists. While administration officials followed its progress with growing concern, some 4,000 Polish Americans, including 2,800 official delegates from 22 states representing a wide spectrum of organizations, convened in Buffalo in May to formally inaugurate the Polish American Congress as a lobbying organization designed to increase the effectiveness of Polonia's political clout. While the Polish National Alliance played a leading role in the formation of the Polish American Congress, and PNA President Charles Rozmarek was elected the first head of the new organization, the congress was founded on "a federal principle," with member groups retaining their autonomy and sending representatives based on their membership to participate in a governing body.[28]

Placing a priority on supporting demands for the reestablishment of the pre–1939 Polish borders and for official recognition of the London government-in-exile, Rozmarek nevertheless chose to adopt a moderate stance in his keynote address. Although attacking the Soviet policy toward Poland, he refused to criticize Roosevelt and also attempted to quell the administration's fears that the Polish American Congress would become a partisan Republican political movement. The new organization, he emphasized, would cooperate with the

Democratic administration's war effort and support a foreign policy based on the principles articulated by the president in the Atlantic Charter. The Polish American Congress, according to Rozmarek, would exert moral rather than political force.

To communicate its position to the administration, the Polish American Congress drafted a special memorandum to President Roosevelt and appointed a committee to deliver it to him personally. In a thinly veiled reference to the Soviet Union, the missive read in part: "We hold that the comradeship in arms impose upon the United States full moral responsibility . . . for the deeds and aims of our Allies."[29] Despite the surface rhetoric, this was viewed by Rozmarek and his colleagues as a compromise because there was no demand for an immediate American commitment to support Polish claims against the Soviet Union.

Soviet reaction to the formation of the Polish American Congress was immediate and vehement. *Pravda* denounced its leaders as Fascists and referred to the organization as "Hitler's Polish agency." Despite the moderate tone of Rozmarek's overtures, the reaction of Democrats at home was hardly less dramatic. Roosevelt and his advisors remained uneasy about the political orientation of the new congress. Democrats noted with concern that the leaders of the Polish American Congress included KNAPP's Maximilian Węgrzynek, the ultranationalistic editor of the New York newspaper *Nowy Świat* and a vocal Dewey supporter, and Frank Januszewski, editor of Detroit's pro-Republican and anti-administration *Dziennik Polski* and a member of the Michigan State Republican Committee. Cordell Hull expressed concern that *Dziennik Polski* was "outspoken in its criticism of both the Polish Government-in-exile and the Soviet Government and represents the ultranationalistic Polish groups in this country."[30] A number of other prominent Republicans were in the congress's ranks, and its National Committee had vetoed a statement of support for Roosevelt. One Roosevelt aid went so far as to note that "one cannot help in detecting a terrific resentment against the Administration."[31]

The Roosevelt administration was particularly sensitive to its vulnerability on the question of postwar Polish borders. Since the president had already given his secret approval at Teheran to the postwar annexation of some 37 percent of Polish territory by the Soviet Union, he and his advisors were deeply concerned that any leak of this information would alienate Polish American voters.[32] Roosevelt was particularly uneasy about a visit by Polish Premier Stanisław Mikołajczyk planned for the summer of 1944. Although he agreed to extend an official invitation in May, he predicated the invitation on the condition "that the prime minister make no public speeches and establish no contacts with Polish Americans."[33] With no alternative, Mikołajczyk agreed.

He and Ambassador Ciechanowski met several times with the president between June 7 and 14. The Poles asked Roosevelt for an increase in aid to the Polish underground, while the president pressed them to accommodate Soviet demands that the Poles eliminate anti-Soviet leaders from their government, accept the revision of their eastern border in favor of the Soviet Union, and have Polish leaders visit Moscow. Roosevelt was willing to extend additional aid, he pointedly told the Poles, but only on the condition of a quid pro quo regarding Soviet demands. In fact, when supplemental appropriations were eventually approved for the Polish underground, it was "conditional upon the Polish Underground forces' activities being closely coordinated with the military opera-

tions of the Soviet Army."³⁴ Although Roosevelt tempered his demand with elo-
quent public statements about the need for Allied unity, the contributions of
Poland to the war effort, and his own "moral" support for Polish independence,
the two Poles recognized this for what it was, as did Neil Sandberg, who correctly concluded that the president's statements "were intended to be a sop to the
only minority group he feared—the seven million Polish-Americans who . . . the
President said voted as a solid unit."³⁵

Thus finessing Mikołajczyk's visit to his own advantage, Roosevelt was still
faced with the potential political challenge of the Polish American Congress.
When its National Committee attempted to make an appointment with
Roosevelt to deliver its memorandum it was told that the president was "too
busy." When Congressmen Lesiński, Wasielewski, and Mruk met with similar
rebuff, the Poles asked Mayor Edward J. Kelly of Chicago to be their envoy, but
he, too, was turned away. Frustrated at this obvious slight, Rozmarek appealed
to Kelly once again in a letter dated September 9, which the Pole concluded with
a thinly veiled political threat: "I earnestly hope that the six million Americans
of Polish descent throughout these United States, represented by their duly
elected delegates at the congress, will not be required to suffer a keen disappointment by having their unanimous request ignored by the Chief Executive in
the White House, to whom they have always felt very friendly."³⁶

In the midst of this domestic political turmoil the Red Army pushed the
retreating Nazis back into Poland in late July. The Poles, still unaware their
interests had already been compromised at Teheran, wanted to present the Red
Army with a liberated Warsaw and gain political advantages that could be used
at the postwar bargaining table. Thus, motivated by political concerns and urged
into rebellion by radio broadcasts from the Red Army promising its assistance,
the Polish Home Army began an uprising on August 1. Although it encouraged
the Poles to rebel and throw out the German occupiers, the Red Army, which the
Poles in Warsaw could clearly hear just a short distance away across the Vistula
River, did nothing to support those fighting against tremendous odds in the
Polish capital. Worse still, the Soviets, seeking to have the Germans eliminate
for them any Polish leadership capable of opposing their plans for postwar
expansion, openly obstructed British and American efforts to provide the uprising with aid.³⁷

When news of the Warsaw Uprising reached the United States, Polish
American leaders pleaded with the Roosevelt administration to assist the Home
Army with or without the cooperation of the Soviet Union. The Polish American
press published repeated calls for assistance, and leaders went so far as to
threaten to vote Republican if no efforts were undertaken. Despite the obvious
vulnerability of Roosevelt on the Polish issue, particularly with the Warsaw
Uprising in progress and Stalin refusing aid, the Republicans made little effort
to capitalize on the situation for political advantage. The Republican platform
contained no strong statement on Poland and the candidate, Governor Thomas
E. Dewey of New York, failed to court the Polish vote in any serious manner.

The Warsaw Uprising lasted 63 bloody days from August through October
1944. Initially, it received little press coverage. While some articles praised the
Poles' heroism, most echoed the sentiments of *Time*, which informed its readers
that the situation was both hopeless and useless, as "the Poles were a 19th-
Century army fighting a 20th-Century war."³⁸ At a time when Allies were

appearing victorious, noted David Januszewski, this was viewed as a defeat and relegated to back pages. *Newsweek, Time* and the *New Republic* all labeled the uprising premature, and few if any felt that it could succeed. On August 28 *Newsweek* praised air crews flying the dangerous 1,750 mile round trip from Italy to Warsaw to drop supplies to the beleaguered Poles, but the magazine never raised the obvious question of why flights did not land in "Allied" territory in the Soviet Union. Although *Time* did ask that question, it informed its readers that "the answer was not immediately forthcoming."[39]

As Warsaw fought and bled, Stalin moved to consolidate his grip on postwar Poland by forming a Polish government in Lublin and refusing to deal with the London Poles. But this, too, raised no alarm among the American public or its politicians. Some questions did begin to appear in the American press about the role of the Soviet Union in the uprising—or, more appropriately, about its inactivity. On September 4 *Time* informed its readers that "So far the Russians, some ten miles away, have dropped nothing."[40] Several publications carried the news that the Soviets, "for political reasons," refused to cooperate with the Polish underground. Yet there was no outcry from an American public much more preoccupied with its own loved ones in uniform than with a situation in Eastern Europe that it knew or cared little about. When the uprising eventually failed, many American periodicals bemoaned the tragedy, but most blamed it on the Polish high command.

Given the Roosevelt administration's refusal to offer public guarantees of Polish borders or freedom in a postwar world, its refusal to support an investigation into the Katyn atrocity, and its refusal to press the Soviets to give aid to the Polish insurgents in Warsaw, many Polish American leaders become increasingly wary of the president's motives. Yet the Republicans generally remained silent, failing to mention Poland in their campaign platform, opposing legislation to admit displaced persons—including many Poles—into the United States, and generally offering little political alternative. Finally, on October 8, Dewey bid for Polonia's support by attacking Roosevelt's evasiveness on Poland, accusing the administration of planning to yield Poland to the Soviets, and promising to firmly oppose Soviet expansion in Eastern Europe. As this political pressure rose, Roosevelt was virtually forced to meet with the Poles or run the risk of losing their vital support in the upcoming election.[41]

Making the most of the occasion, the president chose to receive the Poles on October 11, Pułaski Day, in an obvious attempt to curry their favor. With a clear eye toward political imagery, Roosevelt met Rozmarek and the other members of the delegation in a room whose wall was decorated with a large map of Poland, its prewar boundaries clearly marked in heavy dark ink. Photographs were taken that the Democrats later circulated to the press, giving the impression that the president supported the reestablishment of Poland's prewar boundaries. In fact, the participants in the meeting described Roosevelt as "genial" but "vague" when it came to any statement of firm support for Polish concerns. Although he made general pronouncements that "Poland must be reconstituted as a great nation," and that it should be "one of the bulwarks of the structure upon which we hope to build a permanent peace,"[42] Roosevelt did not offer concrete plans or commitments. Indeed, he could not, having already conceded those interests to the Soviets at Teheran the previous year. Instead, he explained his public silence on Poland by indicating that he could issue no public statement for fear of alien-

President Franklin D. Roosevelt meets with leaders of the Polish American Congress led by Charles Rozmarek (right) in October 1944. This photograph, showing Poland's prewar borders, was among others circulated by Democrats to bolster FDR's standing among Polish Americans prior to the 1944 election. Polish National Alliance.

ating the Soviets, a vital ally in the struggle against Nazi Germany, and Soviet supporters in the United States.

Apparently uneasy about Roosevelt's reluctance to make a definitive statement on Poland, Rozmarek sent a telegram to Mikołajczyk on October 20, 1944, pleading with him to uphold the Polish cause and not cave in to demands from Stalin on the border issue or the composition of the Polish government. "I urge you, on behalf of the Polish organizations in America," he implored, "to defend without further compromise the essential rights of full sovereignty, territorial integrity and the honor of the Polish nation. We earnestly warn you against taking communists into your Cabinet because it would be the beginning of the loss of Polish independence."[43] At the same time, both the Polish American Congress and the influential *Chicago Tribune* spoke highly of the Republican challenger's statement on behalf of Poland, and the newspaper went so far as to accuse Roosevelt and Churchill of abandoning Poland in secret negotiations culminating in an agreement to give approximately one-half of its territory to the Soviet Union. Roosevelt, no doubt greatly distressed by the leak of information on Teheran, remained silent.

On October 28 the president journeyed to Chicago, where he "showed considerable skill in cultivating the Polish-American vote. He realized that Chicago was its 'greatest center,' and he often spoke warmly of Polish-Americans."[44] Dramatically meeting with Rozmarek in his private railway car, Roosevelt "put on one of his most brilliant political performances." He "spoke eloquently of the agony of Warsaw" and of the "Atlantic Charter and its meaning to Poland," and he proclaimed to his entranced audience that while there remained some differences that could not be settled until the war was won, "Poland, the country most severely brutalized by the Nazis, would emerge from its terrible ordeal to assume a leading place in a reconstituted Europe."[45] Rozmarek was clearly affected. "The President's captivating personality, boundless confidence, and total mastery touched Rozmarek deeply. Later that evening, before 125,000 people in Soldier Field, Roosevelt reiterated that the ideals of the Atlantic Charter would be realized."[46]

As president of the Polish National Alliance and the new Polish American Congress, Rozmarek was arguably the strongest political leader Polonia had ever seen. He was powerful enough to bring diverse Polish American organizations together in a movement to unite their political voices, he participated in political discussions with the leaders of Poland's government-in-exile, and he could obtain an audience with the president of the United States. His word meant something, and Polonia would respond to his lead. If ever Polonia was poised to exercise a real impact on American policy, it was in October 1944. Yet on the day after his meeting with Roosevelt Rozmarek informed a reporter from the *New York Times*, and an apprehensive Polonia, that "during the visit of the Polish-American Congress delegates to the White House on Oct. 11 and during my conversation with the President on Oct. 28 in Chicago he assured me that he will carry out the pledge of the Democratic Party with respect to our foreign policy and that he will see to it that Poland is treated justly at the peace conference. Because I am convinced of his sincerity I shall vote for him on Nov. 7 for President of the United States of America."[47]

Rozmarek provided what Roosevelt desired most, an endorsement for a fourth term. The Democratic National Committee made sure that Rozmarek's words were disseminated throughout the American and Polish-language press, providing it with the campaign edge it sought, while Rozmarek failed to receive any firm commitment in return. In retrospect, it is obvious that Rozmarek had no influence on Roosevelt's policies at all, other than to cause him to devise strategies for ensuring the domestic support of Polish American voters. To later generations of Polish Americans it became painfully clear that, as Sadler concluded, Rozmarek

> was a politician, not a statesman, a leader who became well versed in the intricacies of intra-Polonia politics but remained a neophyte in the tortured compromises of international coalitions. . . . Roosevelt treated Rozmarek as a peddler of Polish votes and a hopeless chauvinist to be wooed but not consulted, as Woodrow Wilson and Colonel Edward M. House had treated the towering Paderewski during the First World War. In fact, even as Roosevelt spoke movingly about Poland with Rozmarek in the railroad car, he knew that Churchill had already sealed the fate of Poland at the Moscow negotiations. To Roosevelt, that lack of candor was not dishonesty but a manifestation of traditional ethnic politics. While he presented Rozmarek with inspiring generalizations about Polish heroism, he asked Churchill to keep the Moscow settlement secret until after the election. Ever solicitous of the President's fate in an election year, Churchill was happy to comply.[48]

Continuing the last-minute political offensive begun so successfully by the president in Chicago, the popular New York senator Robert Wagner appeared at the United Polish Clubs in New York City two days before the election, stating flatly: "I believe with every fiber in my being that the complete independence of Poland—the complete restoration and protection of its boundaries reflecting the history and aspirations of the Polish people—is one of the things for which we are fighting this war. . . . I know that this has always been the aim and intent of the Administration of Franklin Roosevelt."[49] With this, their trust in the Roosevelt administration, forged in the depths of the Depression, still unbroken by the border issue, by Katyn, by the failure to aid the Warsaw Uprising, or by the president's equivocation, traditionally Democratic Polish America gave Roosevelt more than 90 percent of its votes on election day. Although the president carried the day, as Robert Szymczak noted in a thoughtful study of this period, "Roosevelt's manipulation of Polish-Americans for political purposes was destined to become a cause for bitterness which came into full force a short time later."[50]

seven

The Cold War, 1945–1954

In the spring of 1945, with the war in Europe nearly over, a poll conducted by *Public Opinion Quarterly* indicated that Americans generally "had a good deal of trust in Moscow."[1] In the heady atmosphere of impending victory, the average citizen, influenced by the attempts of the U.S. government to cement Allied unity during the war, harbored positive feelings toward the Soviets as companions in the great crusade against Nazi aggression. For Poles, and Polish Americans, this attitude made the presentation of their case all the more difficult.[2]

During the war a higher percentage of Polish citizens—Christians, Jews, and others alike—were killed than any other nation except Yugoslavia. Murdered in the streets, gassed in concentration camps, and killed on the battlefields, Poles suffered long and contributed much to the Allied victory. It was the Polish underground, generally considered to be the foremost such organization of the war, that provided England with the secrets of the German Enigma coding machine and the dreaded "buzz-bombs" hurled against British cities. Polish airmen of the Kościuszko Squadron shot down more German planes than any other Allied squadron of *any* nationality during the pivotal Battle of Britain. Polish sailors helped protect convoys in the North Atlantic from German submarines and participated in the D-Day invasion. Polish soldiers fought in defense of France in 1940, at Narvik and Tobruk, at Normandy and the Falaise Gap. Poles captured the crucial German positions at Monte Cassino in the Italian campaign, liberated Bologna, and fought in the bloody Battle of Arnhem. Poland was, in every respect, a contributing member of the Allied coalition, fully deserving of every opportunity for participation and consideration in the postwar political process; but in 1945 the assault on Poland that began with the German onslaught in 1939 was continued by Poland's allies.

As reluctant as they were to "die for Danzig" in 1939, the western Allies proved even more reluctant to honor their commitments to Poland in 1945. It was Winston Churchill who forced Mikołajczyk to accept a new government dominated by pro-Soviet delegates on the threat of withdrawing British support for the London government. It was Franklin Roosevelt who played down misgivings about Soviet intentions and determined to placate Stalin.

Yalta

The bitter end for Poles and their Polish American kin came at Yalta in February 1945. There the Big Three met to formalize the secret protocols agreed to at Teheran. At Yalta, Poland was stripped of some 70,000 square miles of territory, land that was at the same time recognized by the victors as belonging to the Soviet Union. Although Poland was later "compensated" with 40,000 square miles of German territory east of the Oder and Neisse Rivers at the Potsdam Conference in the summer of 1945, it remained the only Allied nation to suffer a loss of territory and population by being on the winning side in the conflict. At the same time the land concessions were made, the Lublin government was officially recognized on the Soviet promise that free Polish elections would be held in the future. As before, the only serious concern Roosevelt impressed on Stalin was his concern about the effects of a settlement on the Polish vote at home.

Returning from Yalta, Churchill spoke in the House of Commons on the need for the Poles to accept the border solution dictated by the Big Three. As if to reassure the Poles that all was not lost, he referred to the "promise" of free elections, stating in his steady, reassuring voice: "I know of no government which stands to its obligations more solidly than the Soviet Government."[3]

News of Yalta sent shock waves through Polonia. Rozmarek was devastated. "Having trusted President Roosevelt on the basis of his pledge to preserve Polish independence," Szymczak wrote, "Rozmarek and his associates were literally taken aback by the virtual casting off of the legal Polish government. The February 1945 Yalta accords occasioned a chorus of protests not only from Polish circles in London, but also from the emotional voice of the Polish-American Congress."[4] Belatedly, the congress vigorously protested the new "partition" of Poland, sending a lengthy memorandum of concern to both the president and congressional leaders. While some of the latter responded, support was mostly limited to those who represented districts with a high proportion of Polish Americans who were no doubt worried about the political consequences if they appeared unconcerned. Most responsive were Republicans who at last sensed a political issue that might be turned to their advantage. Yet aside from the potential for partisan domestic politics, it was already too late to save Poland.

When the Poles were not invited to the San Francisco Conference to discuss plans for formation of the United Nations, they appealed to Britain, the United States, and China in a note dated March 12, 1945, that stands as a chilling prelude of events to come: "The Polish Government wishes to state, considering all that Poland has suffered in the War, that the noninvitation to the San Francisco Conference of Poland whose constitutional President and Government are generally recognized by all the United Nations with the exception of only one of the Powers, and also by the neutral states, is the first disquieting case of the application of the right of veto of great powers which has been made even before the United Nations have approved or accepted the proposals concerning an International Security Organization."[5]

This cartoon, which appeared in *Dziennik Związkowy* on the fifth anniversary of the Yalta agreement, depicts Joseph Stalin presenting his demands at Yalta and Franklin D. Roosevelt being influenced to "agree to everything."

When the United Nations convened at the San Francisco Conference to draft the Charter of the United Nations Organization, the cause of Poland was championed by leaders of the now outraged Polish American Congress. Befriended and assisted by Senator Arthur Vandenberg, they scored a notable success when they were able to prevent the seating of the Soviet-led Lublin Government. The victory, however, was short-lived; soon after the U.S. government, caving in to Soviet demands, recognized the Soviet-sponsored Polish Provisional Government of National Unity, thereby sealing the fate of the legitimate Polish government in London that had steadfastly supported the Allied cause throughout the war.

"No matter from what angle one studies Western diplomacy in the first half of 1945," Thackrah concluded, "an objective observer cannot escape the fact that the Big Three, in their post war settlement of Europe, disregarded the Atlantic Charter and the Four Freedoms [repeatedly advocated by FDR during the war: freedom of speech, freedom of worship, freedom from want, freedom from fear]. Considering the military help Poland gave to the Allied cause in the Second World War, Poland deserved far better than what she actually received from her more fortunately situated Allies." The American people generally agreed. A poll conducted in 1945 showed that 67 percent of the population felt the Yalta agreements were not "fair" to Poland.[6]

Belatedly, the Polish American Congress used the little leverage it had—largely a public appeal to moral indignation over the Yalta "sellout"—to plead the case of Poland before whoever would listen. Rozmarek attempted to rally American support by couching his appeals in traditional American values. He insisted, in the words of Stephen Garrett, "that fundamentally they were interested in the establishment in Poland of a free press, parliamentary institutions, secure civil liberties, and the free enterprise system."[7] By this time, however, Rozmarek's efforts were far too little and far too late.

Refugees from Soviet Oppression

Although outrage over Yalta dominated Polish American rhetoric in 1945, there were other issues that drew Poles together. One major concern was the large number of Polish veterans and displaced persons in Western Europe in need of assistance. By July 1945 there were 230,000 members of the Polish armed forces in the West, as well as more than 1 million civilians, including an estimated 770,000 Polish displaced persons in Western Germany alone.[8] To assist these unfortunates, a substantial number of whom did not want to return to a communist-dominated Poland, the Polish American Congress and its various member organizations conducted fundraising drives and sponsored the collection of food, clothing, medical supplies, and other items for shipment to Poles stranded in Western Europe and to the destitute people of Poland. These organizations were joined in their endeavor by the Catholic League for Religious Assistance to Poland sponsored by the Polish American Catholic bishops, the War Relief Services of the National Catholic Welfare Conference, the Red Cross, and various other organizations.[9]

In conjunction with the refugee issue, the Polish American Congress also lobbied for special legislation to allow Poles into the United States in numbers above the limited restrictions of the immigration quotas. One Congressman suggested that Polish veterans be enlisted in the U.S. Army so that its strength might be maintained without the necessity of military conscription, while another wanted to invite "these hardy soldiers" to settle the harsh wilderness of Alaska. In general, however, there was little support in Congress in the immediate postwar years for loosening the immigration quotas. One serious problem that the Polish American Congress faced, and one possible reason for the lack of sympathy on the refugee issue, was that there were at that time no Polish Americans in the U.S. Senate and fewer than a dozen in the House of Representatives. With no one in the Senate, in particular, to act as a spokesperson in foreign policy debates, Polonia was at a distinct disadvantage. Further, although Senator Vandenberg took up the Polish

American cause, he was a Republican and therefore did not have ready access to the Democratic-controlled White House and State Department.

In 1946 Rozmarek, along with Polish historian Oskar Halecki and New York KNAPP leader Ignatius Nurkiewicz, lobbied on behalf of the Polish cause at the Paris Peace Conference attended by the foreign ministers of the major Allied powers, but they achieved no notable success. Indeed, their best opportunity appeared to be at home, where the Republicans were suddenly awakening to the political potential of the Polish question as the Cold War began to replace the open hostilities of World War II. In the same year that Rozmarek's delegation traveled to Paris, Republican political strategists determined to capitalize in the 1948 election on Polish American disaffection over Yalta, the refugee issue, and the failure of the Soviets to hold the promised "free" elections in Poland.

Before the campaign began, however, the Soviets announced that elections would be held in January 1947. The elections, when they occurred, proved fraudulent. Arthur Bliss Lane, the U.S. ambassador to Poland, was so incensed over the blatant manipulation of the election by the communists that he resigned his post so he "could talk and write publicly about the perpetration of an intentional fraud which has effectively condemned the Polish people to a loss of freedom and independence."[10] Lane became an instant hero throughout Polonia.

In December 1947 Mikołajczyk was forced to flee Poland to avoid communist retribution. He came to Chicago, where he conferred at length with Rozmarek, who promised "a concerted action," but little of substance resulted other than the generation of political ammunition for the Republicans. According to Januszewski, "The Soviet policy of aggrandizement, the faked referendum, and the faked elections in Poland in 1947 seemed to have played into the hands of the Republicans as more and more Americans were becoming aware of the Communist danger."[11] In fact, the Republican challenger, Governor Thomas Dewey of New York, condemned the Yalta agreement and told enthusiastic audiences throughout the country that Poland's plight was the direct result of Roosevelt's "secret diplomacy."[12]

The Election of 1948

Truman was certainly in a poor political situation as the 1948 election drew near. Inheriting the "Polish question" from the Roosevelt administration, he fell heir to the shock of Yalta and the cries of sellout raised throughout Polonia. Despite this handicap, and the deteriorating international situation in general, Truman did have some positive achievements to use in the political war for reelection. The first of these was a reputation for being tough on communism, some of which was earned in a well-publicized incident when he administered a severe tongue-lashing to Ambassador Molotov over the Soviet Union's failure to abide by the Yalta agreements for free elections in Poland. The lack of a consistent U.S. foreign policy on Eastern Europe was remedied in March 1947 with the announcement of the Truman Doctrine, while the Democrats included in their platform a plank on Poland, maintaining that "the United States had traditionally been in sympathy with the efforts of subjugated countries to attain their

Arthur Bliss Lane, U.S. ambassador to Poland, resigned his post and became a staunch supporter of Polish interests because of what he considered to be the failure of Roosevelt and Truman to live up to commitments on Polish issues.

independence, and to establish a democratic form of government. Poland is an outstanding example. After a century and a half of subjugation, it was resurrected after the First World War by our Democratic President Woodrow Wilson. We look forward to the development of these countries as prosperous, free, and democratic fellow members of the United Nations."[13]

Another factor weighing in Truman's favor was his support for European refugees. By 1948 there were still hundreds of thousands of displaced persons in Europe. Truman's willingness to support legislation to admit thousands of displaced persons into the United States met with favor among Poles and other ethnic groups originating in Eastern Europe. In June 1948, with strong support from the president, Congress passed Public Law 744, providing for the admission into the country of more than 200,000 displaced persons from camps in Germany, Austria, and Italy. Truman's support for the admission of displaced persons was a significant plus in Polish American eyes.

Still another important factor in the election was the Democratic party's recognition of the importance of ethnic voters. Democratic planners calculated that there were 35 million white Americans of foreign origin in 1948, with more than 11 million of foreign birth. The census reported that 21 million people claimed a mother tongue other than English, of whom 11 million were eligible to vote. Surprisingly, these people "constituted more than a quarter of the total electorate."[14] Recognizing the tremendous importance of this voting bloc, J. Howard McGrath, chair of the Democratic National Committee, hired Democratic political advisor Michael Cieplinski in 1944 to direct the Nationalities Division of the Democratic National Committee. Cieplinski organized 20 nationality committees, printed campaign literature in each native language, and publicized Democratic policies and candidates in the foreign language press and radio. Showing particular sensitivity, he developed policy statements on issues of concern to each group, appointed important ethnic leaders to positions in the nationality committees, placed advertisements in the foreign language press, and consulted ethnic leaders on how to recruit their compatriots. So successful was he that the director of public relations for the Democratic National Committee asserted that when Rozmarek finally came out in support of Dewey just before the election, "he delivered to the Republicans one vote, his own."[15]

In 1944 Polish Americans had supported the Democrats en masse, but by 1948 there was a great deal of disillusion because of the many betrayals of the Roosevelt years. Nevertheless, the government's support for Polish relief efforts, the admittance of Polish displaced persons, increasing anti-communist rhetoric, and the herculean efforts of Cieplinski persuaded most Polish Americans to remain loyal to Truman. With their support he was able to win a narrow victory over Dewey, despite most predictions of a Republican victory.[16]

Although the Republicans appreciated the potential influence of the Polish American vote and made some attempts to curry favor among the group during the 1948 elections, their general policy was to avoid excessive emphasis on foreign policy issues in an effort to show bipartisanship in that important arena. They also opposed initiatives designed to ease immigration requirements for refugees. Naturally, these policies left them unable to exploit the fallout from Yalta, Katyn, the Polish elections, and refugee issues that were central to winning support from Polish American voters. Following Dewey's defeat, however, "the Republicans reassessed the policy of deemphasizing foreign affairs and determined to concentrate more specifically and vocally on Yalta and other foreign affairs issues in the future." In the wake of the 1948 elections, Republicans began a concerted effort to develop foreign policy issues, particularly those of importance to Eastern Europeans, for use in future domestic political struggles. Republican politicians and would-be candidates took advantage of every opportunity, responding to statements of Democratic incumbents, issuing policy opinions in the media, and appearing as speakers at Polish American celebrations, where they strongly condemned the Yalta agreements and the general conduct of foreign policy by the Democratic administration. This new political initiative reached a peak when, on March 28, 1950, Republican Robert Hale introduced into the House of Representatives a resolution calling for "the repudiation of Yalta." Henceforth, calls for the liberation of the "captive nations" became a source of great eloquence for Republican politicians.[17]

The Katyn Investigation

Soon, however, another initiative surfaced that also provided considerable fodder for Republican rhetoric. Having had no influence on the Yalta agreement and stung by the duplicity of two successive Democratic administrations on the key issues of recognition of the postwar government and the lack of truly free elections in Poland, Rozmarek belatedly awoke to the realization that he had been used by politicians seeking his support in return for naught but empty assurances. If nothing else could be done, Rozmarek finally determined to use the resources of the Polish American Congress to expose the true nature of Stalinism through a renewed campaign to investigate the Katyn affair. In April 1949 he sent a telegram to Warren Austin, U.S. ambassador to the United Nations, requesting that the Katyn issue be brought before the General Assembly. "We beg you," Rozmarek pleaded, "in the name of justice, decency and humanity to raise the issue . . . and demand an immediate and impartial investigation of one of the world's most heinous crimes."[18] Predictably, nothing of consequence resulted from this overture because the U.S. State Department, concerned more for the international repercussions of such a move on Cold War diplomacy, was unwilling to reopen the case.

This time, however, Katyn would not be so easily dismissed. Rebuffed by "official" government representatives, Rozmarek refocused his efforts on congressmen whose electoral districts held large Polish American constituencies. This strategy yielded dividends as early as July 1949, when Republican Representative George A. Dondero of Michigan, no doubt concerned about the potential defection of Democratic voters among his sizable Polish American constituency, read an article on Katyn into the *Congressional Record*. In the wake of this beginning, Vincent Basinski, head of the Indiana Division of the Polish American Congress, held a mass meeting in Gary, Indiana, on September 18, 1949. Democratic Representative Ray Madden of Indiana delivered an impassioned plea for an investigation of Katyn, after which the meeting passed a resolution calling for the "establishment of a duly constituted international tribunal, having as its end, purpose, and sole function the impartial investigation of the mass murder and the just meting out of full punishment to those found guilty and responsible for the Katyn Forest Massacre, . . . so inhumanly brutal and so brutally inhuman, as to be without parallel in the many shameful records of man's inhumanity to man."[19] Although most of those in Congress remained uninformed about the massacre, the actions of Dondero and Madden, spurred by the renewed energy of Rozmarek and his associates, "opened the door for such action."[20]

Further support for a Katyn investigation came from a growing number of journalists and editors. Julius Epstein, for example, published a series of investigative articles in the *New York Herald-Tribune*. When the articles proved popular, Epstein offered to write an objective analysis of the evidence for the Voice of America. After waiting some three months for a response, he was finally informed that the government-funded broadcaster was not interested, the reasons being that Katyn "would create too much hatred against Stalin among the Poles and that the [desk chief] hadn't gotten the green light from Washington to use anything . . . about Katyn."[21] Thwarted in this effort, Epstein pursued the matter further in the summer of 1949 when he contacted Arthur Bliss Lane about the possibility of lending his weight to calls for a Katyn investigation.

Lane, a vocal opponent of U.S. policy toward postwar Poland, proved of invaluable assistance to Rozmarek and other Polish American leaders in the formation of what became the American Committee for the Investigation of the Katyn Massacre.[22] Joined by a number of prominent Americans and funded with an initial grant of $5,000 from the Polish American Congress and donations that arrived daily from all over the world, the committee was formally organized at a meeting held at the Waldorf Astoria Hotel in New York on November 21, 1949.

One of Lane's first activities as a member of the new committee was to apply to the Internal Revenue Service for a federal tax-exempt status as a nonprofit educational organization, a request that was denied on the grounds that the committee had "no educational value."[23] Frustrated by this rebuff and deeply suspicious that the State Department was attempting to cover up the truth about Katyn for political purposes, Lane condemned the IRS reply as "the most cynical letter I had ever been written by an official of the United States Government."[24] Nevertheless, the committee began its work in earnest, interviewing former Polish prisoners of the Soviets, London government officials, and Soviet defectors and building an extensive file of information on Katyn. In the process, Lane's status among Polish Americans rose to that of a national hero.

Given the new Republican attitude toward foreign policy issues and the involvement of Democrats Dondero and Madden in the early stages of the new movement for a Katyn investigation, GOP planners picked up their efforts to assert a leadership role in the Katyn movement. During the fall of 1949 Republican spokespersons added loud voices to the call for action on Katyn, and in 1951 they established an Ethnic Origins Division to work on both the national and state levels. Headed by the former director of the Republican National Committee, A. B. Hermann, its Foreign Language Group was led by Arthur Bliss Lane, who was specifically assigned to develop effective communications with the foreign language groups in the next elections.

Because of the work of the committee, there was a growing public awareness of, and in many cases a growing indignation over Katyn. In light of this public pressure, Republican candidates began taking increasing advantage of the situation to make inroads into Democratic-controlled areas. In Chicago, for example, Republican Timothy P. Sheehan ran successfully in the 1950 congressional election in a heavily Polish, Democratic district by focusing on Yalta, Katyn, and other Polish American concerns and promising that if elected he would initiate in Congress an investigation of the entire Katyn episode. When elected, Sheehan introduced into the U.S. House of Representatives on June 26, 1951, House Resolution 282, calling for a "select committee to be composed of thirteen members of the House of Representatives to be appointed by the Speaker" for the purpose of conducting "a full and complete investigation and study of all aspects of the massacre" of Poles in the Katyn Forest. The resolution languished in the Democratic-controlled House Rules Committee all summer. No doubt this was due to Democratic fears that the Katyn issue might quickly take on anti-administration overtones, as it had done in the election of its sponsor in Chicago.[25]

Despite the shelving of the Sheehan bill, Polonia rallied to its support. The Polish National Alliance organs—*Dziennik Związkowy* and *Zgoda*—were vocal in their support for Sheehan's initiative. Due in large part to this media coverage and to growing support among the general public, the House Rules Committee was "deluged with requests of citizens asking for an investigation"[26] of Katyn. In the face of this growing public interest and the political potential it foretold, Madden reintroduced a bill in September 1951 as HR 390, calling for a select committee "to conduct a full and complete investigation of the massacre of thousands of Polish officers in a mass grave in the Katyn forest."[27] In a stirring speech in favor of the resolution, Sheehan likened the Katyn investigation to the moral duty of the United States to prosecute Japanese and Nazi war criminals. With the 1952 election campaign only months away and the Cold War escalating, the introduction of HR 390 sparked a rush among politicians to join the Katyn bandwagon, resulting in a unanimous vote of 398 to 0 in favor of the bill.

The establishment of the congressional committee to investigate Katyn was a major political victory for Polonia. "Never before had Congress deemed it proper for the legislative branch of the American Government to investigate a specific war crime committed on foreign territory against non-Americans during a time when the United States was not involved in the conflict," noted Szymczak. Polish American reaction to the establishment of the congressional committee was immediate and vocal. *Dziennik Chicagoski* featured a bold headline: "INQUIRY OF THE KATYN CRIME!" Józef Wiewora, editor of *Zgoda*, told his readers that "the realization of the long sought dream of an investigation of Katyn was definitely considered a victory for Polonia."[28] Most attributed the establishment of the Congressional committee to Lane's efforts, and his stock among Polish Americans increased even further.

With the adoption of HR 390 the Lane committee disbanded, turning its substantial files over to the congressional investigation. The members of the Katyn committee were chosen by Speaker Sam Rayburn, with each having a substantial Polish American constituency. The committee began its formal task on February 4, 1952, with President Truman issuing a formal endorsement of formal endorsement of the proceedings and ordering all U.S. government agencies to cooperate fully in the investigation. The committee issued invitations to the Soviet Union, the Soviet-dominated government in Poland, West Germany, and the Polish government-in-exile in London to participate, but the Soviet Union and its Warsaw Pact allies refused. Nevertheless, the committee moved forward, receiving further support on March 11 when the House passed HR 539, allowing the committee to examine witnesses abroad, and upped its initial appropriation of $20,000 to $100,000.

After months of interviews, review of documents, and other investigations, the committee issued an interim report (House Report 2430) on July 2, 1952. Its preliminary conclusions, coming amid heightening Cold War tensions, could be seen as nothing less than political dynamite: "This committee unanimously agrees that evidence dealing with the first phase of its investigation proves conclusively and irrevocably that the Soviet N.K.V.D. (People's Commissariat of Internal Affairs) committed the massacre of Polish Army officers in the Katyn Forest near Smolensk, Russia, not later than the spring of 1940. . . . There can be no doubt this massacre was a calculated plot to eliminate all Polish leaders who subsequently would have opposed the Soviet's plans for communizing Poland."[29]

The explosiveness of the committee's conclusions did not end with its condemnation of the Soviet Union. Following the interim report, the committee went on "to establish why the Katyn massacre with all of its ramifications never was adequately revealed to the American people and the rest of the world . . . and why this crime was not adjudicated at the Nuremberg Trials."[30] In this, it reached the clear conclusion that wartime diplomacy doomed the truth about Katyn because of the western Allies' need to be on good terms with the Soviet Union. The committee concluded that the Roosevelt administration knew fairly early that the Soviets were implicated in the Katyn crime. According to the committee, "All these [reports] were brushed aside, on the theory that pressing the search would irritate Soviet Russia and thus hinder the prosecution of the war to a successful conclusion."[31] If the truth about Katyn had been known in 1943, the committee concluded, "the Kremlin's hand would not have been so strong at the Yalta Conference, and many of the concessions made . . . would have been obviated."[32] Finally, in a statement fraught with domestic political overtones, the committee directly accused the Roosevelt administration of adopting a policy that "military necessity required the sacrifice of loyal allies and our own principles in order to keep Soviet Russia from making a separate peace with the Nazis."[33]

"For Polonia," Szymczak concluded, "the victory was significant: they had finally been vindicated in their decade-long indictment of the Kremlin for the atrocity."[34] That it was a moral victory could not be doubted—but to what advantage? Poland remained under communist domination, while Polonia, though perceived as a potent political force at election time, continued to be treated in pejorative fashion with much rhetoric and little of substance save the personal favors showered on its leaders to maintain their political loyalty. Clearly, it was at best a pyrrhic victory.

The Election of 1952

As the weeks wore on in 1952 and election politics intensified, Katyn contin-ued to be an important political concern for candidates of both political par-ties. Yalta, the closing of the Iron Curtain in Eastern Europe, the loss of China, and recurring Republican cries of "appeasement" placed Truman and the Democratic-controlled Congress on the defensive. Political pressure increased significantly with the shrill calls of Senator Joseph McCarthy for a repudiation of the Yalta agreements and the elimination of "communist sympathizers" from government office.

On May 4, 1952, 150,000 people jammed Humboldt Park in Chicago to commemorate the Polish Constitution of May 3, 1791, with speeches by Rozmarek and Vice President Alben Barkley. The vice president praised the work of the Katyn committee and Poland's progressive constitution of 1791, and he made much of the Truman administration's admission of 150,000 Polish exiles to the United States. Rozmarek, however, used the occasion to exact a token revenge for Roosevelt's betrayal of his support during the war. With Barkley forced to sit on the podium in silent unease, Rozmarek bitterly criticized the Yalta "appeasement" and chastised the Democratic administra-tions for their failure to live up to their commitments to Poland, the Atlantic Charter, and FDR's Four Freedoms.

Rozmarek continued his political assault at the annual convention of the Polish American Congress held in Atlantic City on Memorial Day. There he informed 2,000 delegates, in Szymczak's words, "that American foreign policy was directly responsible for the plight of Poland."[35] If Roosevelt had not with-held the truth about Katyn, Rozmarek argued, the Yalta sellout could not have occurred. Clearly, he concluded, the Roosevelt administration was influenced by Communists.

Although these comments were made to a small Polish American audience, they were given wide circulation by both the ethnic and the mainstream American media. In the months that followed, the perception that Poland had been "betrayed" reached a zenith among both Polish Americans and the general public. Armed with the conclusions of the Katyn Committee, virtually everyone blamed the Democrats for the loss of Eastern Europe and the other failures of American foreign policy during the Cold War. The major beneficiary of this out-rage was, of course, the Republican party.

The Republicans made considerable use of Yalta and Katyn during the 1952 election campaign. Their national platform specifically pledged to repudiate Yalta, a commitment reaffirmed by candidates Dwight Eisenhower and Richard Nixon, particularly in speeches to large Polish American audiences in the major northeast-ern cities. The theme of Democratic betrayal, coupled with the Republican pledge to repudiate Yalta, was prominently covered in Polish-language newspapers and rein-forced by political advertisements paid by the Republican National Committee.

The result of the intense political campaigning was a significant change in voting patterns among Polish Americans. Bitterly disappointed by the fate of their ancestral land, the failure of American foreign policy to forestall commu-nist advances in the Cold War, and the now obvious betrayal of their support by the Democratic party, more than half of the Polish American vote in 1952 went to Dwight Eisenhower, a figure of great personal popularity whom Polish Americans felt would honor Republican commitments to repudiate Yalta. Studies by historians and political scientists indicate that the defection of Polonia from the Democratic fold was a pivotal event in the Republican victory in 1952.[36]

Yet once again Polonia's hopes, aspirations, and trust were unwarranted. Despite its pledges during the 1952 election campaign, once in office the Republican administration abandoned its commitment to repudiate Yalta and "roll back the Iron Curtain."[37] On February 10, 1953, the U.S. ambassador to the United Nations, Henry Cabot Lodge, Jr., presented a 2,363 page report on the Katyn investigation to the UN Secretary General. Neither the president nor the State Department issued any formal statement, and the administration failed to call for a UN investigation or action. Given the pressing demands of the Korean War and the administration's desire to obtain Soviet assistance in breaking the stalemate at the Panmunjom peace talks, Eisenhower chose to allow the Katyn issue to conclude with the submission of the report. At a press conference on February 17, 1953, the president made it clear that "by no means" did he believe it "feasible or desirable that the U.S. should take any action saying that everything that was agreed to at such and such a place or time was repudiated."[38] This policy was explained further on February 18 when Secretary of State John Foster Dulles announced that the administration's policy would be to "reject dramatically" any Soviet violations of the Yalta agreements, while avoiding any "actual repudiation."[39] Soon after, House Joint Resolution 200 was submitted, stating that the wartime agreements "have been perverted to bring about the subjugation of free peoples."[40] It did not, however, speak of repudiation and, according to Athan Theoharis, "the wording of the resolution amounted basically to a reaffirmation of earlier Democratic defenses of the Yalta diplomacy."[41] The Republican leadership in the House killed the bill in committee, and "at no time after March, 1953, did the Eisenhower Administration or the Congressional leadership press for either reconsideration of the resolution or for enactment of any other resolution specifically repudiating Yalta."[42] With this, Yalta, Katyn, and the other issues of interest to Polonia were largely forgotten.

In 1954 the Ethnic Origins Division protested the lack of patronage accorded it and the failure of the administration to fulfill platform pledges from the 1952 campaign. In response, the division was informed that the White House was opposed to the "organization of Nationality Groups," and the following summer the Republican National Committee abolished the Nationalities Division. In 1956, with the approach of the presidential election, a new Nationalities Advisory Group was formed with A. B. Hermann again as its head. Lane was invited to lead a reconstituted Nationalities Division, but he refused, citing the failure of the administration to live up to its promises.

The territorial and political integrity of prewar Poland and the prosecution of the Katyn war crime were significant issues among Polish Americans during World War II and the Cold War years that followed. In retrospect, it is clear that while both Democrats and Republicans were concerned about the potential political impact of the "Polish vote," neither allowed this concern to affect the conduct of American foreign policy. Equally clear is the ineffectiveness of

Polonia's leadership in orchestrating any meaningful commitment on the national scene in return for Polonia's substantial political support. In the end, the tragic result was best described by Robert Szymczak, who concluded, "For all the moral righteousness of the Polish grievance against the Soviet Union for Katyn and other crimes, reality dictates that reasons of state will prevail. In that sense, the Polish soldiers lying in the Katyn Wood are not only the victims of Soviet bullets, but the fortunes of history."[43]

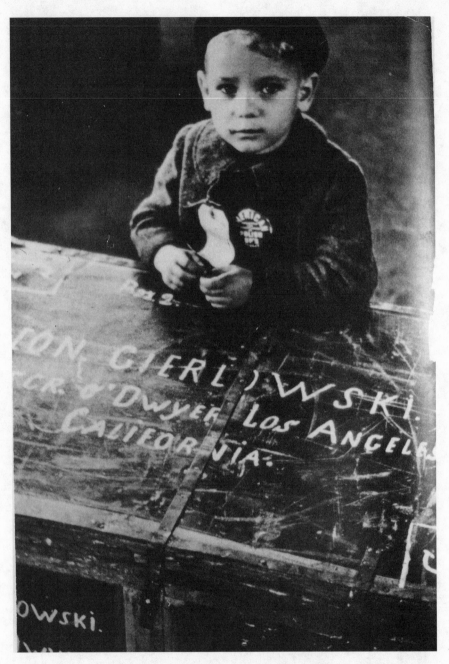

Thousands of Polish refugees entered the United States during the 1950s under special legislation allowing for the admittance of displaced persons and members of the Polish armed forces during World War II. Polish Institute of Arts and Sciences of America.

eight

Restructuring Polonia, 1946–1980

W orld War II had a tremendous impact on Polonia, exerting a multitude of pressures for change. The war brought new immigrants to America who both strengthened Polonia and created new schisms. Rising expectations engendered by wartime travels and new opportunities provided an impetus for third- and fourth-generation Polonians to look beyond the confines of the ethnic community, thereby setting in motion a migration of the young away from the established centers of Polonia. At the same time, new federal policies focusing on urban renewal and civil rights threatened further fragmentation of traditional communities. Finally, the long record of political betrayal at the national level caused Poles to look more to local politics to address their concerns and to become more independent in their support for national candidates.

Exiles and Postwar Immigrants

One of the immediate effects of the war was the influx of a new wave of political emigrés beginning with the Nazi invasion of Poland in 1939. The dislocations created by the invasion and the subsequent Soviet move into Poland were severe. Data from the Polish Embassy in Moscow show that during the period of the Nazi-Soviet friendship pact, September 1939 to June 1941, some 1,692,000 Poles, Jews, Ukrainians, and Belorussians were forcibly deported from Poland to the Soviet Union. Between 1936 and 1977, in addition to the 101,000 Poles admitted to the United States under the quota system, 19,430 arrived as refugees and 135,302 as displaced persons under special legislation enacted between 1954 and 1977.[1]

The Poles who arrived in American during the war and its immediate aftermath had grown to adulthood in an independent Poland and tended to be very protective of Polish freedom and culture. Among their number, particularly in the months immediately following the Nazi invasion, were a high percentage of intellectuals and professionals. Initially, many found they needed additional education or certification before they could practice their professions in the United States, some having to accept menial jobs to support themselves until they could obtain positions in their chosen fields. For the most part, however, they were able to assimilate quite rapidly.[2]

According to Jan Kowalik, "The many Polish refugee intellectuals driven ashore to America intensified and enriched the activities of younger generations of Americans of Polish descent, creating new organizations, and accelerating a trend toward a renaissance of ethnic self-consciousness."[3] One of their first contributions to the preservation of Polish culture and intellectual life in the United States took shape in December 1941 when refugee scholars led by the historian Oskar Halecki met in New York to discuss means by which they could organize to carry on their scholarly activities in exile. The group, drawn largely from members of the prewar *Polska Akademia Umiejętności* (Polish Academy of Arts and Sciences) in Kraków, included such international luminaries as historian Jan Kucharzewski, literary scholar Wacław Lednicki, anthropologist Bronisław Malinowski, jurist Rafał Taubenschlag, chemist Wojciech Świętosławski, and sociologist Feliks Gross. In short order the scholars determined to form an American branch of the *Akademia* to "continue Polish scientific activities," to "spread knowledge about Poland and Polish culture in the United States," and to "deepen cultural relations between Poland and America." The scholars elected Halecki their first president, with Malinowski serving as vice president.

The new association was reorganized on May 15, 1942, as the *Polski Instytut Naukowy w Ameryce* (Polish Institute of Arts and Sciences in America). Within three years the Polish Institute began publishing the *PIAS Bulletin* and established branches in Chicago and Montreal. Rapidly becoming a focus for Polish intellectual life in America, the Polish Institute embarked on an ambitious campaign to establish a research library, to conduct public lectures, to sponsor scholarly conferences, to publish books, and to provide support for members seeking assistance with the requirements of unfamiliar government or professional bureaucracy. In 1956 the institute began publishing the respected scholarly journal the *Polish Review.* It sponsored four major international conferences, held in 1966, 1971, 1975, and 1992, and established a stipend program to provide financial assistance for Polish scholars visiting the United States.[4] The Polish Institute remains a major center for Polish American intellectual life, numbering in excess of 1,300 members in 1990 and continuing to provide a wide variety of venues and support for intellectual exchange.

An early and unique contribution of the Polish Institute was the establishment of its Commission for Research on Polish Immigration. Formed on December 1, 1942, under the chairmanship of Mieczysław Haiman, the purpose of the commission was "to gather documents pertaining to the life and activities of American Polonia, catalogue the materials dealing with the history of Polonia and begin research into the history, structure and evolution of the Polish community in America." In 1944 the commission began publishing the journal *Polish American Studies,* and in 1948 it reorganized as an independent organization called the Polish American Historical Association. As such, it continues to publish its scholarly journal, while also issuing a quarterly *PAHA Newsletter,* assisting with the publication of books on Polish America, sponsoring an annual meeting, and contributing in other ways to the development of scholarship and the dissemination of information about the Polish experience in America.

On July 4, 1943, another group of scholars specializing in the study of modern Polish history met in New York City to found the Józef Piłsudski Institute of America for Research in the Modern History of Poland, which today maintains a reference library, archives, photographic collection, films, and other historical materials focusing on Poland in the twentieth century.

Taken together, the new organizations brought to Polonia an impetus toward cultural and intellectual development. Yet their effect on mainstream Polonia was limited, as the exiles who formed the founding nuclei of these new organizations maintained a European orientation and made little if any effort to reach out to mainstream Polonia. Generally, the postwar immigrants either remained aloof from the established organized Polonia, or in some instances sought to wrest control of groups from the Polish Americans who then held the elective offices. As Robert Hill observed, "To the upwardly mobile, and now middle-aged, sons and daughters of ex-peasants and mill workers the new Polish emigres have symbolized more than unblemished, prideful 'Polishness.' They are also apt to use their superior education and particularly their anti-Communist, 'hero-in-exile' credentials to take over leadership of local Polish-American organizations."[5] In the end, the gulf between Poles and Polish Americans, between the educated postwar emigrés and the sons and daughters of the mill workers, proved nearly unbridgeable. As late as 1990, Polish American organizations in general tended to number among their leadership either immigrant Poles or native-born Polish Americans. Of the institutions created by the post-1939 political exiles, as late as 1990 the Polish Institute of Arts and Sciences was nearly unique in including a balance of both Polish and American born members among its officers and board of directors. Most organizations remained largely unintegrated.

While they established significant organizations, the wartime exiles proved to be only the initial phase of Polish postwar emigration. At the conclusion of the war, hundreds of thousands of Poles—largely veterans of the Polish armed-forces-in-exile and displaced persons—found themselves in Western Europe, many in the large, poorly supported refugee camps. It has been estimated that by the end of 1946 some 730,000 Poles returned to Poland, while about 240,000, mostly veterans of the Polish army, preferred to stay in the west.[6]

The refugee question quickly became a potent issue among Polish Americans. A variety of groups, including Catholic relief organizations, the Red Cross, and a plethora of Polish American organizations, conducted fund-raising to support European relief efforts aimed at easing the plight of these unfortunates whom political circumstances robbed of both victory and homeland. At the same time, led by the Polish American Congress, lobbyists sought to influence the U.S. government to modify its strict quota system to permit the entrance of refugees from the communist areas in Eastern Europe. As a direct result of these efforts, Congress finally passed the Displaced Persons Act in 1948 and a special law in 1950 allowing Polish veterans into the country. Thus, between 1945 and 1954 some 178,000 Poles entered the country, with another 75,000 gaining entry between 1955 and 1966.[7]

Despite the momentary opening of America's doors, the restrictive quota system remained basically unchanged. The McCarran-Walter Act of 1952, enacted over President Truman's veto, retained the infamous nationality quotas. Arguing against this as a "discriminatory policy," Truman cited the sad plight of 138,000 Polish refugees seeking to fill but 6,524 places. It remained, however, for the Immigration and Nationality Act of 1965 to reverse the policy adopted in 1921.

The Poles who came to the United States after World War II added greatly to the heterogeneity of Polonia. Those who arrived during the 1950s, like their counterparts of the 1940s, were primarily political refugees escaping an occupying regime. Although this generation of Polish immigrants contained a cross-section of Polish life, it included a higher proportion of intellectuals, scientists, journalists and exiled leaders of opposition political movements than previous eras. A study by Danuta Mostwin revealed that 16.3 percent were executives, 29.5 percent professionals or semiprofessionals, 16.6 percent skilled workers, and only 16.3 percent unskilled workers.[8]

The result was that, unlike the earlier mass migration, the postwar arrivals tended to be better off financially and did not migrate because of economic reasons. Rather, more than 50 percent migrated because of actual political persecution, another 20 percent fled because of anticipated persecution, and still another 20 percent were political refugees who stated that their primary reason for leaving was opposition to the political regime.[9] Unlike their earlier compatriots, they also came with the trauma of war, Nazi occupation, and Soviet rule sharply etched in their consciousness. "Their personalities, attitudes toward the world and man were shaped by this tragic past; many of their kin and friends paid with their lives; they were the survivors," explained Feliks Gross.

Research by Maurice R. Davie indicates that, also unlike their predecessors, 96.5 percent of these postwar immigrants came to the United States with the intention of staying in America to take advantage of its freedom and opportunity. Further, although they stayed mainly in the same northeastern urban areas as did the turn-of-the-century immigrants, they did not settle within the established Polonia settlements, according to Polzin. Rather, most of the newcomers chose to reside among the general American population instead of the ethnic communities.[10] They came, Polzin concluded, "to escape from a country in which one's life was constantly threatened; where a peaceful life, with even minimal freedom to develop intellectually, culturally, and economically, was blocked."[11] As one immigrant explained, "For the sake of my children who are of school age, I want to stay in the United States. Here we feel like human beings and are not persecuted. Here we can speak our own language if we want, read our Polish newspapers, visit our friends, and go about our business."[12]

The postwar immigrants were indeed different from those who came during the war as well as from those who formed the great majority of Polish America. While organized Polonia long held as one of its major goals the preservation of Polish history and culture, the degree of "Americanization" among second- and third-generation Polish Americans became abundantly clear with the arrival of these new immigrants. To the leaders of Polonia, the newcomers were often regarded as "pushy upstarts," representatives of an educated class that threatened their status as community leaders. Further, the general success of the new immigrants was often resented by the older settlers, who felt that the newcomers should work as long and hard to succeed as had they and their ancestors. To the immigrants, the established Polonia was only marginally Polish, speaking a broken, unsophisticated Polish American dialect and knowing little of Poland beyond the superficial celebration of holidays and anniversaries that had long since lost their original significance and become mere social events. The new arrivals could not rely solely on Polonia, as the earlier immigrants had, as a means of cushioning their transition into a new culture.

The postwar immigrants faced the same impediments to success as had the earlier arrivals: the language barrier, unfamiliar customs and values, generally unsympathetic or hostile Americans, significantly different business and professional customs, and differences between Polish and American education systems. But, according to Polzin, the "most disconcerting problem" continued to be the mutual suspicion and misunderstanding between the new and old immigrants that eventually led to "mutual rejection, so that the new immigration formed its own organizations, cultural and otherwise, rather than join those already established."[13] Polzin attributed this to the differences in socioeconomic status between the two groups.

While the influx of these new immigrants changed the collective face of Polonia, other forces also worked to redefine the Polish American community. In terms of numbers alone, Polonia continued to grow in the postwar years. The 1950 census counted 861,184 people residing in the United States who were born in Poland and 1,925,015 with one or both parents born in Poland. By 1960 the number of Polish-born decreased slightly and those with one or both parents born in Poland increased, yielding figures of 747,000 and 2,031,000, respectively. In the same year, in Standard Metropolitan Statistical Areas with a population of 1 million or more and a "foreign" population of 25 percent, Poles ranked as follows: 21 percent of the "foreign" population in Buffalo, 17 percent in Chicago, 16.8 percent in Detroit, 16.4 percent in Milwaukee, 12.9 percent in Cleveland, 11.8 percent in Pittsburgh, 9.8 percent in New York City, 9.1 percent in Philadelphia, and 3.8 percent in Boston. In 1969 the U.S. government estimated there were 4,021,000 ethnically Polish Americans, 60.2 percent of whom claimed Polish as their mother tongue and 92.6 percent of whom usually spoke English. Polish Americans argued strenuously that this was an underestimate, maintaining that a more accurate figure would be 6–10 million. Estimates varied due to differences in definition, but Polonia's leaders argued that use of a general ethnological definition, regardless of language, sentiments, degree of ethnic stock, and other subjective factors, would yield about 10 million. When defined culturally, including only those actively conscious of their heritage, an accurate estimate would be 6–7 million.[14]

Cultural Renewal

Not all of the interest in cultural and intellectual matters in postwar Polonia emanated from the new arrivals. In this era the established Polonia continued to maintain an interest in Polish heritage and culture. In 1948 a significant event occurred when, on the initiative of Thaddeus Slesinski, 16 clubs representing 14 cities formed the American Council of Polish Cultural Clubs. This organization held its first national convention in 1949 and in 1953 sponsored a conference at the University of Notre Dame, where it adopted a constitution calling for the promotion of Polish culture in America, cooperation with other Polonia organizations, formation of new clubs, and development of materials representative of Polish cultural heritage.[15]

The creation of a national umbrella organization to promote Polish culture in America was a major influence on the preservation of ethnic heritage among Polish Americans. At the same time, the Polish government, anxious to increase ties with the United States, sponsored an international congress of Poles from abroad in Warsaw in 1955. One result of this effort to reestablish contact with Poles worldwide was the creation of the Society for Relations with the Emigration. Although the new society planned a series of cultural exchanges, the vicissitudes of the Cold War frequently prevented them. In 1961, for example, *Mazowsze,* the internationally renowned Polish Folk Song and Dance Company of Warsaw, visited the United States and, despite protests by anti-communist groups, played to large audiences, drawing heavily among Polish Americans. Additional exchanges were precluded by the rise in Cold War tensions, but in 1969 cultural exchanges with Poland received new impetus. In that year the U.S. State Department announced the resumption of limited exchanges with Poland. Seizing on this new opportunity, the Polish Laboratory Theater debuted in New York City and the Kościuszko Foundation announced plans for a college study program in Poland. Despite new protests from anti-communists, these efforts generally met with support from the Polish American community. In the same year, Karol Cardinal Wojtyła of Kraków, who became Pope in 1978, visited 15 American cities, evoking great displays of ethnic pride among the Poles at each stop.[16]

The decade beginning in 1970 witnessed a general renaissance in ethnic interest in the United States. In the midst of this upsurge, Michael Novak argued that white ethnics, particularly those whose ancestors migrated from Southern and Eastern Europe, were embarking on an ethnic revival. In *The Rise of the Unmeltable Ethnics,* Novak described an increasing collective sense of ethnic consciousness among these traditionally ignored and underrepresented peoples. He attributed this to a reaction against the poor treatment they habitually received from politicians and, as Obidinski explained, "the arrogant disdain of intellectuals and liberals."[17] For decades Poles accepted, and in some cases believed, stereotypes of themselves as less intelligent, less talented, and less creative. The Polish ethnic communities tended to lead insular lives, asking little of their elected representatives and expecting less. By the 1960s, however, the growing encroachment of other groups on their traditional neighborhoods provoked widespread defensive reactions among Poles and other traditional white "have nots."

As a part of this new collective awareness, Poles and other white ethnic groups descended from turn-of-the-century immigrants began to take a renewed interest and pride in their historical and cultural heritage. This increasing sense of ethnicity gave the appearance of fulfilling "Hansen's Law," an observation by immigration historian Marcus L. Hansen that while the offspring of the immigrants (the second generation) wish to forget the Old World traditions, the third generation wants to remember them.[18] The renewed interest in ethnic heritage can be seen in the fact that there were more doctorate degrees awarded to people studying the immigrant past of Polish Americans during the 1970s than in any previous decade, books on Poland and Polonia became available in growing numbers, families began reviving dormant ethnic customs, and ethnic festivals became popular and widely attended events. This growing sense of ethnic self-worth was greatly buoyed by the positive role models of such international figures as Leon Jaworski in the Watergate investigation, the election of Karol Cardinal Wojtyła as Pope John Paul II, the role of Zbigniew Brzeziński as national security advisor to President Jimmy Carter, the growth of the Solidarity movement, and the awarding of the Nobel Peace Prize to Lech Wałęsa. Each of these events, combined with increasing Polish American success

During the 1970s an ethnic revival led to renewed interest in celebrations such as this one on Pułaski Day in Rochester, New York. Behind the children in traditional Polish costumes stand veterans of the Polish Army (left) and Polish veterans of the U.S. armed forces (right).

in the workplace, in education, and in local politics, did much to raise the status of Polonia and induce many who heretofore denied their Polish heritage to embrace it.

Concurrent with the rise in ethnic awareness among Poles was an increasing number of public events that provided opportunities for non-Poles to learn about Polish history and culture. In literature, W. S. Kuniczak's novel *The 1,000 Hour Day* (1966), based on the Nazi invasion of Poland in 1939, and Jerzy Kosiński's novel *Steps* (1968), which won the National Book Award, introduced Americans to Polish topics. The Library of Congress sponsored a highly success-ful exhibit of Polish folklore, the Jurzykowski Foundation of New York City endowed a chair in Polish language and literature at Harvard University, and the Orchard Lake Schools, in cooperation with Edward Piszek, president of Mrs. Paul's Foods, inaugurated a large public relations campaign called "Project Pole" designed to increase public awareness of Polish contributions to America and to world civilization. The 1970s also witnessed a steady increase in interest in Polish poster art, literature, and theater in America. The Slavic Cultural Center on Long Island was instrumental in staging various plays, Polish dramas were staged in many cities throughout the country, and Andrzej Wajda films enjoyed popularity among both Polish Americans and avant garde film groups.

In addition to these indigenous initiatives, frequent tours of the Polish folk groups *Mazowsze* and *Śląsk* drew large audiences of Poles and non-Poles alike. The Warsaw Chamber Opera and the Poznań Boys Choir were each well received, and educational programs were inaugurated between various American and Polish universities.[19] A new age of Polish ethnic awareness indeed dawned during the 1970s.

The Changing Face of Polonia

Following World War II the Polish communities in America, despite the influx of new immigrants, began to decrease in size and cultural uniqueness. The war uprooted Polish Americans from the insular environment of their ethnic neighborhoods, exposing them to Americans of other ethnic backgrounds, to other areas of the country and the world, and to other cultures and ways of life. The result was an increase in social and economic expectations among the younger generation of Polish Americans. When they returned from the war many sought jobs outside the ethnic community, while others eagerly took advantage of the G.I. Bill and other opportunities hitherto unavailable. Slowly, they began to rise up the socioeconomic ladder and move to the growing suburbs. When they did, they seldom established new Polish organizations and often greatly reduced or severed ties with their old affiliations.

In this changing milieu, the old established organizations generally continued to focus on Polish issues rather than on the new needs of the changing Polish American community. Consequently, Polish Americans gradually abandoned the old institutions for new insurance companies, professional organizations, and social clubs that better met the needs of an emerging class of *Americans*.

In keeping with the changing role of the Polish American family from the extended economic unit of rural Poland and the turn-of-the-century factory system to a more contemporary nuclear unit, Polish American family size continued the sharp decline that began in the 1930s. A study by Eugene Obidinski found that the mean family size for the immigrant generation was 6.2 and the second generation 3.2; by 1969 it had decreased to 2.7. The national average in 1969 was 3.1. Further evidence of this declining birth rate can be seen in a study of Pittsburgh by Michael Crawford and Evelyn Goldstein. They found that the birth rate in the "Polish Hill" community fell from a high of 41 per thousand in 1907 to 8.3 per thousand in 1969. The same study showed that the mean number of children per female was 4.4 during the first generation and 2.58 during the third.

Other aspects of Polish American family life persisted, however. John L. Thomas, using data from some 300 parishes in Chicago, found that "monogamous indissoluble marriage was a basic value of Poles. Matrimony was considered a Sacrament of union, effective until death."[20] Among all the groups studied, Polish families exhibited the lowest rates of separation and divorce of any ethnic group. He concluded that "the conjugal bond is more stable among Polish Americans than among American Catholics of comparable socioeconomic status."[21] To account for this he theorized that the strong religious beliefs of Poles contributed positively to preservation of the family system in America.[22]

Indeed, despite moves, new opportunities, and a more complex and changing life, one factor that remained relatively constant was Polish adherence to religious beliefs. Research by John Simpson suggests that 80 percent of second-generation Polonians attended church services regularly, a figure nearly equaled by the 79 percent attendance rate of the third generation. This conclusion is supported by Donald Pienkos who, in a 1973 study of Milwaukee Poles found that 74 percent of those surveyed considered themselves to be "strongly religious," compared with only 41 percent of non-Poles. Two studies by Andrew Greeley suggest a similar conclusion. In 1973 he found that "among Catholics in the academic profession, Polish Americans ranked highest in weekly church attendance, with ninety one percent claiming they performed this religious function."[23] In another study in the following year he found "Polish respondents to be the most likely to stress loyalty to the Catholic Faith."[24] Together, the results of these studies, as Pienkos noted, "point to the persistence of Polish ethnic culture" in America.[25]

Although church attendance remained high among Polish Americans, changing residential patterns led to changes in attendance patterns as well. As the original urban immigrant communities began to dwindle in numbers, an interesting phenomenon began to occur as Poles living in suburban areas often traveled into the cities, many driving some distance, to attend services and celebrate holidays in the old Polish parishes with which they now had no other link. Documented by several scholarly studies, this phenomenon clearly suggests the continued interest in ethnic heritage and religious values among Polish Americans in the generation following World War II.

Stanislaus Blejwas, who studied parishes in Connecticut, noted that the more enlightened Polish pastors viewed education as a road to both socioeconomic progress and "transmission of cultural values."[26] The continued observance of Polish Masses and traditional holidays, and the sponsoring of "Polish schools" for children, often after actual parish membership had changed dramatically, no doubt provided Polish American suburbanites with a source of ethnic identification that was otherwise unavailable. This explanation is supported by Paul Wrobel who concluded from his study of Detroit that "the parish performs an important social function by providing an opportunity for Polish Americans to interact with one another. As a result of that interaction, linkages among nuclear families are established and maintained, and an ethnic community is formed and sustained."[27]

The Polish parish, then, despite changing neighborhoods and the movement of the third and fourth generations to the suburbs, continued to serve as a link between Polish Americans who wished to preserve their heritage. Yet Ewa Morawska found that the rationale for attending ethnic parishes differed noticeably between the immigrant and subsequent generations. The immigrants usually pointed to "a sense of *national duty*" to explain their attendance, while the second, third, and fourth generation indicated that they maintained ties with the ethnic parish for "religious and/or *social-recreational* reasons." Morawska's findings appear to support the general conclusion that later generations of Polish Americans continued to exhibit high instances of church attendance, primarily as a means of maintaining religious traditions and social relationships with other Polonians.[28]

While church attendance remained high among Polish Americans in the generation following World War II, religious life nevertheless underwent significant change. The Polish nature of many parishes became suspect as migrations and changing demographics reduced the Polish presence in many of the traditional urban neighborhoods. By 1970, many of the smaller Polish parishes had already undergone a dramatic change, conducting services in English and catering to new ethnic groups. Even in the larger city parishes, urban renewal and changing demographics made the future viability of Polish parishes problematic.

As this change took place, the role and status of the priest also underwent a metamorphosis. In the early part of the century the priest's standing within the Polish community was high. The Church served as a center of both religious and social life, with the pastor being consulted on every major decision, from potential marriages to industrial strikes. By 1970, while the priest was still looked upon as a religious leader, his role in the secular lives of his parishioners, and consequently his socioeconomic status, declined seriously. The rise of parish councils further diluted the authority of the parish priest, and a serious decline in the number of new seminarians resulted in an increasingly aging clergy. Where replacements were available, they were often third-generation Polonians who no longer felt that the preservation of Polish culture was a special aspect of their religious mission.[29]

Another casualty of the changing times was the Polish parochial school system. In 1953 the Felician Sisters, the largest of the Polish teaching orders, operated 250 elementary schools, 28 high schools, three junior colleges, and one senior college with a total enrollment in excess of 85,000 students. Two years later, the Sisters of the Holy Family of Nazareth reported operating 10 hospitals, 81 elementary schools, 15 secondary schools, 7 postsecondary schools, and 2 colleges. The contribution of these and other orders to the socialization of incoming immigrants into American society, to the education of immigrant children, and to the preservation of cultural and social values was inestimable during the early years of the twentieth century. The influence of parochial schools continued to be significant in the postwar era, as seen in a national study by Andrew Greeley and Peter H. Rossi in 1966. They concluded that 73 percent of children of Polish extraction had some parochial school background. By then, however, the decline of Polish parochial education was already at hand. As Poles gradually moved out of the urban ethnic enclaves and away from their traditional parish schools, the changing demographics of traditional neighborhoods altered the ethnic nature of many schools and the declining number of religious vocations decreased the number of priests and nuns available as teachers. With this, Polish parochial schools found it increasingly difficult to staff classrooms. Many began hiring laypersons to fill the gaps, but qualified lay teachers increased expenses, leading in many cases to unbalanced budgets and steady economic decline to the point where schools were no longer viable. Some parishes resorted to hiring unqualified teachers, but as educational standards declined because of this dubious expedient, enrollments also declined as parents sought a better opportunity for their children in suburban public schools.[30]

The decline of the Polish parish school was a significant change for Polonia. As Wrobel eloquently explained in his analysis of Detroit, the fears of those worried about the future of the Polish ethnic community crystallized around the issue of the parochial school. "Many believe the future of this Polish-American community is dependent on what happens to the school in the years to come. If it remains open, people argue, current residents with children will stay, and the neighborhood will attract young Polish-American families. But if the school closes, parents will move to the suburbs, where their children can get a Catholic education, and the neighborhood will lose its appeal for Polish Americans with school-age youngsters."[31]

Ironically, while the size and influence of the Polish American ethnic parish began to decline, the hierarchy of the Roman Catholic Church began to respond to some of the issues that split Poles into anti-clerical and independent movements earlier in the century. In 1952 the Apostolic Constitution *Exsul Familia* guaranteed, for the first time, "the rights of immigrants to proper pastoral care in their own language and traditions."[32] Further, the Church became much more receptive to Polish American priests. One tangible symbol of this was the elevation of John Joseph Krol, auxiliary bishop of Cleveland, to the Archdiocese of Philadelphia in 1961. The eleventh Polish American bishop, he became the first to lead a major Roman Catholic diocese in America. Eight years later, he gained elevation to the College of Cardinals.

Further evidence of the Poles' growth in status within the Church, and within American society, came during the celebration of the millennium of Poland's existence as a nation in 1966. President Lyndon Johnson issued a proclamation on May 3 commemorating the occasion, and the U.S. Postal Service issued a special commemorative stamp. Although the Polish government refused to allow the Polish primate, Stefan Cardinal Wyszyński, to visit the United States because of Cold War tensions, a crowd of 135,000 attended the dedication of the Polish Catholic shrine at Doylestown, Pennsylvania. President Johnson delivered the major address, "emphasizing the heritage of freedom for Poles and other minorities in America."[33]

Despite the tendency to move away from ethnic neighborhoods, Polish Americans appeared to retain other facets of their ethnicity. A study of Buffalo, for example, indicated that 49 percent of Polish Americans who went on to college prior to 1960 attended religious-affiliated institutions, no doubt owing to the influence of parochial education and religion on their lives. Of those who began college in 1960 or after, 48 percent, nearly the same proportion as the earlier group, went to religious affiliated colleges. By means of comparison, only 19 percent of a non-Polish control group attended religious colleges. While 40 percent of Poles went to public colleges, 54 percent of the control group did so. Only 6 percent of the Poles enrolled in the more expensive nonreligious private colleges, while 11 percent of the control group did. Polish Americans also chose to remain closer to their own neighborhoods than did others, with 34 percent going "away" to college as opposed to 59 percent of the control group. Interestingly, the same study showed that 56 percent of Poles received scholarships to attend college, while only 30 percent of the others did.[34] This data is no doubt a reflection of the continuing ties to religion, family, and neighborhood ingrained in Polish American youth, while also reflecting increased interest and competitiveness in education among the third and fourth generations.

While Polish Americans began to take advantage of educational opportunities in increasing numbers between 1945 and 1965, education did not always translate into increased socioeconomic status. The data accumulated by Obidinski in Buffalo suggest that by the mid-1960s Polish Americans in that community failed to achieve significant upward occupational mobility. By then, only 4 percent of Buffalo's Polish American workers occupied professional positions, compared with 8.3 percent of the general population. Similarly, only 4.4 percent of Poles held managerial positions, compared with 7.2 percent of the community at large. Further evidence of this can be seen in a study of 106 corporations in Chicago that indicated "102 had no Polish Americans as directors and 97 had no Polish American officers. Although Poles constituted 6.9 percent of the area population, only 0.3 percent of directors and 0.7 percent of officers were Polish American."[35]

Despite this appearance of relative economic stagnation, other evidence from the same period suggested that some upward movement was beginning to take place. A National Opinion Research Center questionnaire distributed in 1964 reported that white-collar jobs rose from 12 percent among first- and second-generation Polish Americans to 34 percent in the third. Conversely, there was a decline in blue-collar jobs from 77 percent to 65 percent, and in farm occupations from 11 percent to 1 percent. In education, while 85 percent of the second generation reported level of education as eighth grade or below, this fell to only 25 percent in the third generation. Of the second generation, only 13 percent completed at least one year of high school and 2 percent went on to college. In the third generation these figures increased significantly to 51 percent and 24 percent, respectively.[36]

The Challenge of Changing Neighborhoods

One of the more significant problems to face Polonia during this period of restructuring was the changing racial composition of old Polish ethnic neighborhoods. Competition for housing, jobs, and services between black and white residents in the urban cities of the northeast was a part of city life since before the Civil War. This friction was exacerbated by the rapid increase in the urban black population during World War I as the need for industrial workers created more employment opportunities. In Chicago, for example, 1.9 percent of the population was black in 1900. This grew steadily to 4.1 percent in 1920 and 8.2 percent in 1940. Following World War II there was a rapid increase—to 22.8 percent in 1960 and 32.7 percent in 1970—a total of 1.1 million people. With the decrease in manufacturing jobs in the early 1960s, competition for jobs, housing, and services became severe between the black inhabitants and the descendants of European immigrants.[37]

By the 1960s, a large number of affluent and middle-class white residents of northern cities began a mass exodus to the suburbs to escape rising crime rates, increased violence, and physical deterioration in the inner cities. In their wake they left the blue-collar ethnic neighborhoods in a state of serious erosion. Unscrupulous real estate agents, feeding on these fears, encouraged people to sell at below market values in order to "escape" before values fell even further. "Steering" became a common practice as agents encouraged white couples to purchase property in the suburbs while attempting to "steer" blacks toward hitherto Polish sections. The results of these practices were falling property values, the movement of the younger generation of Polonians to the suburbs, and a serious erosion of the "Polishness" of older neighborhoods.[38]

In Chicago, as in other northern cities, Polish, Italian, and other European ethnic neighborhoods became, as Joseph Parot suggested, "a buffer zone" between the largely black urban areas and predominantly white suburbia. To black leaders, the ethnic areas appeared to be blocking black aspirations for better housing. Polish leaders perceived the increased pressure from blacks as a threat to their traditional neighborhoods and their way of life. Since "neither side appears capable of cultural integration," as Parot observed, a clash was inevitable.

The cultural and economic pressures present in the cities soon boiled over into overt conflict. In 1966 Rev. Martin Luther King, Jr., led a series of demonstrations in Chicago aimed at promoting open housing. Some of these demonstrations entered Polish areas, giving rise to fears of violence and destruction among the inhabitants. The result was a series of confrontations that made newscasts and press headlines across the country. The Chicago disturbances were followed by major riots in 1967 in areas such as Detroit and Newark with large black and Polish populations. In the following year, when the flag at a Chicago school was lowered following the assassination of Dr. King, the president of the local Polish Homeowners' Association raised it to the top of the pole, nearly sparking a riot.

On the surface, the conflicts erupting in America's urban areas during the mid-1960s appeared to be a simple case of racism. Given the building socioeconomic pressure, it was, as Parot noted, inevitable that some conflict occur. Nevertheless, when it did, "since these lines of contact occurred so often in Polish and Italian neighborhoods, it appeared to observers that these 'New Immigration' pockets stood in the way of black expansion; it appeared that the 'New Immigration' settlements were saturated with hostile racists."[39] To the liberal civil rights activists and journalists who flocked to participate in and report on the Chicago demonstrations, the Poles who protested the invasion of their neighborhoods along Milwaukee and Archer Avenues were "hardhats," a term laced "with all its racist implications and overtones."[40]

The rush to label Poles as racists, however, reflects a lack of the very sensitivity and understanding that liberal activists professed so vocally to deplore. Rather than attempt to understand *both* sides of the conflict, liberal activists, the media, and the general public preferred the simple, if inaccurate, explanation that Poles were obviously racists. "Everybody calls us racists; just because we want to live in a Polish-American neighborhood," complained one Detroit resident. "I don't mind if a Black family moves in next door or across the street. Right now there are four Black families on our street and there ain't no problems for anyone. . . . But when you ask me if I would be happy with a majority of Blacks in the neighborhood, I would have to say no. . . . If we had a majority of Blacks, then the neighborhood wouldn't be the same any more. It wouldn't be a Polish neighborhood."[41]

To Poles, family and community ties were important traditional values they brought with them from the Old World and preserved in the ethnic enclaves they established in America. Well into the third and fourth generations, Polish Americans continued to attend ethnic churches in large numbers, to support ethnic festivals, and to promote ethnic values in their offspring. By the 1960s, however, Poles often found their neighborhoods slated for "urban renewal" projects that seriously threatened their traditional values and way of life. In both Detroit and Chicago, new expressways cut wide swaths through Polish neighborhoods, fracturing their integrity and sending countless families looking for alternate housing. At the same time, federal, state, and local programs designed to promote integration were perceived as another threat to neighborhood integrity. Urban ethnics recognized early that practices such as "redlining, panic peddling and a dual real estate market usually mean that the integrated neighborhood is merely a transition from an all-white to an all-black neighborhood. . . . And that in turn means that the white people who do not want to move are forced out by social and economic dynamics over which they have no control."[42]

Tax monies raised from the working-class ethnic neighborhoods populated by European groups were used to purchase and tear down whole blocks of traditionally ethnic neighborhoods, replacing them with low income housing reserved for blacks, Hispanics, and other nonwhite groups. With their "long history of oppression and betrayal by strangers," as Greeley explained, Poles reacted defensively to these various incursions. In Pittsburgh, for example, when the federal government's Model Cities Program attempted to provide assistance, the local Polish community refused to participate because it had not been consulted on the project and feared that it would be used only for the benefit of outside political interests. Instead, the Poles organized a local committee to improve the neighborhood without the help of "outsiders."[43]

Polish urban residents found the same form of double standard at work within the Church. In Detroit, Wrobel found that the parish school of St. Thaddeus depended heavily on proceeds from the annual parish festival to meet its operating expenses. With the rise of the civil rights movement, however, the Archdiocese of Detroit required that a portion of all proceeds from these festivals be relinquished to enable the diocese to fund special programs for designated minorities. "Here is where simple economics becomes complicated by political and social forces," Wrobel explained. "For the archdiocese provides financial assistance to inner-city Black parishes, including support for schools. The parishioners of St. Thaddeus resent that. They are aware Black parishes have financial problems, and support their right to receive aid. Their argument, however, is that the problems of St. Thaddeus seem to go unrecognized by members of the church hierarchy in Detroit. Parishioners say, 'We need help too; we have to put on a festival to raise money for the school, so why can't we keep what we earn?'"[44]

To their residents, Polish American neighborhoods were "communities" within the otherwise anonymous confines of a large metropolis. They were home to family and friends, places where social and cultural activities necessary to their way of life occurred, they were a point of both group identification and individuality. As Greeley argued,

> Those who write off as racist all those poor benighted white ethnics who are uneasy about neighborhood change simply cannot grasp how the concepts of "defended neighborhood" or "social turf" can be important to anyone. If you are worried about your neighborhood, your street, your block, your property, then by definition you are a racist—a definition usually made by someone living in a fashionable, safe, upper middle-class suburb. The intellectual and cultural elites of the country simply cannot understand that there are many people who have no objection to racial integration, no resistance to blacks as neighbors or as parents of children who go to school with your children, yet still have very powerful fears of what racial change does to a neighborhood.[45]

In a seminal work on the neighborhood as a community, sociologist Gerald Suttles maintained that "the neighborhood is by definition a place to be defended. The boundaries of the neighborhood are the boundaries of an important segment of one's life. One defends these boundaries because any threat to them is a threat to something that is seen as indispensable to life. Neighborhood is social turf, the place where one lives with one's family and friends."[46] The neighborhood is a "safe," familiar place where one can be at ease with ones own, a necessary place that provides a sense of identity crucial to the psychological well-being of urban residents. The fact that Polish Americans, and other European ethnic groups, sought to preserve the unique nature of their neighborhoods did not mean that they were racists. "While that conclusion is misleading," Wrobel pointed out, "arguments for preserving ethnic communality and a distinct subculture do clash with the democratic ideal that every American should be free to live wherever he pleases. Yet this perplexing problem will not be solved by dismissing the concerns of one group and being attentive to another."[47]

Despite a stereotypical label as racists, there is evidence to suggest this perception of Polish Americans is inaccurate. In 1973, for example, Thomas Pavlak published research in *Public Opinion Quarterly* suggesting that Poles were no more or less racially prejudiced than any other ethnic group studied. To the extent that Poles did display prejudice, Pavlak concluded it was due to the respondents' social class and proximity of residence to blacks. Further, despite the fears and pressures of urban change, Poles sometimes supported collective action with other racial groups. In 1968, a conference of Polish priests in the Archdiocese of Detroit called upon all Polish Americans to support equal rights for all Americans and the maintenance of interracial harmony. In the same year, Polish and black leaders established a Black-Polish Conference to promote cooperation and understanding between the city's two largest ethnic groups. One result of this initiative was a decrease in misunderstanding and tension between the groups. This can be seen in a subsequent mayoral campaign between a Pole, Roman Gribbs, and a liberal black candidate. The campaign, in which Gribbs was victorious, was noticeably devoid of overt racial confrontation.

In 1968, the thinly veiled racist overtures of George Wallace in the Wisconsin primary apparently made little impression among Polish Americans. Studies of the election results indicate that Wallace received significantly fewer votes in heavily Polish American districts than he did in the affluent suburbs. Further studies indicate that Wallace received little support from Polish Americans in any of his campaigns.[48]

In another political campaign that received much attention in 1969, a Polish American candidate ran for mayor of Buffalo on a campaign that stressed maintenance of de facto segregation in the local schools. When she lost by the largest margin in the city's history, analysts interpreted her defeat "as a rejection of a campaign based on the themes of 'law and order' and opposition to busing inner-city pupils to previously all-white schools."[49] The fact that Polish Americans voted overwhelmingly against one of their own points to a rejection of racial politics.

Finally, as Greeley explained, there is the instance of Chicago, where Poles and Hispanics have been able to coexist in relative peacefulness in the traditionally Polish "Stanisławowo" area. "I do not wish to make a case for any great and intimate friendship between the Polish and the Latino communities," Greeley stated, "but they have managed to survive alongside one another in relative peace, occupying a neighborhood which both claim to be theirs and which both have made common cause to defend against the city and federal governments."[50]

The Challenge of Negative Stereotyping

Another serious challenge to Polish Americans in the decade of the 1970s was the increase in anti-Polish sentiments in the United States. Historian Oscar Handlin noted that ethnicity is a temporary state for each new immigrant group. Through the process of acculturation the importance of historical traditions and cultural differences gradually diminish until assimilation eventually occurs.[51] Yet for some groups in American society stereotypical views are more pervasive and immutable than for others. In general, the more numerous and threatening the dominant group perceives the ethnic population to be, the more demeaning and lasting are the negative stereotypes about that group. The Irish and the Germans, as the largest and most "threatening" of the nineteenth-century immigrant groups, suffered from negative stereotypes for decades. Between the period from 1880 to 1920, the largest European immigrant nationalities were Italians and Poles; the negative stereotypes for these groups were widespread and lasting.

For Poles, the threat was from what Obidinski described as "a pervasive stereotype which pictures the Polish American as a relatively unsophisticated, complacent, and intellectually defective creature whose hard physical labor compensated for a lack of mental ability." Although this stereotype had little basis in fact, even for the immigrant generation, it became an "accepted" way of viewing this new, numerically large group that competed with preexisting residents of the northeastern cities for jobs, housing, and services.[52]

By the late 1960s, Polish Americans were making dramatic progress in family income, education, and other socioeconomic indicators. Poles were competing with the older residents for suburban housing, college scholarships, and leadership positions in local political and social organizations. By this time, too, the civil rights movement was successful in making overt discrimination against blacks, Hispanics, and other racial groups increasingly taboo. Probably for a combination of these reasons, coupled with the failure or refusal of the legal system to offer equal protection to European ethnic groups, Poles became a target for a pervasive wave of so-called "Polish jokes" that blanketed the country.

In an intriguing analysis of the problem, Obidinski explained that these "jokes" were a "form of symbolic aggression."[53] At the beginning of the century Polish immigrants were subjected to spitting, name calling, physical violence, and other abuses. "The jokes," Obidinski wrote, "probably are a newer, more socially acceptable form of assault than were the sticks and stones of the past."[54] Although the original stereotype of Poles was not valid, the characterizations contained in these vocal assaults "are the illegitimate offspring of the original peasant stereotype. The 'Polish' individuals described in the jokes are naive, stupid, stubborn, and narrow-minded, but otherwise harmless."[55] As Obidinski further noted, "Humor at the expense of particular ethnic groups is neither new nor surprising and any complete catalog of ethnic derision would include the Irish jokes, Jewish jokes, Italian jokes, and 'colored' jokes as well as associated epithets."[56]

These degrading stereotypes were far from harmless. The constant derision, often publicly disseminated through the mass media, caused serious identity crises, feelings of inadequacy, and low self-esteem for many Polish Americans. Further, the jokes counteracted the real advances of Poles in American society by ascribing to them a very low social status, considerably lower than their socioeconomic standing would otherwise dictate.

The reactions of Polish Americans to these assaults varied widely, as they did among people in other groups. Traditionally, in times of great anti-Polish or anti-immigrant sentiment, many Polish Americans attempted to avoid negative stereotyping by retreating to the comforting confines of the ethnic community, while others coped by leaving ethnic residential areas and organizations, denying their heritage, and changing their names to blend into the general society.[57] By the late 1960s, Poles began to react quite differently, taking a new militant posture against these insulting portrayals. Strong protests from Polish American groups were lodged with the Columbia Broadcasting System, Hallmark Cards, various publishers, and the sponsors of movies and television productions featuring Burt Reynolds, Joan Rivers, and other celebrities who publicly demeaned Polish Americans.

Eventually, the rise of Solidarność, the election of a Pole as Pope, and positive domestic role models such as Zbigniew Brzeziński, coupled with an increasingly positive Polish American self-image that led to vociferous protests, legal actions, and threats of economic boycott, eventually forced the most blatantly offensive "jokes" underground. The result was that by the mid-1980s there was a noticeable decrease in at least the public manifestations of these demeaning stereotypical images.

Restructuring Political Alignments

While the educational and economic status of Polonia between 1945 and 1990 increased, its political structure remained ambiguous. For more than a decade, from 1940 through 1952, both major political parties vigorously courted the Polish American vote in national, state, and local elections. The experience, however, was one that led to much frustration and alienation from the political process rather than an increasing interest in it. The long-standing betrayal of Polish American concerns by the Democrats, followed as it was by the failure of the Eisenhower administration to make good on its pledge to repudiate Yalta, disillusioned many Polish Americans and refocused their attention on the traditional ethnic local political scene and away from national affairs.

To a certain extent, Polish American interest in national politics revived during the campaign of John F. Kennedy in 1960. Kennedy, who cultivated his Irish heritage to political benefit, also made serious efforts to revive the Democratic coalition of ethnics, blue collar workers, blacks and urbanites that formed the backbone of Democratic success under Franklin Roosevelt. Kennedy's overtures impressed Polonia, as did his Roman Catholic background. A study of the 1960 election by Stanley Wagner suggests that Kennedy's victory was due in larger part to class issues than to ethnicity or religion, but, given the retention of ethnic and religious identification among Poles, these cannot be easily divorced from socioeconomic "class" issues. In any event, Polish Americans returned to the Democratic fold in large numbers in 1960, giving Kennedy 78 percent of their vote in key industrial states with many electoral votes.[58]

Much to the surprise of many accustomed to political promises all too easily forgotten, Polish Americans generally fared well under the Kennedy administration, which appointed John Gronouski as postmaster general, the first Polish American to hold Cabinet rank, and took a renewed national interest in the condition of the cities. By the mid-1960s, the increasing deterioration of the cities and the encroachment of highways, urban renewal and new ethnic groups were serious concerns for urban Polish Americans. As a result of their support for John F. Kennedy and Lyndon Johnson's promises during the 1964 election campaign to address the deterioration of the cities, Johnson won 77 percent of the Polish American vote in his successful run for the presidency.[59]

Polish American voters, however, were less loyal to the Democratic party than they had been. In particular, by the end of the 1960s a renewed interest in ethnicity appears to have been a major factor in Polish American voting patterns. In fact, a study by Robert Lorinskas, Brett Hawkins and Stephen Edwards published in 1969 "found that Polish-Americans residing in urban localities were predisposed to vote for fictitious candidates with Polish surnames, regardless of these alleged candidates' party label and regardless of the respondents' own perceived ethnic ties." This conclusion was supported by Walter Borowiec in a study of 83 Buffalo Polish American politicians published in 1974. Borowiec found that "the largest portion of his respondents believed that a candidate's nationality was still the single strongest factor influencing the choice of Polish-American voters. Ethnicity was perceived by these politicians to be more important than these candidates' actual effectiveness in performing services for their constituents, their own campaign efforts, and three times more significant than their party label."[60] While it would be easy to ascribe this phenomenon to the realm of ethnic politics, no doubt the two decades of betrayal by both political parties between 1940 and 1960 played a role in convincing Polish American voters that it was best to cast their lot with a fellow ethnic, regardless of party affiliation.

The politics of Polish America in the era of political scandals, economic reorientation, and the dramatic political changes in Eastern Europe is a topic of continuing interest to the major political parties. A 1971 study by Andrew Greeley indicates that Polish Americans continue to be strongly Democratic in orientation, with 77 percent identifying with that party. Yet Polonia is neither politically homogeneous nor passively compliant. Greeley also found a distinct tendency for Polish American affiliation with the Democratic party to decrease into the third generation. He found that although 77 percent of all Polish Americans claimed to be Democrats, a small but significant number of middle-class Poles tend to be more conservative and to affiliate with the Republican party. This conclusion is supported by Donald Pienkos, who found in a survey of Milwaukee Polonia that 67 percent of working-class respondents were Democrats and 3 percent Republicans, while of the more educated Polish Americans holding professional or skilled occupations 23 percent were Democrats, 23 percent Republicans, and the remainder "independent."[61]

Although there has been an increasing trend since the 1970s for Polish Americans to drift away from the Democratic party to become either Republicans or independents, a strong majority remains committed to the party of

Franklin Roosevelt and John Kennedy. But this does not mean that Poles always vote along party lines. In 1968 Republicans made serious inroads into the "Polish vote" owing to the disaffection of Poles over rising urban violence and the continuing deterioration of the cities. Thus encouraged, the Republicans established in 1971 a Heritage Group Section under a Hungarian refugee named Laszlo Pasztor. In October of that year the section published the first issue of *GOP Nationalities News.* These initiatives, Stephen A. Garrett concluded, were "clearly evidence that the Nixon administration now saw an historic opportunity to woo the ethnic vote away from its traditional Democratic affiliation."[62]

When Edmund Muskie's campaign collapsed in 1972, eliminating a potential unifying ethnic presence at the head of the Democratic ticket, the way was clear for Republican gains. Focusing on the domestic ethnic concerns of law and order and the preservation of traditional values, and largely ignoring the "enslaved" nations theme, Nixon took advantage of a cordial meeting with Polish American leaders in the White House to promise to appoint more Poles to federal positions. Given the work of the Heritage Group Section, the warmth of Nixon's hospitality to the representatives of Polonia, and the president's promise of support for Poles aspiring to federal jobs, Polonia defected in large numbers to the Republican fold in 1972. Subsequent to the campaign, however, Nixon's promises proved as elusive as Roosevelt's commitment to the Atlantic Charter and the Four Freedoms a generation earlier.[63]

During the 20 years between 1970 and 1990 Polish Americans generally remained loyal to the Democratic party. Their influence on government as a group, however, was not strong. There were some political successes, as when Representative Roman Pucinski led a successful effort to pass the Ethnic Heritage Studies Act, or when Poles joined with other groups to successfully lobby for continuing support for Radio Free Europe. In general, however, serious Polish political influence on the national scene remained illusory. By 1976 there were only 7 Polish Americans in the House of Representatives, down from a high of 15 in 1958. Although some—such as Pucinski, Daniel Rostenkowski, who became chair of the powerful Ways and Means Committee, and Barbara Mikulski—commanded great individual influence, there was no significant integrated Polish American pressure on either domestic or foreign affairs. The Polish American Congress publicized at great lengths throughout Polonia its ability to gain presidential audiences and appointments to "blue ribbon" committees, but the committees were largely ceremonial and the incumbents, regardless of party, were able to disregard legitimate Polish American concerns with relative impunity. Aloysius Mazewski, president of the Polish American Congress and Polish National Alliance and the de facto leader of Polonia, proved no more adept at national politics than did his precursors, settling for the personal gratification of largely honorific appointments rather that any meaningful political concessions.

Aside from the Republican victory in 1972, the single occasion when Polonia rose to speak with a relatively unified and significant voice was in the presidential election of 1976. The fate of friends and relatives in Poland living under harsh communist domination continued to be a strong, if sometimes latent, concern in Polonia. In 1975 President Gerald Ford began a campaign to decrease Cold War tensions when he changed the wording of a proposed speech to eliminate remarks that might offend the Soviet Union. As originally drafted, a presidential speech to be delivered shortly before the signing of the Helsinki Treaty of European Security and Cooperation stated: "United States policy supports the aspirations for freedom and national independence of the peoples of Eastern Europe by any peaceful means."[64] The meaning and impact of this statement were dramatically undermined when the wording was changed to read: "United States policy supports the aspirations for freedom and national independence of peoples everywhere."[65] While this change received scant attention at the time, it signaled the beginning of a series of "soft" statements on Eastern Europe culminating in Ford's insistence, during a televised presidential debate in 1976, that Eastern Europe was no longer under Soviet domination. The reaction of Poles was immediate and outspoken. Taking the lead in a chorus of protest from virtually every ethnic group with roots in Eastern Europe, Poles loudly condemned Ford's naivete, giving their overwhelming support to his Democratic challenger, Jimmy Carter.

In the decades between 1945 and 1975 a new generation of Polish Americans came to maturity. Together with the older Polonia and the new arrivals they faced the uncertainty of economic fluctuations, the challenges of threatened neighborhoods and negative stereotyping, intermarriage and the movement of the younger generations to suburbia, and the opportunities of the postwar world. In the process of dealing with these forces they reevaluated old political allegiances, revised or even abandoned some of their traditional institutions, and pursued new avenues to success in mainstream America. Although Polonia had changed, it retained a sense of self-identity manifested in continuing interest in its heritage and culture and occasional collective action when group interests were in jeopardy.

nine

Defining the Future

Henryk Sienkiewicz titled one of his novels on the early Christian era *Quo Vadis*—where are you going? The same question could well be asked of Polonia as it embarks on its second century of existence since the beginning of mass migration in the 1880s.

The 1970 U.S. Census reported 2,437,938 people claiming Polish as their mother tongue. This figure increased slightly from 2,416,000 in 1940. A study by the Census Bureau in 1971 reported that 5 million people claimed both parents to be of Polish origin.[1] The question that bedeviled those who conducted research on Polonia during the Progressive Era remains: How do we count Polish Americans? Should we consider anyone descended from one or more Polish immigrants? Or should we consider only those who identify with Polish heritage and culture? Depending on the answer to that question, Polonia in 1990 can be estimated to include anywhere from 4 million to 15 million people.

The census of 1980 attempted to answer a number of questions relating to ethnicity, including in its questionnaire an opportunity for respondents to indicate their ethnic origin. Based on responses to these questions on ethnic self-identification, the census projected 8,228,037 people with Polish ethnicity.[2]

The Solidarność Era

One of the most important events in determining the future of Polish immigration to America since the nationality quotas were made permanent in 1924 was the Immigration Act of 1965. Eliminating the discriminatory quota system that guided American policy for more than 40 years, the new legislation gave priority to immigrants with skills and to the reunification of families. The elimination of the old quota system was consistent with the emphasis on civil rights legislation during the 1960s, for it removed the discrimination against immigrants from Eastern and Southern Europe. As a result, Polish immigration since 1965 was steady, if moderate, and contained a large number of professionals and intellectuals.[3]

The great majority of the post-1965 immigrants were younger people who grew up and were educated in communist Poland, giving them perspectives and expectations different from those who came before them. Feliks Gross identified four distinct categories within the post-1965 group. The first of these included skilled workers who saw in America opportunities for freedom and economic advancement, a group that Gross labeled the "new economic immigrants." Unlike the immigrants who came "for bread" at the beginning of the century, they were not marginally educated peasants but professionals and skilled artisans who easily found employment in the United States. Given their socialization in a very restrictive society, they were sometimes critical of the excessive freedoms in America that led to violence, self-indulgence, and a fixation on money. The second category included idealists disillusioned with the communist system who sought in America the fulfillment of their utopian dreams. They remained committed to the working-class philosophy, but favored humanistic and democratic principles as a means of achieving their goals. Third were the scholars, generally creative and prominent individuals who suffered discrimination in Poland because of their liberal political outlook. Most of these were successful in finding positions in American universities, where they pursued their respective specializations. The final group consisted of Polish students; young people seeking a better future. They knew little of prewar Poland except through their education and cared little about the political legacies of that period.

Despite such basic differences in age and outlook, the post-1965 immigrants shared a number of general characteristics. As Polzin summarized them: they included a large number of intellectuals, professionals, white-collar workers, and scientists; they migrated primarily to find freedom; few expected to return to Poland; they included a high proportion of women and children; they were largely urban dwellers; they often brought money with them; they sought professional positions in competition with other Americans; they joined American rather than Polish ethnic organizations; they valued education; and they sought citizenship early.[4]

For the most part, the new arrivals were educated and assimilated quickly into American society. Although some rose rapidly to positions of prominence in scholarly and professional organizations, for the most part they did not mix well with the established Polonia that they often regarded as crude and uneducated. The new arrivals generally eschewed older Polonia organizations, creating their own or taking control of organizations established by the postwar exiles. Polonia, in turn, looked to the new arrivals to join their social clubs and take part in Polish American activities. When they did not, Polonians generally viewed the new arrivals as distant and selfish, feeling, as earlier Polish Americans had about the postwar immigrants, that they expected to "get ahead" too quickly without "paying their dues."

Then, too, there was the recurring chasm between the working class and the more affluent and intellectual classes. Adopting the hostility and insecurity of the working-class perspective, Charles Keil noted that there were really two separate and distinct Polonias, "the pretending Polonia of the polonaise and the real Polonia of the polka."[5] In a clear differentiation based on socioeconomic class, he bemoaned the "legendary Polonia managed by professionals" who pretend to be ethnic while "upholding their heritage" and "lording it over their inferiors."[6] In contrast, he praised the "real" Polonia of working-class Polish Americans who "live their ethnic identities without much boasting and would just like to be left alone."[7]

Another example of this modern manifestation of the schisms that have traditionally split Polonia can be seen in the Miłosz-Blejwas exchange in the pages of the *New York Times*. In 1987 an interview with Nobel laureate Czesław Miłosz appeared in the *New York Times Book Review* in which the poet, a recent emigré to America, bemoaned "the incredible cultural crudeness of Polish-Americans." He explained, "It's probably that some civilizations do not shape people so they have enough resilience to be able to stand on their own two feet outside their ghetto." In a letter of response, Stanislaus Blejwas, a professor of history, asked pointedly, "why a poet, an individual concerned with human values, resorts to that intolerant prejudice unique to intellectuals, namely, the contemptuous condemnation of the masses who do not read or understand him?"[8]

At its base level, the Miłosz-Blejwas debate was a difference over "culture," it was a conflict between the culture of the newly arrived Poles and that of the old, misshapen cultural elements that survived from the rural, less educated, turn-of-the-century immigrants. It was also a reflection of the long-standing gulf within Polonia between the peasant culture familiar to the working class and the gentry perspective of the intellectuals. In this, it represented in a sense a lingering manifestation of the old class divisions between the *lud* and the *szlachta*, the people and the gentry.

The Socioeconomic Status of Polonia

The dramatic shift in the U.S. economy, with the loss of tens of thousands of manufacturing jobs, caused a great dislocation within Polonia. The large Polish community in Chicago had retained its vitality over the years to a great extent because of the stability of jobs in the railroad, steel, and stockyard industries. Generations of Polish Americans had found employment in the mines of West Virginia and Pennsylvania, the steel mills of Pennsylvania, Ohio, and the Midwest, and the textile mills of New England and New York. Their decline threatened Polonia's socioeconomic status and fractured its communities as residents gradually relocated to find employment.

Despite these dislocations, the new opportunities offered by the postwar years combined to yield a dramatic increase in Polonia's economic status. Buoyed to some extent by the influx of educated Poles after 1940 and by the opportunities resulting from the G.I. Bill and the social legislation of the Kennedy-Johnson years, the socioeconomic status of Polonia showed significant improvement between 1960 and 1990. By 1970 the annual median income of Polish Americans was $12,275. This was not only greater than the mean for all groups at that time but surpassed that of the Italians, Irish, British, Germans, and the other major European groups. Further proof of the increase in Polish American economic status can be found in a 1976 study by sociologist Eugene Obidinski. After assigning the families studied to one of three groups based on income level—above $15,000, between $6,000 and $14,999, and $5,999 or less—he found that "the percentage of native born Polish American families at the high rank exceeded those of other groups and the percentage of Polish families in the low rank level was less than that for other groups.[9]

The 1980 U.S. Census provided further evidence of Polonia's progress up the economic ladder. A review of data on male workers showed a high percentage of Polish Americans holding professional and technical jobs, being considerably above the national mean in both categories of employment. Further, while the mean national income was $16,105, that for Polish American males was

$18,095. When total family income is considered, Polish Americans ranked third highest. At the same time, the percentage of Polish Americans below the poverty level was the lowest of any group studied.[10]

By 1990 the median income level of Polish American families had risen dramatically to $41,700, compared with a national average of $35,225. While 10 percent of American families existed below the poverty level in 1990, only 4.3 percent of Polish American families found themselves in this condition.[11] A 1991 study of the Detroit area by John J. Bukowczyk and Peter D. Slavcheff found that most Polish Americans there were "no longer members of the working class" but held "a variety of jobs, including professional and managerial positions."[12] Clearly, Polish Americans had not only become integrated into the U.S. economy but had become increasingly successful.

In the area of education, Polonia also exhibited progress. The 1970 U.S. Census showed that in terms of the median number of years of schooling completed, Polish Americans over 35 years of age ranked lower than most groups. By comparison, the younger generation, aged 25–34, who had the advantage of postwar education programs and federal financial aid, ranked slightly higher than the rest of the groups. The 1980 U.S. Census indicated further gains. Polish Americans ranked above the national average in the number of years of schooling and percentage with college degrees. Of those Polish Americans between the ages of 18 and 25, 85.8 percent held high school diplomas, compared with a national average of 78.7 percent. In the same age group, 9.7 percent of Polish Americans held college degrees, compared with a national average of 7.0 percent.[13] By 1990 the U.S. Census showed that 11.4 percent of Polish Americans aged 18–24 had attained a baccalaureate or higher degree, compared with 7.6 percent of the general population. Among people aged 25 and above, 14.1 percent of Polish Americans have a baccalaureate or higher degree, compared with 13.1 percent of the general population.[14] The increasing percentage of educated Polish Americans in these younger age groups illustrates the educational strides made in Polonia between 1970 and 1990.

Is There Still a Polonia?

One of the questions debated by historians, sociologists, and other scholars is the degree to which Polonia can still be identified as an ethnic community. While some insist that it remains a vibrant community intent on preserving its ethnic traditions, others believe that Polonia exists in memory only, with the real essence of ethnic identity having long since given way to assimilation. Pointing to the cultural differences between Polish Americans and the Polish immigrants arriving in the postwar era, David Januszewski concluded, "it is clear that the immigrants did not successfully resist assimilation. When the second wave of Polish immigrants arrived after World War II, they came to the urban Polonia no doubt expecting to find Poles very much like themselves. What they found, however, were people who had become very much American since their settlement here."[15] Donald Pienkos disagreed, arguing that "past researchers have mistaken 'acculturation' (an ethnic group's adjustment to life in America, mastery of the English language, and so forth) with 'assimilation' (loss of ethnic group consciousness in favor of total adherence to the norms of the dominant culture)." He maintained that "while ethnics may gradually adapt to American conditions and become fluent in English, they continue to settle together in ethnic neighborhoods, intermarry, and identify with fellow ethnics who seek political office."[16]

Neil Sandberg addressed the problem of ethnic identification in a work on the Polish community in Los Angeles, providing a definition of Polish ethnicity that can be used to shed light on the question of Polonia's continuing existence. According to Sandberg, ethnicity can be defined by the relative presence of a combination of traits including religion, culture, and nationality. To be properly considered a legitimate ethnic group—that is, a recognizable subculture within American society—the first trait that must be exhibited is a clear religious focus as seen in the presence of ethnic parishes functioning as religious and social centers. Second, there must be a shared culture of values, beliefs, and traditional practices handed down from generation to generation. Third, there must be a feeling of nationality—a mutual sense of kinship, group responsibility, and group identity between those of similar background.[17]

Is there still a Polonia in the 1990s? The first criteria to be considered is religion. In a study of the persistence of ethnic parishes, Roger Stump compared the national parishes in existence in 1940 with those recognizably ethnic in 1980. He found that of the three largest groups of national parishes in 1940—German, Italian, and Polish—only 38 percent of German parishes were still functioning in 1980, whereas 76 percent of Italian and Polish parishes were still active. He also noted that this phenomenon was *not* characteristic of only the larger urban parishes but was also reflected in smaller parishes, presumably more susceptible to change.[18]

Other evidence suggests that Polish ethnic parishes have not only survived but flourished. A study of Italian and Polish neighborhoods in Detroit, Baltimore, and Providence, Rhode Island, by John Carlisi in 1978–79 indicated that Polish families "scored strongly on both church affiliation and the desire to send their children to parochial schools."[19]

In his comprehensive study of Detroit, Paul Wrobel found "a vibrant Polish American community," which he attributed largely to the fact that "a Roman Catholic parish serves as a source of social organization in an urban neighborhood."[20] Wrobel found that the parish was not restricted to a religious role but also served a significant function as a focal point for social relationships. The church bulletin contained a lengthy schedule of events, sometimes with two or three per evening, that included meetings of parish societies, scout meetings, senior citizens events, a teen club, bingo, a liturgy meeting, confessions and Mass in Polish, and a variety of other religious and secular events.[21]

As a result of his observations of parish life, Wrobel concluded that from a sociological perspective "the web of relationships formed among its members is of major importance. A social network links nuclear families together so that no parishioner remains a stranger and so that a neighborhood becomes a community, an identifiable geographic and social unit."[22] Clearly, Wrobel's conclusions, supported by studies of other Polish ethnic parishes in Buffalo, Chicago, Los Angeles, New Britain (Connecticut), Pittsburgh, and Rochester (New York) show that the religious criteria in Sandberg's definition are fulfilled.

If we concede that there is still a Polish aspect to religious and social observance, the next question is whether a unique culture still exists. Obviously, there are few if any areas in the United States today that are self-sustaining Polish

American communities, ethnic enclaves such as those of 1910 where a person could be born, raised, educated, live, work, and play among fellow ethnics without ever having to learn English or adopt either the internal or external culture of the dominant group. Nevertheless, we can still detect a recognizable Polish American culture.

Tracing "Polish" cultural traits in America is sometimes difficult, especially given the increasing generations since the original mass migration and the fact that many of the "Polish" values that the original immigrants manifested in unique traditions have been adapted to the American environment to the point of being all but unrecognizable. As Robert Hill observed, Polish Americans "share many cultural components with most other citizens of the National State: respect for national symbols, the wisdom of the common man, equality, capitalism, individualism, achievement, law and order, pragmatism, and the value of the American dream." Thus, being "typically Polish" is often to be "typically" American.[23]

Nonetheless, some common cultural characteristics can still be observed. One interesting study that sheds light on the presence and transmission of Polish cultural traits is a project undertaken by Danuta Mostwin, in which she studied 480 people aged 60 and above from five nationalities in Baltimore and Washington. She found that the Poles "retained the characteristics of an agricultural, traditional family" more than any of the other groups. Although they no longer lived in the extended family home as did the immigrants of 1900, "they nevertheless retained a strong tendency for daily contact with them."[24] She concluded that "two key variables determine the degree of need for intimacy with one's own children: tradition and education."[25] In this sense, both the tradition of the rural Polish extended family and the influence of the parochial education combined to reinforce Polish values among Polish Americans.

Mostwin also found that, in keeping with the values of the original immigrants and their children, most elderly Poles were reluctant to seek public assistance, some considering it a "disgrace," and tended more than the other groups to rely on the traditional support of family members and children. Further, Poles exhibited a clear interest in passing on to their offspring *both* their American and their Polish cultural values and traditions. "The unique constellation of the three environments—the heritage of the country of origin, the ethnic community, and American society—combine to create a Polish American subculture," she concluded. "The values of this subculture and not the 'pure values' of the country of origin constitute the acting force in fulfilling the need for survival."[26]

Although Mostwin's study dealt with older Polish Americans of the second generation, who might be expected to be more ethnically oriented, research by other scholars identified the same phenomenon, if somewhat less pronounced, among the third and fourth generations. In the decades after 1960 the tremendous overcrowding of the cities, the spiraling economic inflation, and the dramatic rise in urban violence, crime, and delinquency combined to produce what Feliks Gross called "processes of social disintegration and anomie, dissolution of family and community ties."[27] To some extent, Polish American families fell victim to the same external forces, yet there is strong evidence that the traditionally strong family values of Polish Americans made them, as a group, less susceptible than others. Paul Wrobel's study of Detroit during this period led him to conclude that there was "compelling evidence" to indicate that Polish American families were particularly resilient. "In this sociocultural milieu," he noted, "the family is a prominent institution. To working-class Polish Americans, nothing is more important. . . . The family, therefore, is a haven, a refuge from the larger society, a source of warmth and affection, a set of relationships in which individuals invest themselves."[28]

A primary means of communication and transmission of heritage is the ethnic press, a segment of Polish American life where a clear demise can be seen. The peak era for Polish periodical publications in America was between 1900 and 1920, when at least one such publication appeared in 27 different states, with 65 percent located in the areas of high Polish American population density—New York, Pennsylvania, Illinois, and Michigan. During this period the cities of New York, Chicago, and Detroit were home to 43 percent of the publications, with the single largest number, not surprisingly, in Chicago.

Still, by 1974 there remained in Polonia some 107 ethnic publications, of which 48 were in Polish, 27 in English, and 32 bilingual. The total circulation of these was estimated at 664,365 copies in 41 cities in 14 states and the District of Columbia. Newspapers comprised 28 percent of the total, with the remaining 72 percent being periodicals. This was a significant change over former years, where the number of newspapers was greater and the ratio of newspapers to periodicals was greatly in favor of the former.

The weight of evidence appears to support the conclusion that Polish Americans, while clearly "American" and no longer "Polish," do maintain an ethnic identity. A study by Melanie Cyganowski and H. A. Ziontz found that 85 percent of Polish Americans who reached adulthood in the postwar era lived in Polish ethnic neighborhoods and 74 percent attended parochial schools. Consequently, they were subject to Polish cultural identification when being raised. "Childhood residency in Polish-American neighborhoods," they concluded, "indicates an exposure to common ethnic experiences."[29] Further, Neil Sandberg's study of Los Angeles Poles concluded that, regardless of socioeconomic class, they believed Polish culture should be preserved and Polish American organizational life maintained. These studies, and others with similar results, seem to support Walter Krolikowski's conclusion that "Poles, although they have lost many of their outward signs of ethnic identity, seem to be here to stay."[30]

Finally, having satisfied the first two of Sandberg's criteria—religion and culture—there remains the question of nationality, of group identity. A survey of 246 Polish Americans in Milwaukee by Donald Pienkos showed that there was indeed an ethnic consciousness, although it varied between individuals based largely upon demographic factors.[31] Pienkos's study indicates that there remains a strong ethnic identification among a significant number of Polish Americans.

The health and vitality of Polonia have traditionally been closely associated with its parishes and fraternal organizations. In financial terms, the strength of Polonia in the 1980s remained undiminished. Frank Renkiewicz estimated that by 1975 Polish American fraternal insurance organizations possessed combined assets in excess of $300 million, making them "the largest system of any produced by the immigration of 1880–1930."[32] Approximately 50 percent of the total assets were controlled by the Polish National Alliance, "the largest private Polish enterprise anywhere." Indeed, by 1980 the PNA claimed $167,355,210 in assets, with 294,761 members in 1,175 lodges.[33]

In Oneida County, New York, local parishes joined forces to raise funds and donations of food, clothing, and medical supplies for the Polish people following the imposition of martial law by the communist government. Continuing interest in the welfare of the homeland is but one typically Polish American ethnic trait. Stanley Babiarz, Eugene Dziedzic and Michael Dziedzic.

While the major fraternal organizations within Polonia have generally remained financially sound, the same cannot be said of their ability to sustain membership. In 1955 the 10 largest fraternals claimed approximately 753,000 members. Twenty years later, although the number of Americans of Polish descent increased, the same organizations numbered only 649,000. Renkiewicz estimated that this was only 10–15 percent of the total Polish American population, and Hill, who studied the Polish Falcon movement, similarly noted that there was clearly an "under-participation in voluntary associations" within Polonia.[34] Apparently, the compelling imperatives that led to the dramatic growth of the major fraternals during the immigrant generation, and their steady increase during the second generation, failed to appeal to the third and fourth generation Poles, whose focus was more on the domestic issues of daily life than sentimental attachments to the Old World.

Renkiewicz identified a number of reasons for the gradual demise of the fraternals. The ever-present factionalism—a bane of Polonia—coupled with the self-interest of leaders who provided themselves with undeserved increases in salary and benefits and settled for personal honors at the expense of Polonia's best interests resulted in a general undermining of confidence in their leadership. Then, too, as the third and fourth generations became more educated, they became increasingly disenchanted with a rigid leadership unwilling or unable to find ways to open its ranks. The educated sons and daughters from later generations could have added not only a badly needed sense of professionalism but a necessary focus on issues of relevance to contemporary Polonia. "Fraternal insurance may still be cheap," Renkiewicz noted, "but the benefit is not nearly so attractive to a generation raised in the post–New Deal welfare state and accustomed to an inflationary economy. Furthermore, institutional Polonia—still heavily influenced by the second generation descendants of the immigrants of 1880–1930 and by the refugees of 1945–55—lags behind the development of the community as a whole."[35] In fact, the financial success of the insurance fraternals may be their ultimate undoing as a force for ethnic preservation and focus. As Renkiewicz speculated, "The centralization of insurance transactions and the declining number of lodges may weaken grass roots interest and ethnic identification. The allure of financial gain, the preoccupation of regulatory agencies and trade associations with fiduciary responsibilities, and the competition of commercial companies seems to increase in proportion to the decline of the fraternals as vital ethnic institutions. Nonprofit status—their special advantage and responsibility—may yet become another form of conventional capitalism."[36] While organized Polonia remains strong in the 1990s, it is obvious that its active members are dwindling.

While there clearly remains a "Polonia" more than 100 years after the beginning of the mass migration, it is equally clear that it is not the Polonia of 1900 or even of 1950. What is unclear is whether there will be any recognizable form of Polonia a century hence. Studies by a number of scholars, including Sandberg, Obidinski, and Pienkos, indicate that overall ethnicity decreases with succeeding generations. As Sandberg noted, there was a leveling off of ethnic cohesiveness in the third and fourth generations. The increasing number of generations from the era of mass migration that gave life to Polonia's ethnic communities, the increasing socioeconomic success of Polish Americans that is dependent on their integration into the mainstream, and the homogenizing effect of mass culture propagated by technological change are all strong factors weighing against the long-term survival of any recognizable Polonia as seen during the first four generations. If "the status-enhancement functions of Polonian communities" is important, Obidinski said, "the influence and relevance of these communities will decline as younger generations of Polish Americans find status and recognition outside the community."[37]

There is little doubt that the traditional form of Polonia is in decline. In New York, traditionally Polish neighborhoods such as St. Mark's Place and the Lower East Side have lost their ethnic character, with, among other changes, the "Dom Polski" (Polish Home) first becoming a night club and most recently an American community center. In Pittsburgh, the population of "Polish Hill" peaked at about 10,000 in the early 1920s and has declined ever since. The remaining communities in Polonia are aging quickly, as the younger generations move out to take advantage of educational and economic opportunities elsewhere. In 1960 Pittsburgh's "Polish Hill" area had a mean age of 33.5 years; by 1970 it was 39.67.[38]

The survey conducted by Pienkos in Milwaukee concluded that a sense of Polish ethnicity still existed, but also found trends toward increased assimilation and a lessening of ethnic knowledge and understanding. Indeed, Pienkos's description of Milwaukee can be applied with increasing frequency to other communities as economic and demographic changes continue to reshape traditional Polish American ethnic enclaves. In Milwaukee, the era of the strong, self-sustaining ethnic community is over. In the words of Ronald Monticone,

"Polonia is no longer as closely knit and many Polish institutions have either disappeared or lost much of their ethnic character. Many Poles have moved out of the city and blacks and Hispanics have moved in. Even in areas that have remained Polish, electoral reforms have diluted their influence."[39] Although candidates with Polish names appear to be winning political office, "the dispersion and assimilation of the Poles indicate that their success no longer depends on their appeal to Polish American voters." Indeed, Pienkos found that the largest number of respondents to his survey were already "assimilated."[40]

The younger generations of Polish Americans, born in the United States, are clearly more assimilated than their ancestors. The majority reside outside traditional Polish areas, have high school diplomas and often some college as well, remain strongly religious, but appear to rank low on political consciousness, with 52.9 percent expressing "no ideological orientation" or attitude toward their congressional representative. Those ethnics who maintain strong ties with Poland or are active in ethnic organizations tend to be older, to live in more exclusively Polish neighborhoods, and to be politically conservative.[41]

In Pienkos's survey, "factor analysis revealed that highly religious persons of Polish heritage were no more likely to identify themselves in ethnic terms than less religious individuals, nor were they apt to possess personal ties with relatives in Poland."[42] Most telling, however, are the revelations of a study of those who belong to ethnic organizations in Milwaukee, presumably Polish Americans who are the most ethnic, the most in touch with their heritage. Only 44.4 percent could identify Edward Gierek as a Polish leader, only 14.5 percent could describe the Oder-Neisse dispute, and only 27.3 percent could correctly define the term "Polonia." Of the assimilated group, the percentages were 17.8, 9.6, and 7.5, respectively.[43]

It is apparent that to fourth- and fifth-generation Polonians, the traditions of their ancestors continue primarily as curiosities, religious ceremonies, or things performed out of habit or tradition whose original meaning has long since vanished. Polonian organizations provide little in the way of status or recognition to upwardly mobile Polish Americans, and people give to them, rather than get from them, as they advance in the professions. Although organized Polonia has made some effort to reach out to its assimilated brethren, it has been largely unsuccessful. Most Polish Americans today are assimilated. They live in suburbs, hold jobs outside the traditional manufacturing fields, and are otherwise barely distinguishable from other Americans. They are not often acknowledged by scholars studying the ethnic neighborhoods of urban America.

It is clear from the evidence that while Polonia still exists in the 1990s, it has evolved considerably over the past century and no longer resembles the typically insular ethnic community established by the immigrant generation. In the future, its survival will depend in large measure on its ability to address the real needs and concerns of Polish Americans rather than the old concerns of Poland and Polish issues, thus making ethnic identification more meaningful in contemporary life than some abstract "tradition."

Notes

one

1. Joseph Wieczerzak, "Pre- and Proto-Ethnics: Poles in the United States before the Immigration 'After Bread'," *Polish Review* 21, no. 3 (1976): 12.

2. Joseph Wieczerzak, "The Polish Insurrection of 1830–1831 in the American Press," *Polish Review* 6, nos. 1–2, (1961), 54, 56.

3. Jerzy Lerski, "Polish Exiles in Mid-Nineteenth Century America," *Polish American Studies* 31, no. 2 (1974): 39, 42; Wieczerzak, "Pre- and Proto-Ethnics," 13–14; Wieczerzak, "Polish Insurrection," 65n4.

4. Wieczerzak, "Pre- and Proto-Ethnics," 17.

5. *Ibid.*, 18.

6. Jerzy Jedlicki, "Land of Hope, Land of Despair: Polish Scholarship and American Immigration," *Reviews in American History,* March 1975, 90.

7. Wieczerzak, "Pre- and Proto-Ethnics," 18.

8. Lerski, "Polish Exiles," 32–33, 35, 41–42, quote from 41; Bélla Vassady, Jr., "The 'Tochman Affair': An Incident in Mid-Nineteenth Century Hungarian Emigration to America," *Polish Review* 25, nos. 3–4 (1980): 17.

9. Joseph Wieczerzak, "American Opinion and the Warsaw Disturbances of 1861," *Polish Review* 7, no. 3 (1962): 81.

10. Information on the exiles of 1846 is based on Lerski, "Polish Exiles," 33–35, 40, 42–43; Polzin, "Polish Americans," 61–62, 104; Salvatore Mondello, "America's Polish Heritage as Viewed by Miecislaus Haiman and the Periodical Press," *Polish Review* 4, nos. 1–2 (1959): 116; Jedlicki, "Land of Hope," 90; T. Lindsay Baker, "The Reverend Leopold Moczygemba: Patriarch of Polonia," *Polish American Studies* 41, no. 1 (1984): 66, 68, 70–71, 76–78, 80; and Brożek, "Polish Migration," 20, 22.

11. Jerzy Lerski, "Jewish-Polish Amity in Lincoln's America," *Polish Review* 18, no. 4 (1974): 45.

12. Jan Kowalik, *The Polish Press in America* (San Francisco: R and E Research, 1978), 2; Eugene Podraza, "The Polish Emigré and the Domestic Press and the American Civil War," *Polish Review* 27, nos. 3–4 (1982): 115–16.

13. Information on Polish-Russian relations is based on Jedlicki, "Land of Hope," 90; Podraza, "Polish Emigré," 115–16; and Wieczerzak, "American Opinion," 74.

14. Wieczerzak, "American Opinion," 74.

15. Lerski, "Polish Exiles," 43.

16. Podraza, "Polish Emigré," 113, 115.

17. *Ibid.,* 118–19.

two

1. Thomas A. Michalski, "The Prussian Crucible: Some Items in the Cultural Baggage of Prussian Polish Immigrants," *Polish American Studies* 42, no. 2 (1985): 6–7.

2. *Ibid.,* 7.

3. *Ibid.,* 6–7.

4. *Ibid.,* 12–13.

5. Robert F. Hill, *Exploring the Dimensions of Ethnicity: A Study of Status, Culture and Identity* (New York: Arno Press, 1980), 114.

6. Michalski, "Prussian Crucible," 14–15.

7. Hill, *Dimensions of Ethnicity,* 115–16.

8. *Ibid.,* 115.

9. Frank A. Renkiewicz, "An Economy of Self-Help: Fraternal Capitalism and the Evolution of Polish America," in *Studies in Ethnicity: The East European Experience in America,* ed. Charles A. Ward, Philip Shashko, and Donald E. Pienkos (Boulder, Colo.: East European Monographs, 1980), 72; Ewa Morawska, "'For Bread with Butter': Life-Worlds of Peasant-Immigrants from East Central Europe, 1880–1914," *Journal of Social History* 17, no. 3 (1984): 388–89.

10. Hill, *Dimensions of Ethnicity,* 114–15; Morawska, "Life-Worlds," 387–89.

11. Morawska, "Life-Worlds," 389.

12. *Ibid.,* 388.

13. *Ibid.*

14. Hill, *Dimensions of Ethnicity,* 116.

15. Theresita Polzin, "The Polish Americans," in *Contemporary American Immigration: Interpretive Essays (European),* ed. Dennis Laurence Cuddy (Boston: Twayne Publishers, 1982), 64; Hill, *Dimensions of Ethnicity,* 113; quote from Richard Zeitlin, "White Eagles in the North Woods: Polish Immigration to Rural Wisconsin, 1857–1900," *Polish Review* 25, no. 1 (1980): 72.

16. Zeitlin, "White Eagles," 69–70.

17. Hill, *Dimensions of Ethnicity,* 110, 116; Helena Znaniecka Lopata, "Polish Immigration to the United States of America: Problems of Estimation and Parameters," *Polish Review* 21, no. 4 (1976): 105.

18. Zeitlin, "White Eagles," 71.

19. Victor R. Greene, "Pre-World War I Polish Emigration to the United States: Motives and Statistics," *Polish Review* 6, no. 3 (1961): 46–47; Bolesław Kumor, "The Catholic Church in the Austrian Partition and Emigration," in *Pastor of the Poles: Polish American Essays Presented to Right Reverend Monsignor John P. Wodarski in Honor of the Fiftieth Anniversary of His Ordination,* ed. Stanislaus A. Blejwas and M. B. Biskupski (New Britain, Conn.: Polish Studies Program Monographs, Central Connecticut State University, 1982), 93.

20. Lopata, "Problems of Estimation," 86; Polzin, "Polish Americans," 61.

21. Lopata, "Problems of Estimation," 89, 92–93.

22. *Ibid.,* 87–88.

23. *Ibid.,* 100, 106–7.

24. J. David Greenstone, "Ethnicity, Class and Discontent: The Case of Polish Peasant Immigrants," *Ethnicity* 2 (1975), 5; Jerzy Jedlicki, "Land of Hope," 93.

25. William I. Thomas and Florian Znaniecki, *The Polish Peasant in Europe and America* (New York: Alfred A. Knopf, 1927); John Bodnar, "Immigration and Modernization: The Case of Slavic Peasants in Industrial America," *Journal of Social History* 10 (1976): 44. For a discussion of the concept of social disorganization see the abridged edition of *The Polish Peasant in Europe and America,* ed. Eli Zaretsky (Urbana and Chicago: University of Illinois Press, 1984), 191–92; for Thomas and Znaniecki's conclusions on the subject, see Zaretsky, 287–90.

26. Ewa Morawska, "The Internal Status Hierarchy in the East European Immigrant Communities of Johnstown, PA, 1890–1930s," *Journal of Social History* 16, no. 1 (1982): 85.

27. Morawska, "Internal Status," 77; William J. Galush, "Faith and Fatherland: Dimensions of Polish-American Ethnoreligion, 1875–1975," in *Immigrants and Religion in Urban America,* ed. Randall M. Miller and Thomas D. Marzik (Philadelphia: Temple University Press, 1977), 87.

28. William J. Galush, "The Polish National Catholic Church: A Survey of Its Origins, Development, and Mission," *Records of the American Catholic Historical Society of Philadelphia* 83, no. 3–4 (1973): 131.

29. Zeitlin, "White Eagles," 76; David G. Januszewski, "Organizational Evolution in a Polish American Community," *Polish American Studies* 43, no. 2 (1985): 47, 49; Helena Znaniecka Lopata, *Polish Americans: Status Competition in an Ethnic Community* (Englewood Cliffs, N.J.: Prentice-Hall, 1976), 47.

30. Theresita Polzin, "The Polish American Family—I: The Sociological Aspects of the Families of Polish Immigrants to America before World War II, and Their Descendants," *Polish Review* 21, no. 3 (1976): 113.

31. Bodnar, "Immigration and Modernization," 47; Richard S. Sorrell, "Life, Work, and Acculturation Patterns of Eastern European Immigrants in Lackawanna, New York: 1900–1922," *Polish Review* 14, no. 4 (1969): 82; Polzin, "Polish American Family," 113.

32. Januszewski, "Organizational Evolution," 51–52.

33. Quote from Greenstone, "Ethnicity," 8; Januszewski, "Organizational Evolution," 52.

34. Hill, *Dimensions of Ethnicity,* 110–11; James S. Pula and Eugene E. Dziedzic, *United We Stand: The Role of Polish Workers in the New York Mills Textile Strikes of 1912 and 1916* (Boulder, Colo.: East European Monographs, 1990), 46.

35. Gromada, "'Goral' Regionalism and Polish Immigration to America," in *Pastor of the Poles,* ed. Blejwas and Biskupski, 105–6.

36. Hill, *Dimensions of Ethnicity,* 111.

37. Janice E. Kleeman, "Polish-American Assimilation: The Interaction of Opportunity and Attitude," *Polish American Studies* 42, no. 1 (1985): 20.

38. Edward R. Kantowicz, "Polish Chicago: Survival through Solidarity," in *The Ethnic Frontier: Essays in the History of Group Survival in Chicago and the Midwest,* ed. Melvin G. Holli and Peter d'A. Jones (New York: William B. Eerdmans, 1977), 182–83; Bodnar, "Immigration and Modernization," 47; quote from Melanie Cyganowski and H. A. Ziontz, "Survey: The Buffalo Polish-American Legal Experience," *Buffalo Law Review* 30, no. 1 (1981): 165.

39. Kleeman, "Assimilation," 20; Sorrell, "Life, Work and Acculturation," 69.

40. Januszewski, "Organizational Evolution," 53.

41. Kleeman, "Assimilation," 19; Polzin, "Polish American Family," 105.

42. Material on the Polish American family is based on Polzin, "Polish American Family," 105–8.

43. Polzin, "Polish American Family," 105.

44. *Ibid.,* 107.

45. *Ibid.*

46. Descriptions of the factory system and immigrant family adaptation are based on Helena Znaniecka Lopata, "Polish American Families," in *Ethnic Families in America: Patterns and Variations,* ed. Charles H. Mindel and Robert W. Habenstein (New York: Elsevier, 1981), 26–30; Frank A. Renkiewicz, "Polish American Workers, 1880–1980," in *Pastor of the Poles,* ed. Blejwas and Biskupski, 118; Michael P. Weber, "East Europeans in Steel Towns: A Comparative Analysis," *Journal of Urban History* 11, no. 3 (May 1985): 297, 300; Hill, *Dimensions of Ethnicity,* 147. Quotation from Morawska, "Internal Status," 97–98.

47. John Bodnar, "The Family Economy and Labor Protest in Industrial America: Hard Coal Miners in the 1930s," in *Hard Coal, Hard Times: Ethnicity and Labor in the Anthracite Region,* ed. David L. Salay (Scranton: Anthracite Museum Press, 1984), 88.

48. Morawska, "Life-Worlds," 396.

49. Morawska, "Internal Status," 97–98; Morawska, "Life-Worlds," *passim.*

50. Boarders tended to be Poles, or sometimes other Slavic immigrants such as Lithuanians, Slovaks, or Ukrainians. Morawska, "Internal Status," 97–98; Morawska, "Life-Worlds," *passim.*

51. Hill, *Dimensions of Ethnicity,* 119; Morawska, "Life-Worlds," 395; Bodnar, "Family Economy," 396.

52. Polzin, "Polish American Family," 111; Bodnar, "Family Economy," 86.

53. Bodnar, "Family Economy," 396.

54. Kleeman, "Assimilation," 20; Bodnar, "Immigration and Modernization," 49.

55. Morawska, "Life-Worlds," 397.

56. *Ibid.,* 391; quote from Morawska, "Internal Status," 76–77.

57. Hill, *Dimensions of Ethnicity,* 118.

58. Morawska, "Internal Status," 86–90, 92.

59. Morawska, "Life-Worlds," 396–97.

three

1. Morawska, "Internal Status," 89–90.

2. Kowalik, *Polish Press,* 39–40.

3. *Ibid.,* 3.

4. *Ibid.,* 6.

5. *Ibid.,* 2–4.

6. *Ibid.,* 4–6.

7. *Ibid.,* 3–5.

8. *Ibid.,* 4.

9. Renkiewicz, "Self-Help," 73–74, quote from 73.

10. Alexander Janta, "Barriers into Bridges: Notes on the Problem of Polish Culture in America," *Polish Review* 2, no. 2–3 (1957): 79.

11. Renkiewicz, "Self-Help," 71.

12. Kantowicz, "Polish Chicago," 185.

13. Joseph Parot, *Polish Catholics in Chicago 1850–1920* (DeKalb: Northern Illinois University Press, 1981), *passim*.

14. Parot, *Polish Catholics, passim*.

15. William J. Galush, "Both Polish and Catholic: Immigrant Clergy in the American Church," *Catholic Historical Review* 70, no. 3 (1984): 412.

16. Januszewski, "Organizational Evolution," 49; Thomas and Znaniecki, *Polish Peasant*, 1602–11.

17. Donald E. Pienkos, *PNA: A Centennial History of the Polish National Alliance of the United States of North America* (Boulder, Colo.: East European Monographs, 1984), 50–51.

18. Renkiewicz, "Self-Help," 74.

19. *Ibid.*, 75.

20. Pienkos, *PNA*, 52–53.

21. Daniel S. Buczek, "The Polish-American Parish as an Americanizing Factor," in *Studies in Ethnicity*, ed. Ward, Shashko, and Pienkos, 161; Pienkos, *PNA*, 50–51; Galush, "Polish and Catholic," 413; Renkiewicz, "Self-Help," 75.

22. Kantowicz, "Polish Chicago," 190.

23. Januszewski, "Organizational Evolution," 49; Thomas and Znaniecki, *Polish Peasant*, 1602–11.

24. Renkiewicz, "Self-Help," 75–76.

25. *Ibid.*, 78.

26. *Ibid.*

27. *Ibid.*, 75.

28. *Ibid.*, 77–78.

29. *Ibid.*, 79.

30. *Ibid.*, 80.

31. *Ibid.*, 81.

32. Renkiewicz, "Self-Help," 81; Stanley R. Pliska, "The 'Polish-American Army' 1917–1921," *Polish Review* 10, no. 3 (1965): 47–48.

33. Renkiewicz, "Self-Help," 82.

34. Galush, "Faith and Fatherland," 85; Daniel S. Buczek, *Immigrant Pastor: The Life of Right Reverend Monsignor Lucyan Bojnowski of New Britain, Conn.* (Waterbury, Conn.: Association of Polish Priests in Connecticut, 1974), *passim*.

35. Galush, "Faith and Fatherland," 85–86; Kantowicz, "Polish Chicago," 193; Galush, "Polish and Catholic," 411; Renkiewicz, "Self-Help," 73.

36. Galush, "Polish National Catholic Church," 131.

37. Anthony Kuzniewski, review of Andrzej Brożek's *Polonia amerykańska, 1854–1939*, *Polish American Studies* 37, no. 2 (1980): 69.

38. Kantowicz, "Polish Chicago," 188; Andrzej Brożek, *Polish Americans: 1854–1939* (Warsaw: Interpress, 1985), 45.

39. Buczek, *Immigrant Pastor, passim*; John J. Bukowczyk, "Mary the Messiah: Polish Immigrant Heresy and the Malleable Ideology of the Roman Catholic Church, 1880–1930," *Journal of American Ethnic History* 4, no. 2 (1985): 5.

40. Bukowczyk, "Mary the Messiah," 8.

41. *Ibid.*

42. Galush, "Faith and Fatherland," 84.

43. Dolores Ann Liptak, "The National Parish: Concept and Consequences for the Diocese of Hartford, 1890–1930," *Catholic Historical Review* 71, no. 1 (1985): 53.

44. Roger W. Stump, "Patterns in the Survival of Catholic National Parishes, 1940–1980," *Journal of Cultural Geography* 7, no. 1 (1986): 78.

45. Galush, "Faith and Fatherland," 89; Greenstone, "Ethnicity," 7.

46. Leslie Woodcock Tentler, "Who Is The Church? Conflict in a Polish Immigrant Parish in Late Nineteenth Century Detroit," *Comparative Studies in Society and History* 25, no. 2 (1983): 245; Kantowicz, "Polish Chicago," 193.

47. Kantowicz, "Polish Chicago," 196–97.

48. Galush, "Polish and Catholic," 415.

49. Daniel S. Buczek, "Polish-Americans and the Roman Catholic Church," *Polish Review* 21, no. 3 (1976): 52–53; Galush, "Polish and Catholic," 417–18.

50. Buczek, "Polish-Americans," 52–54.

51. *Ibid.*, 54.

52. Galush, "Polish National Catholic Church," 133.

53. Galush, "Faith and Fatherland," 90–91; Bukowczyk, "Mary the Messiah," 20.

54. Galush, "Polish National Catholic Church," 134, 136.

55. *Ibid.*, 137.

56. *Ibid.*, 138–39.

57. Bukowczyk, "Mary the Messiah," 19; Galush, "Polish National Catholic Church," 145.

four

1. Hill, *Dimensions of Ethnicity,* 89; Andrzej Brożek, "Polish Ethnic Group in American Labour Movement," *Studia Historiae Oeconomicae* 13 (1978): 173, 177.

2. Weber, "Steel Towns," 292.

3. Henry B. Leonard, "Ethnic Cleavage and Industrial Conflict in Late 19th Century America: The Cleveland Rolling Mill Company Strikes of 1882 and 1885," *Labor History* 20 (1979): 525.

4. Renkiewicz, "Workers," 116–17.

5. This and other references to the New York Mills Corporation are based on Pula and Dziedzic, *United We Stand.*

6. Material and quotations regarding Lackawanna are from Sorrell, "Life, Work, and Acculturation," 68–72.

7. See Pula and Dziedzic, *United We Stand, passim.*

8. Victor R. Greene, "The Polish American Worker to 1930: The 'Hunky' Image in Transition," *Polish Review* 21, no. 3 (1976): 69.

9. Morawska, "Life-Worlds," 387.

10. John J. Bukowczyk, "The Transformation of Working-Class Ethnicity: Corporate Control, Americanization, and the Polish Immigrant Middle Class in Bayonne, New Jersey 1915–1925," *Labor History* 25, no. 1 (1984): 57.

11. Renkiewicz, "Workers," 116; Buczek, "Polish-American Parish," in *Studies in Ethnicity,* ed. Ward, Shashko, and Pienkos, 161.

12. Greene, "Polish American Worker," 76; David Brody, *The Steelworkers in America: The Nonunion Era* (Cambridge, Mass.: Harvard University Press, 1960), *passim.*

13. Leonard, "Ethnic Cleavage," 524; Greene, *The Slavic Community on Strike: Immigrant Labor in Pennsylvania Anthracite* (Notre Dame, Ind.: University of Notre Dame Press, 1968); Donald Cole, *Immigrant City: Lawrence, Massachusetts, 1845–1921* (Chapel Hill, N.C.: University of North Carolina Press, 1963).

14. Bukowczyk, "Bayonne," 53.

15. For the positive response of labor to the Poles see Pula and Dziedzic, *United We Stand, passim;* Renkiewicz, "Workers," 126; Kenneth Fones-Wolf, "Revivalism and Craft Unionism in the Progressive Era: The Syracuse and Auburn Labor Forward Movements of 1913," *New York History,* October 1982, 404–5.

16. Brożek, "American Labour," 176; Donald E. Pienkos, "Politics, Religion, and Change in Polish Milwaukee, 1900–1930," *Wisconsin Magazine of History,* Spring 1978, 143.

17. Material on the Lattimer episode is based on George A. Turner, "Ethnic Responses to the Lattimer Massacre," in *Hard Coal, Hard Times,* ed. Salay, 126–28, 147–48; Brożek, "American Labour," 177.

18. Turner, "Lattimer Massacre." 127.

19. *Ibid.,* 128.

20. *Ibid.,* 127.

21. Material on the Bayonne strike is based on Bukowczyk, "Bayonne," 55, 66, 68.

22. *Ibid.,* 66–67.

23. *Ibid.,* 73.

24. Material on Little Falls is based on Robert E. Snyder, "Women, Wobblies, and Workers' Rights: The 1912 Textile Strike in Little Falls, New York," *New York History,* January 1979, 29, 34, 38, 41, 53.

25. *Ibid.,* 37.

26. *Ibid.,* 39.

27. For the New York Mills strikes see Pula and Dziedzic, *United We Stand.*

28. Material on Polish efforts to assist the homeland is based on M. B. Biskupski and Joseph T. Hapak, "The Polish National Defense Committee in America, 1912–1918: A Dual Review Essay," *Polish American Studies* 44, no. 2 (1987): 70–74; Pliska, "Polish-American Army," 46, 48; Buczek, "Polish-American Parish," 161–62; Bukowczyk, "Mary the Messiah," 22; Renkiewicz, "Self-Help," 84.

29. Biskupski and Hapak, "Review Essay," 71.

30. Kowalik, *Polish Press,* 8.

31. Material on Paderewski is based on M. B. Biskupski, "Paderewski as Leader of American Polonia, 1914–1918," *Polish American Studies* 43, no. 1 (1986): *passim.*

32. Material on Haller's Army in generally based on Pliska, "Polish-American Army," *passim.*

33. Biskupski, "Paderewski as Leader," 39, 45, 53.

34. *Ibid.,* 53; Robert Szymczak, "An Act of Devotion: The Polish Grey Samaritans and the American Relief Effort in Poland, 1919–1921," *Polish American Studies* 43, no. 2 (1986): 14.

35. Biskupski and Hapak, "Review Essay," 75; Galush, "Faith and Fatherland," 94; Renkiewicz, "Self-Help," 84.

36. Pliska, "Polish-American Army," 49–54.

37. *Ibid.,* 54.

38. *Ibid.,* 51.

39. *Ibid.,* 55; Jan Ciechanowski, "Woodrow Wilson in the Spotlight of Versailles," *Polish Review* 1, no. 2–3 (1956): 16; Eugene Kusielewicz, "Wilson and the Polish Cause in Paris," *Polish Review* 1, no. 1 (1956): 64–65.

40. Shawn Aubitz and Gail F. Stern, "Americans All! Ethnic Images in World War I Posters," *Prologue* 19, no. 1 (Spring 1987): 41–42.

41. Buczek, "Polish-Americans," 56; Szymczak, "Act of Devotion," 14.

42. Pliska, "Polish-American Army," 52–53.

43. *Ibid.,* 47, 56; Buczek, "Polish-Americans," 56.

44. Pliska, "Polish-American Army," 57.

45. Ciechanowski, "Woodrow Wilson," 12–13.

46. Szymczak, "Act of Devotion," 15.

47. *Ibid.,* 13.

48. *Ibid.,* 15–16.

49. Marian Andrzej Sosnowski, "Poland and American Polonia in 1919–1920," *Polish Review* 25, no. 3–4 (1980): 10.

50. Szymczak, "Act of Devotion," 16, 18, 22–23; Ludwik Krzyżanowski, "President Hoover—Dispenser of American Largesse to Poland," *Polish Review* 25, no. 3–4 (1980): 105.

51. Szymczak, "Act of Devotion," 20.

52. *Ibid.,* 22.

53. *Ibid.,* 26, 34.

54. Material on the U. S. Immigration Commission is generally based on James S. Pula, "American Immigration Policy and the Dillingham Commission," *Polish American Studies* 37, no. 1 (1980): 5–31.

55. Oscar Handlin, *Immigration as a Factor in American Society* (Englewood Cliffs, N.J.: Prentice-Hall, 1959), 186.

56. John Higham, *Strangers in the Land: Patterns of American Nativism, 1860–1925* (New York: Atheneum, 1970), 164.

57. Anthony J. Kuzniewski, "Boot Straps and Book Learning: Reflections on the Education of Polish Americans," *Polish American Studies* 32, no. 2 (1975): 21–22.

58. Robert A. Divine, *American Immigration Policy 1924–1952* (New Haven: Yale University Press, 1957), 14.

59. T. J. Woofter, *Races and Ethnic Groups in American Life* (New York: McGraw-Hill, 1933), 31.

60. Oscar Handlin, *Race and Nationality in American Life* (Boston: Little, Brown, 1957), 97–98; Pula, "Dillingham Commission," 7–8.

61. Quote from Kleeman, "Assimilation," 15; see also Pula, "Dillingham Commission," 8–13.

62. Karel D. Bicha, "Hunkies: Stereotyping the Slavic Immigrants, 1890–1920," *Journal of American Ethnic History* 2 (Fall 1982): 22–23, 26.

five

1. Kuzniewski, review of Brożek, 70; Kantowicz, "Polish Chicago," 208.

2. The following discussion of demographics is based on Lopata, "Problems of Estimation," 94–95; Lopata, "Families," 18; Lubomir Zyblikiewicz, "U.S. Foreign Policy and the Poles in the West," in *Hyphenated Diplomacy, European Immigration and*

U. S. Foreign Policy, 1914–1984, ed. Helene Christol and Serge Ricard (Aix-en-Provence: Université de Provence, 1985), 75; Edward Kolodziej, "Emigration from II Polish Republic to America on Background of Employment Seeking Emigration Process from Poland: Number and Structures," in *Emigration from Northern, Central, and Southern Europe* (Kraków: Nakładem Uniwersytetu Jagiellonskiego, 1984), 176, 179.

3. Adam Walaszek, *Reemigracja ze Stanów Zjednoczonych do Polski po I wojnie światowej (1914–1924)* (Re-emigration from the United States to Poland after World War I) (Kraków: Państwowe Wydawnictwo Naukowe, 1983), *passim.*

4. Walaszek, *Reemigracja, passim.*

5. Andrew A. Urbanik and Joseph O. Baylen, "The Development of Polish Cultural-Educational Policy towards American Polonia," *Polish American Studies* 41, no. 1 (1984): 6–7; Kuzniewski, review of Brożek, 71.

6. The following discussion of Polish educational and cultural policy toward Polonia is based on Urbanik and Baylen, "Cultural-Education Policy," 5–9, 13–15.

7. *Ibid.,* 9–10.

8. *Ibid.,* 10–11.

9. *Ibid.,* 11.

10. *Ibid.,* 15.

11. *Ibid.,* 17–18.

12. M. B. Biskupski, "Poland in American Foreign Policy, 1918–1945: 'Sentimental' or 'Strategic' Friendship?—A Review Article," *Polish American Studies* 38, no. 2 (1981), 5–15.

13. Urbanik and Baylen, "Cultural-Education Policy," 19.

14. Ibid., 22, 24.

15. Brożek, *Polish Americans,* 191

16. Renkiewicz, "Self-Help," 84.

17. Januszewski, "Organizational Evolution," 56; Renkiewicz, "Self-Help," 85.

18. Morawska, "Life-Worlds," 171; Kowalik, *Polish Press,* 8.

19. Januszewski, "Organizational Evolution," 44–45; Helena Znaniecka Lopata, "The Function of Voluntary Associations in an Ethnic Community: 'Polonia,'" in *Contributions to Urban Sociology,* ed. Ernest W. Burgess and Donald J. Bogue (Chicago: University of Chicago Press, 1964), *passim;* Renkiewicz, "Self-Help," 85–86.

20. Renkiewicz, "Self-Help," 85.

21. Janta, "Barriers into Bridges," 85.

22. Paul Best, "Polish-American Scholarly Organizations," in *Pastor of the Poles,* ed. Blejwas and Biskupski, 154–55.

23. *Pastor of the Poles,* ed. Blejwas and Biskupski, vii.

24. Buczek, "Polish-American Parish," 159.

25. Buczek, "Polish-Americans," 59–60; Buczek, "Polish-American Parishes," 153; Galush, "Faith and Fatherland," 96.

26. Renkiewicz, *Formative Years, passim;* Stump, "National Parishes," 79; Galush, "Faith and Fatherland," 97.

27. Galush, "Faith and Fatherland," 95; Thaddeus C. Radzilowski, "The Second Generation: The Unknown Polonia," *Polish American Studies* 43, no. 1 (1986): 11.

28. Buczek, "Polish-Americans," 58; Konstantin Symmons-Symonolewicz, "A Sociological Analysis of Polish-Americans," *Polish Review* 23, no. 2 (1978): 77–78.

29. Buczek, "Polish-American Parish," 161–62.

30. Edward R. Kantowicz, "The Emergence of the Polish-Democratic Vote in Chicago," *Polish American Studies* 29, no. 1–2 (1972): 72.

31. Feliks Gross, "Notes on the Ethnic Revolution and the Polish Immigration in the U.S.A.," *Polish Review* 21, no. 3 (1976): 159–60; Brożek, "American Labour," 177.

32. Robert Lewis Mikkelsen, "Immigrants in Politics: Poles, Germans, and the Social Democratic Party of Milwaukee," in *Labor Migration in the Atlantic Economies: the European and North American Working Classes During the Period of Industrialization,* ed. Dirk Hoerder (Westport, Conn.: Greenwood Press, 1985), 279.

33. Robert G. Monticone, "Essays on Polish Ethnic Politics," *Polish American Studies* 37, no. 1 (1980): 71.

34. Kantowicz, "The Emergence," 68.

35. Monticone, "Polish Ethnic Politics," 66.

36. *Ibid.,* 66.

37. Kantowicz, "The Emergence," 67.

38. Januszewski, "Organizational Evolution," 53–54; Alfred J. Pike, "Transitional Aspects of Polish-American Music," *Polish Review* 3, no. 3 (1958): 105.

39. Radzilowski, "Second Generation," 10.

40. *Ibid.,* 11.

41. *Ibid.,* 11–12.

42. Niles Carpenter and Daniel Katz, "A Study in the Acculturation of the Polish Group in Buffalo, 1926–1928," *University of Buffalo Studies* 7, no. 4 (June 1929): 89; Eugene E. Obidinski, "Beyond Hansen's Law: Fourth Generation Polonian Identity," *Polish American Studies* 42, no. 1 (1985): 33–34.

43. Buczek, "Polish-American Parish," 160.

44. Polzin, "Polish Americans," 80; quote from Franciszek Lyra, "The Polish Language in the United States: Some Problems and Findings," *Polish Review* 7, no. 2 (1962): 81.

45. Radzilowski, "Second Generation," 8–9.

SIX

1. George H. Janczewski, "The Significance of the Polish Vote in the American National Election Campaign of 1948," *Polish Review* 13, no. 4 (1968): 102.

2. Material on the effort to court the Polish American vote and on U.S. policy that follows, unless otherwise indicated, is based on Fred B. Misse, "Franklin Roosevelt and the Polish Vote in 1944," *Midwest Quarterly* 21 (1980): 319–20; Charles Sadler, "'Political Dynamite': The Chicago Polonia and President Roosevelt in 1944," *Journal* 71, no. 2 (1978): 120, 122–24, 126; Peter H. Irons, "'The Test Is Poland': Polish Americans and the Origins of the Cold War," *Polish American Studies* 30, no. 2 (1973): 11–13, 15, 19–20, 22; Kowalik, *Polish Press,* 10; Robert Szymczak, "A Matter of Honor: Polonia and the Congressional Investigation of the Katyn Forest Massacre," *Polish American Studies* 41, no. 1 (1984): 32; David G. Januszewski, "The Case for the Polish Exile Government in the American Press, 1939–1945," *Polish American Studies* 43, no. 2 (1986): 57–58, 75–76; Zyblikiewicz, "Foreign Policy," 77.

3. Sadler, "Political Dynamite," 120; Irons, "The Test," 12.

4. Sadler, "Political Dynamite," 120.

5. *Ibid.*

6. Szymczak, "Matter of Honor," 32.

7. Sadler, "Political Dynamite," 124; Kowalik, *Polish Press,* 10; Irons, "The Test," 19–20; Szymczak, "Matter of Honor," 32.

8. Sadler, "Political Dynamite," 122, 124.

9. *Ibid.,* 122.

10. *Ibid.*

11. Jack L. Hammersmith, "Franklin Roosevelt, the Polish Question, and the Election of 1944," *Mid-America* 59, no. 1 (1977): 6.

12. Sadler, "Political Dynamite," 123–24.

13. Material on the Katyn atrocity is based on Januszewski, "Exile Government," 58–61; Sadler, "Political Dynamite," 119–20, 125–27; Szymczak, "Matter of Honor," 31, 33; Athan G. Theoharis, "Ethnic Politics and National Policy: Polish-Americans and Yalta," *Intellect,* March 1976, 470–71; Zyblikiewicz, "Foreign Policy," 77–78; Irons, "The Test," 29.

14. Januszewski, "Exile Government," 58–60, 62.

15. *Ibid.,* 63.

16. Szymczak, "Matter of Honor," 31, 35; Zyblikiewicz, "Foreign Policy," 77–78; Hammersmith, "Election of 1944," 8.

17. Sadler, "Political Dynamite," 125.

18. Hammersmith, "Election of 1944," 6; Zyblikiewicz, "Foreign Policy," 77–78.

19. J. R. Thackrah, "Aspects of American and British Policy Towards Poland from the Yalta to the Potsdam Conferences, 1945," *Polish Review* 21, no. 4 (1976): 3, 16, quote from 3; Szymczak, "Matter of Honor," 30.

20. Misse, "Polish Vote," 322.

21. *New York Times,* January 12, 1944.

22. Misse, "Polish Vote," 322.

23. Irons, "The Test," 29.

24. Misse, "Polish Vote," 323–24.

25. Sadler, "Political Dynamite," 125–26; Szymczak, "Matter of Honor," 33.

26. Szymczak, "Matter of Honor," 33.

27. Hammersmith, "Election of 1944," 6.

28. Irons, "The Test," 6; Renkiewicz, "Self-Help," 84; Szymczak, "Matter of Honor," 33; Stephen A. Garrett, "Eastern European Ethnic Groups and American Foreign Policy," *Political Science Quarterly* 92, no. 3 (Summer 1978): 314; Hammersmith, "Election of 1944," 8, 10; Theoharis, "Ethnic Politics," 471; Sadler, "Political Dynamite," 127.

29. Theoharis, "Ethnic Politics," 471; Hammersmith, "Election of 1944," 8.

30. Sadler, "Political Dynamite," 129; Hammersmith, "Election of 1944," 9.

31. Hammersmith, "Election of 1944," 8–9; Sadler, "Political Dynamite," 127, 129.

32. Irons, "The Test," 29.

33. Hammersmith, "Election of 1944," 10.

34. *Ibid.,* 10–12.

35. Misse, "Polish Vote," 324.

36. *Ibid.,* 328.

37. Material on the Warsaw Uprising and its aftermath is based on Hammersmith, "Election of 1944," 13; Januszewski, "Exile Government," 64–65, 67–68, 70–72; Sadler, "Political Dynamite," 129; Misse, "Polish Vote," 326.

38. Sadler, "Political Dynamite," 129; Januszewski, "Exile Government," 67–68.

39. Januszewski, "Exile Government," 70.

40. *Ibid.*

41. Material on the election campaign of 1944 is based on Misse, "Polish Vote," 328–30; Janczewski, "Polish Vote," 109; Theoharis, "Ethnic Politics," 471–72; Garrett, "Eastern European," 314; Zyblikiewicz, "Foreign Policy," 77–78; Szymczak, "Matter of Honor," 35; Hammersmith, "Election of 1944," 14–15; Sadler, "Political Dynamite," 131.

42. Misse, "Polish Vote," 328–29; Theoharis, "Ethnic Politics," 471; Garrett, "Eastern European," 314; Hammersmith, "Election of 1944," 14; Sadler, "Political Dynamite," 131.

43. Sadler, "Political Dynamite," 131.

44. *Ibid.*, 120.

45. Theoharis, "Ethnic Politics," 471; Hammersmith, "Election of 1944," 15; Zyblikiewicz, "Foreign Policy," 77–78; Szymczak, "Matter of Honor," 35; Sadler, "Political Dynamite," 131.

46. Sadler, "Political Dynamite," 131.

47. Theoharis, "Ethnic Politics," 471–72; Misse, "Polish Vote," 330.

48. Sadler, "Political Dynamite," 131.

49. Hammersmith, "Election of 1944," 16.

50. Szymczak, "Matter of Honor," 35.

seven

1. Szymczak, "Matter of Honor," 36.

2. Material on Cold War politics and the election of 1948 is based on Szymczak, "Matter of Honor," 36; Theoharis, "Ethnic Politics," 471–72; Janczewski, "Polish Vote," 102–3, 106, 108; Januczewski, "Exile Government," 96; Sadler, "Political Dynamite," 129, 132; Zyblikiewicz, "Foreign Policy," 76–78, 81–83; Irons, "The Test," 9; Thackrah, "Aspects of," 31.

3. Thackrah, "Aspects of," 12.

4. Szymczak, "Matter of Honor," 35.

5. Thackrah, "Aspects of," 16.

6. *Ibid.*, 31.

7. Garrett, "Eastern European," 315.

8. Zyblikiewicz, "Foreign Policy," 76.

9. Garrett, "Eastern European," 315.

10. Szymczak, "Matter of Honor," 36–38; Arthur Bliss Lane, "How Russia Rules Poland," *Life,* July 14, 1947, 98.

11. Janczewski, "Polish Vote," 102, 105–6.

12. Theoharis, "Ethnic Politics," 472.

13. Irons, "The Test," 5; Zyblikiewicz, "Foreign Policy," 73; Janczewski, "Polish Vote," 102–3, 105–6, 108.

14. Janczewski, "Polish Vote," 106.

15. Theoharis, "Ethnic Politics," 471; Janczewski, "Polish Vote," 108; Sadler, "Political Dynamite," 132.

16. Januczewski, "Polish Vote," 101.

17. Theoharis, "Ethnic Politics," 472.

18. Material on the Katyn investigation is based on Szymczak, "Matter of Honor," 25, 41, 44–45, 47–49, 51–55, 57, 63; Theoharis, "Ethnic Politics," 472–73.

19. Szymczak, "Matter of Honor," 42.

20. *Ibid.*, 42.

21. *Ibid.*, 43.

22. *Ibid.*, 44.

23. *Ibid.*, 45.

24. *Ibid.*

25. *Ibid.*, 47–48.

26. *Ibid.*, 48.

27. *Ibid.*, 25, 49, 51.

28. *Ibid.*, 51–52.

29. *Ibid.*, 58–59.

30. *Ibid.*, 59.

31. *Ibid.*, 60.

32. *Ibid.*

33. *Ibid.*, 60.

34. *Ibid.*, 59.

35. *Ibid.*, 57.

36. Pienkos, "Research on Ethnic Political Behavior among the Polish Americans: A Review of the Literature," *Polish Review* 21, no. 3 (1976): 123–48.

37. Szymczak, "Matter of Honor," 63.

38. Szymczak, "Matter of Honor," 63; Theoharis, "Ethnic Politics," 473.

39. *Ibid.*

40. Theoharis, "Ethnic Politics," 473.

41. *Ibid.*

42. Szymczak, "Matter of Honor," 63; Theoharis, "Ethnic Politics," 473.

43. Szymczak, "Matter of Honor," 64.

eight

1. Polzin, "Polish Americans," 65.

2. *Ibid.*, 65, 77.

3. Kowalik, *Polish Press,* 9.

4. Material on the Polish Institute of Arts and Sciences, the Joseph Piłsudski Institute, and the Polish American Historical Association is from Best, "Scholarly," 155–57, 159–60, 162.

5. Hill, *Dimensions of Ethnicity,* 113.

6. Zyblikiewicz, "Foreign Policy," 81.

7. See Pula, "Dillingham Commission," 13–14.

8. Polzin, "Polish Americans," 70.

9. Polzin, "Polish Americans," 63–64; Gross, "Ethnic Revolution," 161–62.

10. Polzin, "Polish Americans," 63, 70, 81, quote from 63–64.

11. Information on postwar immigration is based on Polzin, "Polish Americans," 71, 74, 77, 82.

12. Polzin, "Polish Americans," 63–64.

13. *Ibid.,* 74, 77, quote from 73.

14. Polzin, "Polish Americans," 62; Hill, *Dimensions of Ethnicity,* 146.

15. Janta, "Barriers into Bridges," 88, 92–93.

16. *Ibid.*

17. Obidinski, "Hansen's Law," 31.

18. *Ibid.*

19. Edward J. Czerwinski, "Notes on Polish Theater in the United States," in *Studies in Ethnicity,* ed. Ward, Shashko, and Pienkos, 211–12.

20. Polzin, "Polish American Family," 117–18.

21. *Ibid.*

22. Information on the Polish family is based on Polzin, "Polish American Family," 109, 117–18; Michael H. Crawford and Evelyn Goldstein, "Demography and Evolution of an Urban Ethnic Community: Polish Hill, Pittsburgh," *American Journal of Physical Anthropology* 43 (1975): 136–37.

23. John Simpson, "Ethnic Groups and Church Attendance in the United States and Canada," in *Ethnicity,* ed. Andrew Greeley and Gregory Baum (New York: Seabury Press, 1978), 17; quote from Donald E. Peinkos, "Research on Ethnic Political Behavior among the Polish-Americans: A Review of the Literature," *Polish Review* 21, no. 3 (1976): 130.

24. Pienkos, "Ethnic Political Behavior," 130.

25. *Ibid.*

26. Stanislaus A. Blejwas, "Pastor of the Poles: The Second Generation," in *Pastor of the Poles,* ed. Blejwas and Biskupski, 15.

27. Paul Wrobel, *Our Way: Family, Parish, and Neighborhood in a Polish-American Community* (Notre Dame, Ind.: University of Notre Dame Press, 1979), 148; Ewa Morawska, "The Poles in Europe and America," in *Ethnicity,* ed. Greeley and Baum, 34; Blejwas, "Pastor," 15.

28. Morawska, "Europe and America," 34.

29. Blejwas, "Pastor," 11–17.

30. Galush, "Faith and Fatherland," 97; Walter P. Krolikowski, "Poles in America: Maintaining the Ties," *Theory into Practice* 20, no. 1 (1981): 56; Wrobel, *Our Way,* 149.

31. Wrobel, *Our Way,* 149.

32. Buczek, "Polish-Americans," 60.

33. *Ibid.*

34. Cyganowski and Ziontz, "Legal Experience," 169–70.

35. Eugene Obidinski, "Polish American Social Standing: Status and Stereotypes," *Polish Review* 21, no. 3 (1976): 99; Kleeman, "Assimilation," 13.

36. Polzin, "Polish American Family," 116.

37. Joseph Parot, "Ethnic Versus Black Metropolis: The Origins of Polish-Black Housing Tensions in Chicago," *Polish American Studies* 29, no. 1–2 (1972): 5, 17, 30.

38. Wrobel, *Our Way,* 150; Renkiewicz, "Self-Help," 86.

39. The analysis of pressures in urban areas is based on Parot, "Housing Tensions," 5, 16, 19, 32.

40. *Ibid.*

41. Wrobel, *Our Way,* 135–36.

42. Hill, *Dimensions of Ethnicity,* 122; Andrew M. Greeley, "Two Other Neighborhoods—Bridgeport and the Stanislowo," in his *Neighborhood* (New York: Seabury Press, 1977), 24–25.

43. Andrew M. Greeley, "Ethnicity and Racial Attitudes: The Case of the Jews and the Poles," *American Journal of Sociology* 80, no. 4, 926; Hill, *Dimensions of Ethnicity,* 122.

44. Wrobel, *Our Way,* 149.

45. Greeley, "Neighborhoods," 24.

46. Suttles quoted in Greeley, "Neighborhoods," 24.

47. Greeley, "Neighborhoods," 24; Wrobel, *Our Way,* 152.

48. Pienkos, "Ethnic Political Behavior," 127, 132n40; Hill, *Dimensions of Ethnicity,* 121–22.

49. Frank Renkiewicz, *The Poles in America 1608–1972* (Dobbs Ferry, N.Y.: Oceana Publications, 1973).

50. Greeley, "Neighborhoods," 41.

51. Hill, *Dimensions of Ethnicity,* 4.

52. Obidinski, "Social Standing," 80.

53. Eugene Obidinski, "American Polonia: Sacred and Profane Aspects," *Polish American Studies* 32, no. 1 (1975): 81.

54. *Ibid.*

55. *Ibid.*

56. *Ibid.,* 12, 81.

57. Obidinski, "Social Standing," 81, 88; Kleeman, "Assimilation," 13, 16; Wrobel, *Our Way,* 147.

58. Stanley Wagner, "The Polish Vote in 1960," *Polish American Studies* 21, no. 1 (1964): 1–9; Gerald Pomper, *Elections in America: Control and Influence in Democratic Politics* (New York: Dodd, Mead, 1968), 72.

59. Pienkos, "Ethnic Political Behavior," 143; Pomper, *Elections in America,* 72.

60. Pienkos, "Ethnic Political Behavior," 129, 131, 134; Walter Borowiec, "Perceptions of Ethnic Voters by Ethnic Politicians," *Ethnicity* 1, no. 3 (November 1974): 267–68; Robert Lorinskas, Brett Hawkins, and Stephen Edwards, "The Persistence of Ethnic Voting in Urban and Rural Areas: Results from Controlled Election Method," *Social Science Quarterly* 49, no. 1 (March 1969): 891–99.

61. Andrew Greeley, *Why Can't They Be Like Us: America's White Ethnics* (New York: E. P. Dutton, 1971), 67.

62. Garrett, "Eastern European," 313.

63. Pienkos, "Ethnic Political Behavior," 131, 140; Garrett, "Eastern European," 313–14.

64. Garrett, "Eastern European," 301.

65. *Ibid.,* 314.

nine

1. Garrett, "Eastern European." 304; Michael J. Mikoś, "Polish in the United States: A Study in Language Change," in *Studies in Ethnicity,* Ward, Shashko, and Pienkos, 1; Pienkos, "Ethnic Political Behavior," 138.

2. John A. Kromkowski, "A Compendium of Social, Economic, and Demographic Indicators for Polish Ancestry and Selected Populations in the United States," *Polish American Studies* 47, no. 2 (1990): 16.

3. Gross, "Ethnic Revolution," 150, 162; Polzin, "Polish Americans," 66–67, 70.

4. Polzin, "Polish Americans," 81.

5. Charles Keil, "Class and Ethnicity in Polish-America," *Journal of Ethnic Studies* 7, no. 2, 37.

6. *Ibid.*

7. *Ibid.*

8. Czesław Miłosz, "Separate Nations: Poetry and the People," *New York Times Book Review,* 11 October 1987, 3–4; Stanislaus Blejwas, "Miłosz and the Polish Americans," *New York Times Book Review,* October 22, 1987, 47. The polemic was continued in Polish in "Polonia w Ameryce," *Akcent* 13, no. 4 (1992): 116–27.

9. Obidinski, "Social Standing," 91; Kromkowski, "A Compendium," 39–46.

10. Kromkowski, "A Compendium," 39–46.

11. *1990 Census of Population: Ancestry of the Population in the United States* (Washington, D.C.: U.S. Department of Commerce, Bureau of the Census, 1993), table 3; comparative population data provided by the National Center for Urban Ethnic Affairs, John Kromkowski, president.

12. John J. Bukowczyk and Peter D. Slavcheff, "Metropolitan Detroit Polish Americans: A Statistical Profile," *Polish American Studies* 38, no. 1 (1991): 59.

13. Kromkowski, "A Compendium," 39, 59; Obidinski, "Social Standing," 93; Mostwin, "Emotional Needs," 269.

14. *1990 Census of Population: Ancestry of the Population in the United States,* table 3; comparative population data provided by the National Center for Urban Ethnic Affairs, John Kromkowski, president.

15. Januszewski, "Organizational Evolution," 43.

16. Pienkos, "Ethnic Political Behavior," 129.

17. Neil C. Sandberg, *Ethnic Identity and Assimilation: The Polish American Community* (New York: Praeger, 1974), *passim.*

18. Stump, "National Parishes," 81.

19. John A. Carlisi, *Drug Abuse in Three Ethnic Neighborhoods* (Washington, D.C.: National Center for Urban Ethnic Affairs, 1979), *passim;* Mostwin, "Emotional Needs," 274.

20. Wrobel, *Our Way,* 3, 145–46.

21. *Ibid.*

22. *Ibid.,* 146.

23. Hill, *Dimensions of Ethnicity,* 96.

24. Mostwin, "Emotional Needs," 266.

25. *Ibid.*

26. *Ibid.,* 267, 269, 270.

27. Gross, "Ethnic Revolution," 152.

28. Wrobel, *Our Way,* 146.

29. Cyganowski and Ziontz, "Legal Experience," 166–67.

30. Quote from Krolikowski, "Maintaining the Ties," 57; Obidinski, "Social Standing," 88; Sandberg, *Ethnic Identity.*

31. Pienkos, "Ethnic Political Behavior," 128.

32. Renkiewicz, "Self-Help," 87.

33. Pienkos, *PNA, passim;* quote from Renkiewicz, "Self-Help," 87.

34. Hill, *Dimensions of Ethnicity,* 92; Pienkos, "Ethnic Political Behavior," 147n86; Renkiewicz, "Self-Help," 87.

35. Renkiewicz, "Self-Help," 87.

36. *Ibid.*

37. Obidinski, "Hansen's Law," 32; Sandberg, *Ethnic Identity,* 68.

38. Gross, "Ethnic Revolution," 152; Crawford and Goldstein, "Polish Hill," 134–35.

39. Pienkos, "Ethnic Orientations among Polish Americans," *International Migration Review* 11, no. 3 (1977): 350.

40. Monticone, "Polish Ethnic Politics," 70; quotes from Pienkos, "Ethnic Orientations," 350.

41. Pienkos, "Ethnic Orientations," 357.

42. *Ibid.,* 354.

43. *Ibid.,* 354, 358.

Selected Bibliography

Aubitz, Shawn, and Gail F. Stern. "Americans All! Ethnic Images in World War I Posters." *Prologue* 19, no. 1 (Spring 1987): 41–45.

Babiński, Grzegorz. "Occupational Mobility of Polish Americans in Selected U.S. Cities after World War Two." In *The Polish Presence in Canada and America,* edited by Frank Renkiewicz, 229–39. Toronto: Multicultural History Society of Ontario, 1982.

Baker, T. Lindsay. "The Reverend Leopold Moczygemba: Patriarch of Polonia." *Polish American Studies* 41, no. 1 (1984): 66–109.

Baran, Alina. "Distribution of the Polish Origin Population in the USA." *Polish Western Affairs* 17 (1976): 139–44.

Barendse, Michael A. *Social Expectations and Perception: The Case of the Slavic Anthracite Workers.* University Park: Pennsylvania State University Press, 1981.

Bernard, William S. *American Immigration Policy—A Reappraisal.* New York: Harper and Bros., 1950.

Best, Paul. "Polish-American Scholarly Organizations." In *Pastor of the Poles: Polish American Essays Presented to Right Reverend Monsignor John Wodarski in Honor of the Fiftieth Anniversary of His Ordination,* edited by Stanislaus A. Blejwas and M. B. Biskupski, 153–65. New Britain, Conn.: Polish Studies Program, Central Connecticut State College, 1982.

Betten, Neil. "Polish American Steelworkers: Americanization through Industry and Labor." *Polish American Studies* 32, no. 2 (1976): 31–42.

Bicha, Karel D. "Hunkies: Stereotyping the Slavic Immigrants, 1890–1920." *Journal of American Ethnic History* 2 (Fall 1982): 16–38.

Biskupski, M. B. "Paderewski as Leader of American Polonia, 1914–1918." *Polish American Studies* 43, no. 1 (1986): 37–56.

———. "Poland in American Foreign Policy, 1918–1945: 'Sentimental' or 'Strategic' Friendship?—A Review Article." *Polish American Studies* 38, no. 2 (1981): 5–15.

———, and Joseph T. Hapak. "The Polish National Defense Committee in America, 1912–1918: A Dual Review Essay." *Polish American Studies* 44, no. 2 (1987): 70–75.

Blejwas, Stanislaus A. "Old and New Polonias: Tensions within an Ethnic Community." *Polish American Studies* 38, no. 2 (1981): 55–83.

———. "Pastor of the Poles: The Second Generation." In *Pastor of the Poles:*

Polish American Essays Presented to Right Reverend Monsignor John Wodarski in Honor of the Fiftieth Anniversary of His Ordination, edited by Stanislaus A. Blejwas and M. B. Biskupski, 1–19. New Britain, Conn.: Polish Studies Program, Central Connecticut State College, 1982.

————. "A Polish Community in Transition." *Polish American Studies* 34, no. 1 (1977): 26–69.

———— and M. B. Biskupski, eds. *Pastor of the Poles: Polish American Essays Presented to Right Reverend Monsignor John Wodarski in Honor of the Fiftieth Anniversary of His Ordination.* New Britain, Conn.: Polish Studies Program, Central Connecticut State College, 1982.

Bodnar, John. "Beyond Ethnicity: Polish Generations in Industrial America." In *The Polish Presence in Canada and America,* edited by Frank Renkiewicz, 139–54. Toronto: Multicultural History Society of Ontario, 1982.

————. "The Family Economy and Labor Protest in Industrial America: Hard Coal Miners in the 1930s." In *Hard Coal, Hard Times: Ethnicity and Labor in the Anthracite Region,* edited by David L. Salay, 78–99. Scranton: Anthracite Museum Press, 1984.

————. *Immigration and Industrialization: Ethnicity in an American Mill Town, 1870–1940.* Pittsburgh: University of Pittsburgh Press, 1977.

————. "Immigration and Modernization: The Case of Slavic Peasants in Industrial America." *Journal of Social History* 10 (1976): 44–71.

————, Roger Simon, and Michael Weber. *Lives of Their Own: Blacks, Italians, and Poles in Pittsburgh, 1900–1960.* Chicago: University of Illinois Press, 1982.

Brody, David. *The Steelworkers in America: The Nonunion Era.* Cambridge, Mass.: Harvard University Press, 1960.

Brożek, Andrzej. *Polish Americans: 1854–1939.* Warsaw: Interpress, 1985.

————. "Polish Ethnic Group in American Labour Movement." *Studia Historiae Oeconomicae* 13 (1978): 173–82.

Buczek, Daniel S. *Immigrant Pastor: The Life of Right Reverend Monsignor Lucyan Bojnowski of New Britain, Conn.* Waterbury, Conn.: Association of Polish Priests in Connecticut, 1974.

————. "Polish American or American? The Polish Parishes in the 1920s." In *The Polish Presence in Canada and America,* edited by Frank Renkiewicz, 185–94. Toronto: Multicultural History Society of Ontario, 1982.

————. "The Polish American Parish as an Americanizing Factor." In *Studies in Ethnicity: The East European Experience in America,* edited by Charles A. Ward, Philip Shashko, and Donald E. Pienkos, 151–65. Boulder, Colo.: East European Monographs, 1980.

————. "Polish American Priests and the American Catholic Hierarchy: A View from the Twenties." *Polish American Studies* 32, no. 1 (1976): 34–43.

————. "Polish-Americans and the Roman Catholic Church." *Polish Review* 21, no. 3 (1976): 39–61.

————. "Three Generations of the Polish Immigrant Church: Changing Styles of Pastoral Leadership." In *Pastor of the Poles: Polish American Essays Presented to Right Reverend Monsignor John Wodarski in Honor of the Fiftieth Anniversary of His Ordination,* edited by Stanislaus A. Blejwas and M. B. Biskupski, 20–36. New Britain, Conn.: Polish Studies Program, Central Connecticut State College, 1982.

Bukowczyk, John J. "Factionalism and the Composition of the Polish

Immigrant Clergy." In *Pastor of the Poles: Polish American Essays Presented to Right Reverend Monsignor John Wodarski in Honor of the Fiftieth Anniversary of His Ordination,* edited by Stanislaus A. Blejwas and M. B. Biskupski, 37–47. New Britain, Conn.: Polish Studies Program, Central Connecticut State College, 1982.

———. "The Immigrant 'Community' Re-examined: Political and Economic Tensions in a Brooklyn Polish Settlement, 1888–1894." *Polish American Studies* 37, no. 2 (1980): 5–16.

———. "Mary the Messiah: Polish Immigrant Heresy and the Malleable Ideology of the Roman Catholic Church, 1880–1930." *Journal of American Ethnic History* 4, no. 2 (1985): 5–32.

———. "The Transformation of Working-Class Ethnicity: Corporate Control, Americanization, and the Polish Immigrant Middle Class in Bayonne, New Jersey 1915–1925." *Labor History* 25, no. 1 (1984): 53–82.

Carlisi, John A. *Drug Abuse in Three Ethnic Neighborhoods.* Washington, D.C.: National Center for Urban Ethnic Affairs, 1979.

Carpenter, Niles, and Daniel Katz, "A Study in the Acculturation of the Polish Group in Buffalo, 1926–1928." *University of Buffalo Studies* 7, no. 4 (June 1929).

Ciechanowski, Jan. "Woodrow Wilson in the Spotlight of Versailles." *Polish Review* 1, no. 2–3 (1956): 12–21.

Cole, Donald. *Immigrant City: Lawrence, Massachusetts, 1845–1921.* Chapel Hill, N.C.: University of North Carolina Press, 1963.

Crawford, Michael H., and Evelyn Goldstein. "Demography and Evolution of an Urban Ethnic Community: Polish Hill, Pittsburgh." *American Journal of Physical Anthropology* 43 (1975), 133–40.

Cyganowski, Melanie, and H. A. Zionts. "Survey: The Buffalo Polish-American Legal Experience." *Buffalo Law Review* 30, no. 1 (1981): 161–84.

Czerwinski, Edward J. "Notes on Polish Theater in the United States." In *Studies in Ethnicity: The East European Experience in America,* edited by Charles A. Ward, Philip Shashko, and Donald E. Pienkos, 211–24. Boulder, Colo.: East European Monographs, 1980.

Divine, Robert A. *American Immigration Policy 1924–1952.* New Haven: Yale University Press, 1957.

Fones-Wolf, Kenneth. "Revivalism and Craft Unionism in the Progressive Era: The Syracuse and Auburn Labor Forward Movements of 1913." *New York History,* October 1982, 389–416.

Galush, William J. "Both Polish and Catholic: Immigrant Clergy in the American Church." *Catholic Historical Review* 70, no. 3 (1984): 407–27.

———. "Faith and Fatherland: Dimensions of Polish-American Ethnoreligion, 1875–1975." In *Immigrants and Religion in Urban America,* edited by Randall M. Miller and Thomas D. Marzik, 84–102. Philadelphia: Temple University Press, 1977.

———. "The Polish National Catholic Church: A Survey of Its Origins, Development and Missions." *Records of the American Catholic Historical Society of Philadelphia* 83, no. 3–4 (1973): 131–49.

Garrett, Stephen A. "Eastern European Ethnic Groups and American Foreign Policy." *Political Science Quarterly* 93, no. 2 (1978): 301–23.

Greeley, Andrew M. "Ethnicity and Racial Attitudes: The Case of the Jews and the Poles." *American Journal of Sociology* 80, no. 4, 909–33.

————. "Two Other Neighborhoods—Bridgeport and the Stanislowo." In Greeley's *Neighborhood,* 21–43. New York: Seabury Press, 1977.

————, and Gregory Baum, eds. *Ethnicity.* New York: Seabury Press, 1978.

Greene, Victor R. "The Polish American Worker to 1930: The 'Hunky' Image in Transition." *Polish Review* 21, no. 3 (1976): 63–78.

————. "Pre–World War I Polish Emigration to the United States: Motives and Statistics." *Polish Review* 6, no. 3 (1961): 45–68.

————. *The Slavic Community on Strike: Immigrant Labor in Pennsylvania Anthracite.* Notre Dame, Ind.: University of Notre Dame Press, 1968.

Greenstone, J. David. "Ethnicity, Class, and Discontent: The Case of Polish Peasant Immigrants." *Ethnicity* 2 (1975): 1–9.

Gromada, Thaddeus V. "'Goral' Regionalism and Polish Immigration to America." In *Pastor of the Poles: Polish American Essays Presented to Right Reverend Monsignor John Wodarski in Honor of the Fiftieth Anniversary of His Ordination,* edited by Stanislaus A. Blejwas and M. B. Biskupski, 105–15. New Britain, Conn.: Polish Studies Program, Central Connecticut State College, 1982.

Gross, Feliks. "Notes on the Ethnic Revolution and the Polish Immigration in the U.S.A." *Polish Review* 21, no. 3 (1976): 149–76.

Hammersmith, Jack L. "Franklin Roosevelt, the Polish Question, and the Election of 1944." *Mid-America* 59, no. 1 (1977): 5–17.

Handlin, Oscar. *Immigration as a Factor in American History.* Englewood Cliffs, N.J.: Prentice-Hall, 1959.

————. *Race and Nationality in American Life.* Boston: Little, Brown, 1957.

Higham, John. *Strangers in the Land: Patterns of American Nativism, 1860–1925.* New York: Atheneum, 1970.

Hill, Robert F. *Exploring the Dimensions of Ethnicity: A Study of Status, Culture, and Identity.* New York: Arno Press, 1980.

Irons, Peter H. "'The Test is Poland': Polish Americans and the Origins of the Cold War." *Polish American Studies* 30, no. 2 (1973): 5–65.

Janczewski, George H. "The Significance of the Polish Vote in the American National Election Campaign of 1948." *Polish Review* 13, no. 4 (1968): 101–9.

Janta, Alexander. "Barriers into Bridges: Notes on the Problem of Polish Culture in America." *Polish Review* 2, no. 2–3 (1957): 79–97.

Januszewski, David G. "The Case for the Polish Exile Government in the American Press, 1939–1945." *Polish American Studies* 43, no. 2 (1986): 57–97.

————. "Organizational Evolution in a Polish American Community." *Polish American Studies* 42, no. 1 (1985): 43–58.

Jedlicki, Jerzy. "Land of Hope, Land of Despair: Polish Scholarship and American Immigration." *Reviews in American History,* March 1975, 87–94.

Kantowicz, Edward R. "The Emergence of the Polish-Democratic Vote in Chicago." *Polish American Studies* 29, no. 1–2 (1972): 67–80.

————. *Polish-American Politics in Chicago, 1888-1940.* Chicago: University of Chicago Press, 1975.

————. "Polish Chicago: Survival Through Solidarity." In *The Ethnic Frontier: Essays in the History of Group Survival in Chicago and the Midwest,* edited by Melvin G. Holli and Peter d'A. Jones, 179–209. New York: William B. Eerdmans, 1977.

Keil, Charles. "Class and Ethnicity in Polish-America." *Journal of Ethnic Studies* 7, no. 2, 37–45.

Kleeman, Janice E. "Polish-American Assimilation: The Interaction of Opportunity and Attitude." *Polish American Studies* 42, no. 1 (1985): 11–26.

Kołodziej, Edward. "Emigration from II Polish Republic to America on Background of Employment Seeking Emigration Process from Poland: Number and Structures." In *Emigration from Northern, Central, and Southern Europe*, 165–84. Kraków: Nakładem Uniwersytetu Jagiellonskiego, 1984.

Kowalik, Jan. *The Polish Press in America*. San Francisco: R & E Research, 1978.

Krolikowski, Walter. "Poles in America: Maintaining the Ties." *Theory into Practice* 20, no. 1 (1981): 52–57.

Kromkowski, John A. "A Compendium of Social, Economic, and Demographic Indicators for Polish Ancestry and Selected Populations in the United States." *Polish American Studies* 47, no. 2 (Autumn 1990): 5–75.

Krzyżanowski, Ludwik. "President Hoover—Dispenser of American Largesse to Poland." *Polish Review* 25, no. 3–4 (1980): 105–8.

Kulikowski, Mark. "A Bibliography on Polish Americans, 1975–1980." *Polish American Studies* 39, no. 2 (1982): 24–85.

Kumor, Rev. Bolesław. "The Catholic Church in the Austrian Partition and Emigration." In *Pastor of the Poles: Polish American Essays Presented to Right Reverend Monsignor John Wodarski in Honor of the Fiftieth Anniversary of His Ordination*, edited by Stanislaus A. Blejwas and M. B. Biskupski, 93–104. New Britain, Conn.: Polish Studies Program, Central Connecticut State College, 1982.

Kusielewicz, Eugene. "Wilson and the Polish Cause at Paris." *Polish Review* 1, no. 1 (1956): 64–79.

Kuzniewski, Anthony. "Boot Straps and Book Learning: Reflections on the Education of Polish Americans." *Polish American Studies* 32, no. 2 (1975): 5–26.

———. Review of Andrzej Brożek's *Polonia amerykańska, 1854–1939*. *Polish American Studies* 37, no. 2 (1980): 68–73.

———. "Wenceslaus Kruszka and the Origins of Polish Roman Catholic Separatism in the United States." In *The Polish Presence in Canada and America*, edited by Frank Renkiewicz, 97–116. Toronto: Multicultural History Society of Ontario, 1982.

Lane, Arthur Bliss. "How Russia Rules Poland." *Life*, July 14, 1947.

Leonard, Henry B. "Ethnic Cleavage and Industrial Conflict in Late Nineteenth Century America: The Cleveland Rolling Mill Company Strikes of 1882 and 1885." *Labor History* 20 (1979): 524–48.

Lerski, Jerzy. "Jewish-Polish Amity in Lincoln's America." *Polish Review* 18, no. 4 (1974): 34–51.

———. "Polish Exiles in Mid-Nineteenth Century America." *Polish American Studies* 31, no. 2 (1974): 30–42.

Liptak, Dolores Ann. "The National Parish: Concept and Consequences for the Diocese of Hartford, 1890–1930." *Catholic Historical Review* 71, no. 1 (1985): 52–64.

Lopata, Helena Znaniecki. "The Function of Voluntary Associations in an Ethnic Community: 'Polonia.'" In *Contributions to Urban Sociology*, edited by Ernest W. Burgess and Donald J. Bogue, 201–23. Chicago: University of Chicago Press, 1964.

———. "Intergenerational Relations in Polonia." In *The Polish Presence in*

Canada and America, edited by Frank Renkiewicz, 271–84. Toronto: Multicultural History Society of Ontario, 1982.

——. "Polish American Families." In *Ethnic Families in America: Patterns and Variations,* edited by Charles H. Mindel and Robert W. Habenstein, 17–42. New York: Elsevier, 1981.

——. *Polish Americans: Status Competition in an Ethnic Community.* Englewood Cliffs, N.J.: Prentice-Hall, 1976.

——. "Polish Immigration to the United States of America: Problems of Estimation and Parameters." *Polish Review* 21, no. 4 (1976): 85–107.

Lyra, Franciszek. "The Polish Language in the United States: Some Problems and Findings." *Polish Review* 7, no. 2 (1962): 81–95.

Michalski, Thomas A. "The Prussian Crucible: Some Items in the Cultural Baggage of Prussian Polish Immigrants." *Polish American Studies* 42, no. 2 (1985): 5–17.

Mikkelsen, Robert Lewis. "Immigrants in Politics: Poles, Germans, and the Social Democratic Party of Milwaukee." In *Labor Migration in the Atlantic Economies: The European and North American Working Classes during the Period of Industrialization,* edited by Dirk Hoerder, 277–95. Westport, Conn.: Greenwood Press, 1985.

Mikoś, Michael J. "Polish in the United States: A Study in Language Change." In *Studies in Ethnicity: The East European Experience in America,* edited by Charles A. Ward, Philip Shashko, and Donald E. Pienkos, 15–26. Boulder, Colo.: East European Monographs, 1980.

Miller, Eugene. "Leo Krzycki—Polish American Labor Leader." *Polish American Studies* 32, no. 2 (1976): 52–64.

Misse, Fred B. "Franklin Roosevelt and the Polish Vote in 1944." *Midwest Quarterly* 21 (1980): 317–32.

Mondello, Salvatore. "America's Polish Heritage as Viewed by Miecislaus Haiman and the Periodical Press." *Polish Review* 4, nos. 1–2 (1959): 105–18.

Monticone, Ronald G. "Essays on Polish Ethnic Politics." *Polish American Studies* 37, no. 1 (1980): 65–72.

Morawska, Ewa. "'For Bread with Butter': Life-Worlds of Peasant-Immigrants from East Central Europe, 1880–1914." *Journal of Social History* 17, no. 3 (1984): 387–404.

——. "The Internal Status Hierarchy in the East European Immigrant Communities of Johnstown, PA, 1890–1930s." *Journal of Social History* 16, no. 1 (1982): 75–107.

——. "The Poles in Europe and America." In *Ethnicity,* edited by Andrew M. Greeley and Gregory Baum, 30–35. New York: Seabury Press, 1978.

Mostwin, Danuta. "Emotional Needs of Elderly Americans of Central and Eastern European Background." In *Ethnicity and Aging. Theory, Research and Policy,* edited by Donald E. Gelfand and Alfred J. Kutzik, 263–76. New York: Springer Publishing Company, 1979.

Obidinski, Eugene. "American Polonia: Sacred and Profane Aspects." *Polish American Studies* 32, no. 1 (1975): 5–18.

——. "Beyond Hansen's Law: Fourth Generation Polonian Identity." *Polish American Studies* 42, no. 1 (1985).

——. "Polish American Social Standing: Status and Stereotypes." *Polish Review* 21, no. 3 (1976): 79–101.

O'Connell, Lucille. "The Lawrence Textile Strike of 1912: The Testimony of Two Polish Women." *Polish American Studies* 36, no. 2 (1979): 44–62.

Orzell, Laurence. "A Minority within a Minority: The Polish National Catholic Church, 1896–1907." *Polish American Studies* 36, no. 1 (1979): 5–32.

———. "The 'National Catholic' Response: Franciszek Hodur and his Followers, 1897–1907." In *The Polish Presence in Canada and America,* edited by Frank Renkiewicz, 117–35. Toronto: Multicultural History Society of Ontario, 1982.

Parot, Joseph. "Ethnic versus Black Metropolis: The Origins of Polish-Black Housing Tensions in Chicago." *Polish American Studies* 29, no. 1–2 (1972): 5–33.

———. *Polish Catholics in Chicago 1850–1920.* DeKalb, Ill.: Northern Illinois University Press, 1981.

———. "The Racial Dilemma in Chicago's Polish Neighborhoods, 1920–1970." *Polish American Studies* 32, no. 2 (1975): 27–37.

Pienkos, Donald E. "Ethnic Orientations Among Polish Americans." *International Migration Review* 11, no. 3 (1977): 350–62.

———. *PNA: A Centennial History of the Polish National Alliance of the United States of America.* Boulder, Colo.: East European Monographs, 1984.

———. "Politics, Religion, and Change in Polish Milwaukee, 1900–1930. *Wisconsin Magazine of History,* Spring 1978, 179–209.

———. "Research on Ethnic Political Behavior among the Polish-Americans: A Review of the Literature." *Polish Review* 21, no. 3 (1976): 123–48.

———. "The Secular Organizations of Polish Americans: The Fraternals' Role in Polonia." In *The Polish Presence in Canada and America,* edited by Frank Renkiewicz, 287–304. Toronto: Multicultural History Society of Ontario, 1982.

Pike, Alfred J. "Transitional Aspects of Polish-American Music." *Polish Review* 3, no. 3 (1958): 104–11.

Pliska, Stanley R. "The 'Polish-American Army' 1917–1921." *Polish Review* 10, no. 3 (1965): 46–59.

Podraza, Eugene. "The Polish Emigré and the Domestic Press and the American Civil War." *Polish Review* 27, nos. 3–4 (1982): 112–21.

Polzin, Theresita. "The Polish American Family—I: The Sociological Aspects of the Families of Polish Immigrants to America before World War II, and Their Descendants." *Polish Review* 21, no. 3 (1976): 103–22.

———. "The Polish Americans." In *Contemporary American Immigration,* Dennis Laurence Cuddy, 59–85. *Interpretive Essays (European).* Boston: Twayne Publishers, 1982.

———. *The Polish Americans: Whence and Whither.* Pulaski, Wis.: Franciscan Press, 1973.

Pomper, Gerald. *Elections in America: Control and Influence in Democratic Politics.* New York: Dodd, Mead, 1968.

Pula, James S. "American Immigration Policy and the Dillingham Commission." *Polish American Studies* 37, no. 1 (1980): 5–31.

———, and Eugene E. Dziedzic. *United We Stand: The Role of Polish Workers in the New York Mills Textile Strikes, 1912 and 1916.* New York: Columbia University Press, East European Monographs, 1990.

Radzilowski, Thaddeus V. "The Competition for Jobs and Racial Stereotypes: Poles and Blacks in Chicago." *Polish American Studies* 32, no. 2 (1976): 5–18.

———. "Ethnic Conflict and the Polish Americans of Detroit, 1921–42." In

The Polish Presence in Canada and America, edited by Frank Renkiewicz, 195–207. Toronto: Multicultural History Society of Ontario, 1982.

———. "Reflections on the History of the Felicians in America." *Polish American Studies* 32, no. 1 (1975): 19–28.

———. "The Second Generation: the Unknown Polonia." *Polish American Studies* 43, no. 1 (1986).

Renkiewicz, Frank. "An Economy of Self-Help: Fraternal Capitalism and the Evolution of Polish America." In *Studies in Ethnicity: The East European Experience in America,* edited by Charles A. Ward, Philip Shashko, and Donald E. Pienkos, 71–91. Boulder, Colo.: East European Monographs, 1980.

———. "Polish American Workers, 1880–1980." In *Pastor of the Poles: Polish American Essays Presented to Right Reverend Monsignor John Wodarski in Honor of the Fiftieth Anniversary of His Ordination,* edited by Stanislaus A. Blejwas and M. B. Biskupski, 116–36. New Britain, Conn.: Polish Studies Program, Central Connecticut State College, 1982.

———, ed. *The Poles in America 1608–1972.* Dobbs Ferry, N.Y.: Oceana Publications, 1973.

———, ed. *The Polish Presence in Canada and America.* Toronto: Multicultural History Society of Ontario, 1982.

Sadler, Charles. "'Political Dynamite': The Chicago Polonia and President Roosevelt in 1944." *Journal* 71, no. 2 (1978): 119–32.

Sandberg, Neil C. "The Changing Polish American." *Polish American Studies* 31, no. 1 (1974): 5–14.

———. *Ethnic Identity and Assimilation: The Polish American Community.* New York: Praeger, 1974.

Sanders, Irwin T., and Ewa Morawska. *Polish American Community Life: A Survey of Research.* Boston: Boston University, 1975.

Shea, John. "Reflections on Ethnic Consciousness and Religious Language." In *Ethnicity,* edited by Andrew M. Greeley and Gregory Baum, 85–90. New York: Seabury Press, 1978.

Simpson, John. "Ethnic Groups and Church Attendance in the United States and Canada." In *Ethnicity,* edited by Andrew M. Greeley and Gregory Baum, 16–22. New York: Seabury Press, 1978.

Snyder, Robert E. "Women, Wobblies, and Workers' Rights: The 1912 Textile Strike in Little Falls, New York." *New York History,* January 1979, 29–57.

Sorrell, Richard S. "Life, Work, and Acculturation Patterns of Eastern European Immigrants in Lackawanna, New York: 1900–1922." *Polish Review* 14, no. 4 (1969): 65–91.

Sosnowski, Marian Andrzej. "Poland and American Polonia in 1919–20." *Polish Review* 25, no. 3–4 (1980): 3–11.

Spustek, Irena. "Immigrant Perceptions of Life in North America." In *The Polish Presence in Canada and America,* edited by Frank Renkiewicz, 11–16. Toronto: Multicultural History Society of Ontario, 1982.

Stump, Roger W. "Patterns in the Survival of Catholic National Parishes, 1940–1980." *Journal of Cultural Geography* 7, no. 1 (1986): 77–97.

Symmons-Symonolewicz, Konstantin. "A Sociological Analysis of Polish-Americans." *Polish Review* 23, no. 2 (1978): 76–79.

Szymczak, Robert. "An Act of Devotion: The Polish Grey Samaritans and the

American Relief Effort in Poland, 1919–1921." *Polish American Studies* 43, no. 2 (1986): 13–36.

————. "A Matter of Honor: Polonia and the Congressional Investigation of the Katyn Forest Massacre." *Polish American Studies* 41, no. 1 (1984): 25–65.

Tentler, Leslie Woodcock. "Who Is the Church? Conflict in a Polish Immigrant Parish in Late Nineteenth-Century Detroit." *Comparative Studies in Society & History* 25, no. 2 (1983): 241–76.

Thackrah, J. R. "Aspects of American and British Policy Towards Poland from the Yalta to the Potsdam Conferences, 1945." *Polish Review* 21, no. 4 (1976): 3–25.

Thackray, Frank W. "To Serve the Cause of Poland: The Polish Grey Samaritans, 1919–1922." *Polish Review* 35, no. 1 (1990): 37–50.

Theoharis, Athan G. "Ethnic Politics and National Policy: Polish-Americans and Yalta." *Intellect*, March 1976, 470–73.

Thomas, William I., and Florian Znaniecki. *The Polish Peasant in Europe and America*. 2 vols. 1918. New York: Alfred A. Knopf, 1927.

Turner, George A. "Ethnic Responses to the Lattimer Massacre." In *Hard Coal, Hard Times: Ethnicity and Labor in the Anthracite Region*, edited by David L. Salay, 126–52. Scranton: Anthracite Museum Press, 1984.

Urbanik, Andrew A., and Joseph O. Baylen. "The Development of Polish Cultural-Educational Policy towards American Polonia." *Polish American Studies* 41, no. 1 (1984).

Vassady, Bélla, Jr. "The 'Tochman Affair': An Incident in Mid-Nineteenth Century Hungarian Emigration to America." *Polish Review* 25, nos. 3–4 (1980): 12–27.

Walaszek, Adam. *Reemigracja ze Stanów Zjednoczonych do Polski po I wojnie Światowej (1914–1924)* (Re-emigration from the United States to Poland after World War I). Kraków: Państwowe Wydawnictwo Naukowe, 1983.

Weber, Michael. "East Europeans in Steel Towns: A Comparative Analysis." *Journal of Urban History* 11, no. 3 (May 1985): 280–313.

Wieczerzak, Joseph. "American Opinion and the Warsaw Disturbances of 1861." *Polish Review* 7, no. 3 (1962): 67–83.

————. "The Polish Insurrection of 1830–1831 in the American Press." *Polish Review* 6, nos. 1–2 (1961): 53–72.

————. "Pre- and Proto-Ethnics: Poles in the United States before the Immigration 'After Bread.'" *Polish Review* 21, no. 3 (1976): 7–38.

Woofter, T. J. *Races and Ethnic Groups in American Life*. New York: McGraw-Hill, 1933.

Wrobel, Paul. *Our Way: Family, Parish, and Neighborhood in a Polish-American Community*. Notre Dame, Ind.: University of Notre Dame, 1979.

Zeitlin, Richard. "White Eagles in the North Woods: Polish Immigration to Rural Wisconsin 1857–1900." *Polish Review* 25, no. 1 (1980): 69–92.

Zyblikiewicz, Lubomir. "U.S. Foreign Policy and the Poles in the West." In *Hyphenated Diplomacy: European Immigration and U.S. Foreign Policy, 1914–1984*, edited by Helene Christol and Serge Ricard, 73–87. Aix-en-Provence: Université de Provence, 1985.

Index

The Author

A native of New York Mills, New York, James S. Pula is dean of Metropolitan College at The Catholic University of America in Washington, D.C. He obtained a B.A. in social sciences from the State University of New York at Albany in 1968, an M.A. and Ph.D. in history from Purdue University in 1970 and 1972, respectively, and did further postgraduate work at the University of Maryland, where he obtained an M.Ed. in 1979. He is editor of *Polish American Studies* and has published numerous books and articles in the fields of immigration history and Polish American studies. He is the recipient of the Mieczysław Haiman Award for contributions to the study of the Polish experience in America and the annual Oskar Halecki Prize for the best book on Polish American history and culture.

The Editor

Thomas J. Archdeacon is professor of history at the University of Wisconsin-Madison, where he has been a member of the faculty since 1972. A native of New York City, he earned his doctorate from Columbia University under the direction of Richard B. Morris. His first book, *New York City, 1664–1710: Conquest and Change* (1976), examines relations between Dutch and English residents of that community during the late seventeenth and early eighteenth centuries. Building on that work, he has increasingly concentrated his research and teaching on topics related to immigration and ethnic-group relations. In 1983 he published *Becoming American: An Ethnic History.*